WOMEN BUILD THE WELFARE STATE

Women Build the Welfare State

PERFORMING CHARITY AND CREATING RIGHTS

IN ARGENTINA, 1880–1955

Donna J. Guy

DUKE UNIVERSITY PRESS   *Durham and London*   2009

© 2009 Duke University Press

All rights reserved

Printed in the United States of
America on acid-free paper ∞

Designed by Amy Ruth Buchanan

Typeset in Cycles by Keystone
Typesetting, Inc.

Library of Congress Cataloging-in-
Publication data appear on the last
printed page of this book.

 *For my Tucumán Family*

Contents

Acknowledgments

Both good fortune and great help from my Argentine friends and co-workers enabled me to expand this book from a discussion of street children to one that looks at feminist and female philanthropic child advocacy and the welfare state. My understanding of both themes would have been far different if I had not finally received permission to research heretofore closed archives. After eight years of persistence and, with the help of Dora Barrancos, then head of the Women's Studies Program at the Universidad Nacional de Buenos Aires and a former legislator for the Government of Buenos Aires, I obtained permission to consult the archives of the government agency charged with monitoring state institutions for children and other legal issues associated with minors and the family. Currently known as the Consejo Nacional de Niñez, Adolescencia y la Familia [the National Council for Childhood, Adolescence and the Family, CNNAF], it holds many of the archival papers of child welfare institutions (including the Society of Beneficence) that are missing from the Archivo General de la Nación [National Archives of Argentina, AGN], as well as more than five hundred thousand files on children who entered state institutions. Significantly, the portion from 1880 to 1955 that I was allowed to consult had approximately fifty thousand files. Since that date the numbers have soared tenfold—a clear indication that the welfare state in Argentina continues to function, albeit in a more limited and poorly financed way. This observation is reaffirmed by the lines of families that queue outside of state agencies. Assisted by my researchers, Fernanda Gil Lozano, Luis Blacha, Laura Moon, and Analía Coccolio, we read these files for two years until a change of government and administration led to the rejection of our request to expand the time frame of our investigation. Throughout our research, we were not allowed to xerox, scan, or photograph files, but rather only transcribe them with computers.

As we sampled the materials, particularly from the 1930s onward, a rich collection of letters emerged concerning the role of philanthropic women and their social workers. In addition, letters from parents to children and from children to parents, social workers' reports on the housing of parents and foster parents, and correspondence related to the children offered a vantage point previously unavailable. In an effort to tell the stories of these people, as well as the institutions, I have quoted freely from the archives so that the children, parents, and agency employees of these institutions have the opportunity to represent themselves alongside the institutional evaluations of them. Clients' names have not been revealed in accordance with the wishes of the Consejo.

Access to provincial archives also permitted me to expand the story of child welfare beyond the city of Buenos Aires. However, the richness of these archives depended upon the wealth of the province or city as well as specific interests of local politicians. Furthermore, not all provinces and cities maintained careful statistics on child abandonment, juvenile delinquency, and women's feminist and philanthropic organizations. For these reasons I have expanded the story to include the provinces of Buenos Aires, Tucumán, and La Pampa, while others have been mentioned according to specific themes.

This project took more than ten years to complete and would have been impossible without considerable financial and intellectual support. The University of Arizona's College of Social and Behavioral Sciences Research Institute offered a number of summer travel grants and a Research Professorship Grant; and the Ohio State University has generously supported this project through my Selective Investment Professor's research fund. I also received funding from the National Endowment for the Humanities and the American Council of Learned Societies. I wish to thank all the staff members at the following institutions: at the Archivo General de La Nación in Argentina, especially Elizabeth Cipoletta and Liliana Crespi; the staff at the Biblioteca Nacional; the Consejo Nacional de Niñez, Adolescencia y la Familia; the Archivo Histórico de la Provincia de Tucumán; the Archivo Histórico de la Pampa; the IWO [Instituto Científico Judío], especially, but not exclusively, Abraham Lichtenbaum; Anita Weinstein of the AMIA archives [Asociación Mutual Israelita Argentina]; the Patronato de la Infancia, the Museo del Templo Libertad; and the Patronato Español, especially Sra. Elsa Insogna. Paul Armony of the Jewish Geneological Association [Asociación de Geneología Judía] helped me obtain information about the Jewish boys' orphanage. My research has been aided over the years by

Kent Darcy, Osvaldo Barreneche, Enrique Sánchez Miñano, Tracy Alexander, Douglas Stuart, and Shijin Wu. Dora Barrancos, Marta Goldberg, Ana María Presta, and my Argentine mother, Sra. Olga Aráoz de Ramos, offered me their knowledge and their hospitality during these many years and helped keep me sane. I am also indebted to Asunción Lavrin, Peter Ross, Sandra Deutsch, Daniel Campi, José Luis Moreno, Lila Caimari, Noemí Girbal de Blacha, Adriana Brodsky, and Ann Blum. Rob Buffington, Ken Andrien, Stephanie Smith, Herbert Kaplan, Susan Deeds, and Stephanie Gilmore read earlier versions of the manuscript and encouraged me to sharpen the focus and rewrite. I, of course, take full responsibility for the work. My wonderful husband, Gary Hearn, deserves special mention, for he has put up with a lot, read most of my drafts, and given me incredible support during the creation of this book.

Introduction

This book examines the complex interrelationships between female philanthropic groups and feminists in their advocacy of child welfare programs and family reforms in Argentina in the late nineteenth century and the first half of the twentieth. Members of female philanthropic groups, who generally were representatives of the middle and upper classes, organized and provided help, often voluntarily, for people poorer than themselves. In contrast, feminists came from all walks of life and organized to promote equal legal, social, and political rights for women. I argue that the activities and conflicts between these two groups provide an excellent historical vantage point for examining the origins and rise of the Argentine welfare state between 1880 and the fall of the Juan Perón government in 1955.

This project began as an effort to understand why Argentine and other Latin American feminists lobbied explicitly to gain greater legal authority over their biological children than did their counterparts in the United States. In my research I discovered that Argentine feminists only rarely addressed the plight and rights of non-biological children and orphans. Instead, they combined the goals of protecting mothers and their biological children at the same time that they supported campaigns for equal political, social, and economic rights. In contrast, elite philanthropic women, who were usually identified as members of the Sociedad de Beneficencia (but by my findings also included middle-class and immigrant women), organized to help poor children who had been orphaned and abandoned. In the political sphere, some of these nonfeminist women supported adoption laws so that married and unmarried women could legally adopt a child, a theme that remained outside most feminist discourse. Why did such differences in attitudes toward child welfare divide Argentine female philanthropists and feminists?

I have taken much inspiration from the recent literature on women and the welfare state in the United States, Europe, and the Middle East.[1] These studies have forged a new understanding of how women fought for both protection and rights within nascent welfare states, ones that often discriminated on the basis of class and race and, in the case of the Middle Eastern countries and many European ones, arose out of both religious and feminist movements in response to similar concerns. However, the publications that have examined both progressive and conservative women's movements rarely touch on the issue of orphanages. As Sonya Michel, an exception to this generalization, noted in her work published in 1999 on U.S. child-care policies, "Parents' use of orphanages for child-caring purposes became so widespread that by the second half of the 19th century, 'half-orphans' (children with one living parent) outnumbered full orphans in most asylums," but such institutions increasingly ran into feelings of "anti-institutional sentiment."[2] The direct links between feminism, the anti-institutional sentiment, and the role of women in these institutions became the focus of my work on the Argentine case, and more recent studies, including works on Latin America, have also begun to fill in this gap. This is particularly true of Christine Ehrick's work on the role of women within the formation of the Uruguayan welfare state.[3]

This scholarship on cases outside Argentina has paid great attention to the role of local groups and policies in the construction of the welfare state, and it has divided the concept of the welfare state into diverse components with different histories. This work has been helpful in bridging the gap between the local and the national, and between charity and state obligations, by arguing that such categories are not mutually exclusive. Young-Sun Hong's study of the Weimar state, supposedly the beginning of the welfare state model, hypothesized that "one of the reasons for the neglect of poor relief and charity in most studies of the development of the welfare state has been the perception that they retained their traditional forms and thus perpetuated their anachronistic existence until they were rendered superfluous by social insurance and social welfare systems during the twentieth century."[4] Hong argued that such "traditional" organizations in Germany proved to be functional rather than anachronistic. Even in the classic Weimar welfare state, many reform groups organized according to religious affiliations "whose political and religious cleavages mirrored those of German society itself."[5]

Lynne Haney, in her study of local institutions and their impact on the welfare state in mid-twentieth-century socialist Hungary, noted that contrary to traditional accounts that posit that the Hungarian socialist regime created an entirely new welfare state, many of the social policies within the new state utilized earlier concepts of welfare and charity rooted in the role of family members. In particular, Haney focused on a 1952 Hungarian law that declared that all children had two parents, which subsequently enabled caseworkers to investigate paternity—a long-standing conundrum of child welfare policy as a whole. Enforcing male paternity recognition involved giving single mothers more political leverage until new full employment laws caused the regime to target the moralization of working mothers. Thus Haney distinguished between the formation of the *welfare state* and what I call *social policies* (what she called welfare regimes), with the latter consisting of policies created to implement welfare reform. Social policies could have consequences unimagined by national lawmakers. Haney clearly delineated the difference between welfare states as opposed to social policies, and she placed the family directly within the range of the welfare state.[6] These two works by Hong and by Haney on European welfare states offer productive avenues for thinking about the Argentine welfare state not only as a concept but also as a historical process.

The historical process in Argentina has often involved women in religious organizations. Within the United States, Maureen Fitzgerald's *Habits of Compassion: Irish Catholic Nuns and the Origins of New York's Welfare System, 1830–1920* directly addressed the role of religious women in the formation of New York's welfare system by examining the links between the Irish order of the Sisters of Charity, their self-defined mandate, and the subsidies they received at the local and state level through the influence of Tammany Hall. The Sisters were female religious figures who opposed Protestant feminists in many ways, and they did not fit the feminist imaginary of women totally submissive to the church. Indeed, the relative independence and social origins of the Sisters who operated in New York made them appear to be middle-class Irish counterparts to Protestant feminists rather than their antithesis, even though they opposed each other's views of charity.[7]

I have drawn on these works to formulate a framework that traces the historical process of welfare state formation. This framework analyzes the ways that social policies evolved over time (as opposed to the national welfare state created in the late 1940s); how public subsidies to philanthropic organizations, often run by women, linked the state to immigrant and religious communities; and how child social policies, often expressed by feminists and female philanthropists, provide insights into historical continuities from the rise of the liberal state until the fall of Juan Perón in 1955. The interplay between philanthropy and feminism expands the universe of political actors to include traditional charitable organizations, immigrant welfare societies, public health specialists, child rights' advocates, and juvenile delinquency specialists. Although the often adversarial relationships of these groups are complicated, they put forward essential elements to the history of the welfare state as it evolved. The intricacies of these relationships justify the imperative for examining female philanthropy and feminism in the rise of the Argentine welfare state, and they provide a unique integrated vantage point from which to challenge a number of assumptions about the ways that welfare states develop.

Although specialists in the history of women and the welfare state have advanced female-focused welfare studies immensely, the field of grand, overarching social theory has been mostly gender neutral or focused on males. Within this category Theda Skocpol's *Protecting Soldiers and Mothers: The Political Origins of Social Policy in the United States*, published in 1992, created a firestorm of controversy by focusing on the origin of maternalist politics and promoting new questions concerning gender and the origins of the welfare state. Unfortunately, it also had the effect of excluding child welfare from these discussions. In this lengthy, brilliant monograph, Skocpol argued that the U.S. welfare system evolved in response to women's clubs and other groups that supported national mothers' pensions ("maternalist" policies), as well as the failure and corruption of the soldiers' pension plans ("paternalist" policies). At the same time she excluded the influence of all male and female "charity" work in the rise of the welfare state because it advocated a needs basis for aid and rarely reached the national level, a claim clearly refuted by others.[8]

Lisa Di Caprio has argued in her book published in 2007 that the French Revolution provided the seeds of the welfare state by providing work for poor women, often after women protested their plight in the streets. This perspective provides a variation of Skocpol's thesis by placing female rather than male workers at the forefront of the secularized welfare state and by directly addressing welfare issues at a very early time.[9]

For specialists in Argentine history, the pathbreaking efforts of Cole Blasier and his studies of the formation of social security systems formed the analytical model of Latin American social welfare until recently. Unless groups had specific national *cajas,* or social security funds, they remained invisible to the Latin American welfare state and often by theorists as well. Thus Blasier created the Latin American antecedent for the Skocpol thesis. A work on social security by Guillermo Alonso published in 2000 has built

upon the Skocpol and Blasier theses. Alonso argued that in the early twentieth century Argentine workers rarely went on strike to demand benefits
from a welfare state. The state therefore had no need to respond to pres-
sures, and early pension plans were devised for government bureaucrats,
not for workers. Thus, Alonso contends, no "welfare state" existed. Equally
important, Argentina fought no international wars that would have created
a large demand for soldiers' pensions. The time has come to meld gender
analysis into the larger sociological and economic models often used in
Latin American studies.[10]

For Argentines who oppose Peronist policies and its original leader, Juan
Perón (1946–1955, 1973–1974), as well as for those who believe in the
staunchly liberal nature of nineteenth-century Argentine society, a thesis
that links female philanthropy to the welfare state may appear to be prob-
lematic. These factions would question how Peronism related to the formation of the liberal state, and whether a welfare state, that is, a complete set
of national programs to provide benefits for all, ever existed in 1940s Argentina. Furthermore, they would never accord child welfare institutions and
campaigns a significant role in the creation of the Argentine welfare state.

José Luis Moreno's wonderful compilation of essays in *Social Politics
before Social Politics (Charity, Beneficence and Social Politics in Buenos Aires,
1800–2000)* paved the way for understanding the history of social policies
and the difficulties in forming a welfare state in Argentina. As the title
implies, social policies rather than the welfare state have determined the
distribution of public beneficence since the colonial period. The essays
record a very long history of such social policies, female volunteerism, and
governmental involvement. How can historians reconcile the existence of
extensive documentation on social policies at every level of the Argentine
state when some argue that Argentina had no real welfare state before
Peronism? And how do we place the role of philanthropy and feminism in
welfare state history?[11]

I have envisioned the Argentine welfare state (which is never explicitly
defined within the Moreno collection) as a process that through a series of
social policies began to form at the local level, particularly in municipal
settings. But it is a process that did not become clearly visible at the national
level until the 1940s. For example, by the 1880s municipal authorities in
Buenos Aires offered free medical care to the indigent, as well as special
education to future mothers, as an effort to deal with the consequences of
extensive European immigration. These efforts paralleled those of philanthropic private citizens, especially women volunteers and female religious

orders. Subsequently organized philanthropies sought additional funding from municipal, state, and national governments. The process of petitioning government officials who allocated such funding, called subsidies or subventions, became a feature of Argentine politics particularly devoted to helping marginal children. The full-blown but still patchy Argentine welfare state only belatedly appeared under Peronism after the national government attempted to end these subsidies and assumed the burden of protecting minors.

This process may be similar in other countries, but most Latin American welfare state history contains neither a component of mother and child welfare nor studies of subsidies. Based upon grand theory, it begins with the implementation of a national set of policies, often in response to economic distress such as the world depression of the 1930s or a result of the emergence of a powerful leader or ideology like Juan Perón and Peronism. The fact that Latin American welfare state history ignores the charity and child rescue movements where female participation became so prevalent makes it difficult to understand the contributions of both female philanthropists and feminists. An exclusive focus on welfare activities at the national level hides the participation of actors at local and state (or in the case of Argentina, provincial) levels. Women's groups often disappear altogether unless they are involved in female suffrage or in campaigns focusing on the rights of mothers. The time has come to recast Latin American and Argentine welfare state history to include the state at all levels as well as all types of women's activities in service to the state. Now is the time to ask whether the welfare state evolved separately from social policies.

I argue that in Argentina what emerged as a Peronist welfare state became the scaffolding built around earlier social policies that offered a disjointed but rather effective edifice comprised of national subsidies to philanthropic groups. The subsidies not only provided funding but also government recognition to literally thousands of child welfare institutions operated by religious, immigrant, and municipal entities. Women led most of the organizations, particularly those focused on orphanages and young girls, and they were staffed with numerous female volunteers or members of female religious orders. Perceived gender-appropriate female roles gave these women the authority to help disadvantaged children. Female volunteerism also reflected the absence of professional jobs that would have increased female participation in the labor force as social workers, doctors, and psychologists in the late nineteenth century and early twentieth. Philanthropy became a time-consuming job and women became central to its unpaid labor force, just as poorly paid female religious workers helped reduce the costs of paid labor.

From the early nineteenth century onward, diverse Argentine women's philanthropic and feminist groups opened up workshops, orphanages, milk programs, and juvenile reform schools. They ranged from the Sociedad de Beneficencia [Society of Beneficence] founded in 1823, the most famous and most highly subsidized agency, to lesser-known Catholic, Jewish, and Muslim organizations, immigrant-sponsored orphanages, and finally to the Eva Perón Foundation, a charity founded by the wife of President Juan Perón in 1948.

Initially, the high rates of illegitimacy and infant abandonment during the era of massive European immigration to Argentina between 1880 and 1914 served to mobilize immigrant, religious, and municipal organizations as well as politicians and public health specialists. Local groups, usually but not exclusively operated by female philanthropists, set up child-care institutions, and political groups granted municipal, provincial, and national subsidies to care for abandoned infants. After 1914, public officials shifted their concerns to support state institutions and new legal reforms for juvenile delinquents, a topic that remained in the public mind throughout the twentieth century. Female philanthropists responded accordingly by providing funding and personnel for such entities.

Feminists participated in this process by promoting civil code reforms to give mothers more custody rights over their children, as well as the right to control the use of their own salaries. Unlike U.S. feminists, they did not all see private patriarchy as the root cause of their malaise. State codes created inequities and feminists decided they needed to force the state to change laws. Furthermore, as women demanded entry into Argentine universities, their presence as teachers and students in the early twentieth century prepared the next generation of female professionals who eventually replaced unpaid voluntary female workers.

By the 1940s the expanding welfare state, along with the decreased importance of affiliation with immigrant communities, led many female philanthropic institutions to close down. A new generation of feminists and male and female political activists championed child welfare at the same time that they continued to insist on increased rights for women. Most children benefited from these campaigns because feminists believed that all mothers needed equal legal rights to protect and govern their children whereas under Argentine law only fathers exercised such rights. Furthermore, the number of orphans decreased, although single mothers continued to have economic burdens that sent their children into the streets only to be castigated by police disapproval of children working in public spaces. Thus in different ways feminists and female philanthropists worked for common goals—ensuring the welfare of mothers and children.

The rise of the Peronist welfare state has been a contentious issue for traditional historians. Contemporary Argentine feminist scholars also disagree over the meaning of the Peronist welfare state for women. A controversy emerged over the definition of the Peronist welfare state and whether it had both maternalist (mother-focused) and pro-natalist components that demanded women become mothers. Some viewed Peronism as an Argentine version of fascism. They looked at assorted child- and mother-focused laws and presented them as a Foucauldian discourse of state power demanding that women stay at home and have babies. Others, like Dora Barrancos, pointed out that contraceptives had been available throughout the period, and many typical extreme pro-natalist laws based on eugenics did not became a central focus of the Peronist tradition. A study of Peronist public health propaganda published in 2003 has supported Barrancos's views.[12]

Another way to approach the history of the Argentine welfare state and its relationship to female philanthropy and feminists has analyzed what volunteer women received in lieu of wages and compares it to what feminism offered. Welfare state history has ignored the unpaid labor of mothers and daughters, as well as that of female charity volunteers, even though an analysis of these contributions is fundamental to understanding the origins of gender inequality. Reversing this trend, Daniel Giménez's *Gender, Pensions and Social Citizenship in Latin America*, influenced by Pierre Bordieu, argued that salaries formed only one form of compensation for women's social work. Giménez contended that alternative compensation must be considered, since "there is no reason why care cannot be exchanged for other forms of payment, including both material and symbolic goods (social position, among others)."[13] Although Giménez did not specifically address the contributions of women's philanthropic groups in Argentina, his hypothesis provides a new way to explore their contributions.

In the Argentine case, the accrual of social status and community recognition, along with an opportunity to perform good works outside the home, something that I call the "performance of charity," initially led immigrant and native-born women to engage in welfare activities. For them, charity became an empowering experience. Married women, who were particularly limited by patriarchal authority, found philanthropy to be one of the few acceptable work options for middle- and upper-class women. The new status of philanthropic women became embodied in the substantial edifices they constructed for child welfare as well as the number of children aided. Subsequently Argentine feminists supported reforms enacted in 1926 that permitted married women to work without their husbands' permission and keep their salaries. They also campaigned for equal access to higher education and wages to improve the conditions of female laborers outside the home. Within the home, feminists believed that married women needed equal rights to govern and protect their children, while philanthropic women promoted marriage rather than consensual relations. Together, despite ideological and class antagonisms, the commitment by female philanthropists and feminists to mothers and child welfare underpinned the logic of the child-focused components of the Peronist welfare state. Peronism created new agencies to promote child welfare in which women received salaries commensurate to their education and job description. Perón also opened public universities to all students at no cost, thereby creating an educated labor force that would eventually need less help from the state.

This child-focused, gendered approach to Argentine history offers new insights revealing surprising continuities as well as shifts of social policies from the 1880s to the first Peronist era (1946–1955). Studies of political parties and the personalities of leaders obscure such relationships. Indeed, traditional Argentine history abounds with stories of the rise of political parties and their male leaders, and it privileges male-dominated political history. Such an approach makes it difficult to view continuities in Argentine social practices and policies, and it often ignores the reactions of adult inhabitants, citizens, and minors, both male and female.

The major watersheds in modern Argentine history as currently constructed begin with the formation of the nation-state, which evolved through several periods including independence from Spain (1810–1816); the Rivadavian era of early liberal rule (1823–1826) based upon reforms implemented by Bernadino Rivadavia as minister of government for the province of Buenos Aires and, for one year (1826) as national president; civil wars and the dictatorship of Juan Manuel de Rosas (1829–1852); and the struggle between Buenos Aires and the interior provinces for control of the nation-state (1852–1880). More modern Argentine history has been based upon the political party history that began in the 1870s with the creation of the first political party, the Partido Autonomista Nacional (PAN), led by Julio Roca. The second, much shorter, era involved the Argentine experiment in democratic practices. It encompassed the rise of the first middle-class party, the Unión Cívica Radical [the Radical Civic Union] and its leader Hipólito Yrigoyen (1916–1922, 1928–1930). This second phase also includes smaller parties, especially the Argentine Socialist Party led by Juan B. Justo. A military coup in 1930 led by José F. Uriburu interrupted political party history and led to thirteen years of dictatorship and corrupt political administration from a military-political alliance called the Concordancia [Concordance], organized by Agustín P. Justo. And then, in 1946, Juan Perón rose to power from within the military and created an alliance with labor unions that led to Peronism and the Peronist Party. This movement lasted until 1955 and another military coup that ushered in years of economic and political instabilities. This periodization reveals little about the similarities and differences in social policies and attitudes toward child welfare, as well as the welfare state itself; instead, it embeds Argentine history with person-alistic politics.

Originally written by the liberal victors of the nineteenth-century civil wars, traditional historiography reveled in the liberal triumph of male poli-ticians in the late nineteenth century and the early twentieth. Furthermore it made the study of the welfare state particularly difficult because it ig-nored the liberals' support of Catholic philanthropic institutions. Later historiographical battles between conservative (the liberal PAN), Marxist, socialist, and Peronist advocates have focused more on ruptures between political eras than on their similarities. They ignored the reality that the Argentine national government, as early as the 1880s when it "resolved" the church-state controversy by eliminating religious education from the public schools, began to subsidize religious philanthropic and educational institutions. The national government paid for the construction of new churches as well as hospitals and orphanages. Subsidies continued under the more politically disreputable alliance of the Concordancia of the 1930s. This also proved to be an important moment to begin the expansion of the social security pension system. Later military regimes have been studied from the perspective of human rights and not for the dismantling of the welfare state and the privatization of the social security system, a pro-cess that continued under subsequent democratic governments. Indeed, the study of social policies and the welfare state in Argentina uncovers a se-ries of political relationships that political parties of all stripes would prefer to ignore. Particularly important for this work, these ties reveal strong links between the social policies of traditional parties and Peronism—often iden-tified as a deeply divisive political ideology.

Scholars who believe that a modern welfare state really existed in Argentina attribute it to Juan Perón and his wife Eva. During his administration, Perón created two Five-Year Plans to implement political, social, and economic goals. His welfare state goals emerged in the second plan, formulated in 1951. By this time, fewer women joined philanthropic organizations because they preferred wages to status. Equally important, the age of European immigration began to fade in the minds of Argentine inhabitants and thus fewer people joined the organizations and paid dues. Instead they joined labor unions and supported political parties. These social realities enabled Perón to link his political philosophy of social justice and his wife Eva's public commitment to welfare and her performance of public love to a long-standing concern about street children and child welfare. Together the Peróns reshaped, modernized, and nationalized—but did not totally replace —the existing child welfare organizations.

In many ways Perón's welfare state relied more on rhetoric and performance than on strong institutional roots. The high costs of the welfare state contributed to Perón's willingness to continue Eva's philanthropy rather than bureaucratize the entire system. He became reluctant to close down most philanthropies and relied instead on refusing to pay out the vast subsidies that his political cronies advocated. After Eva died, however, Perón's administration began to back away from her system of philanthropy to individuals. With all of these tensions and inconsistencies, it is easy to dismiss Perón's programs as falling short of a welfare state. The absence of a firm institutional base also facilitated the actions of subsequent political leaders who privatized pension funds and dismantled much of what existed as a welfare state. Nonetheless, state-subsidized child welfare has persisted as a critical focus of government policy.

 CHAPTER 1

Female Philanthropy and
Feminism before the Welfare State

FAMILY LAW AND THE POLITICS OF NAMES

Before Argentina's independence from Spain, orphaned children were cared for by male and female members of religious organizations. Following independence, however, secular women began to replace or to supervise female religious members, and as early as 1823 liberal reformers acknowledged their reliance on unpaid female philanthropic work. Thus modern female philanthropy in Argentina appeared with the formation of the modern nation-state.

The Argentine version of liberalism, however, severely restricted the custody rights of married women over their own children at the same time that it acknowledged and subsidized the Society of Beneficence. How could feminists overcome patriarchal laws so that married women had custody rights over their children, and what role did female philanthropists play in this process? Upon first glance, such outcomes might seem unexpected given the strong legal position of fathers and husbands, both in a private sense and a public one. The women who joined the organizations dedicated to child welfare and feminist causes could not until 1947 rely on female suffrage. Nevertheless, by that time women, particularly single mothers, had been accorded many rights earlier denied to them, and they had been providing child welfare facilities for more than one hundred years. Both feminists and female philanthropists played crucial roles in the expansion of women's legal rights over children.

The legal status of women in Argentina, inscribed in the first civil code in effect after 1871, accorded married women few legal rights within the family. Judges and the police always suspected that unwed mothers acted irresponsibly or immorally, and their children suffered the stigma of illegitimacy if the father refused to recognize them. Only legally married mothers could protect their legitimate children with access to equal inheritance and a mandated right to receive clothing, food, and shelter from the family patriarch. Married women, however, had difficulty obtaining redress for grievances and exercised no custody rights over their children. If they were so poor that they could declare themselves paupers, married women could take irresponsible but legitimate fathers to court to demand food for themselves and their offspring. These legal realities provided the rationale for female philanthropists as well as feminists to demand that the government, either local or national, do more to provide women with the legal apparatus to protect themselves and their children.

Early legislative efforts to modify the legal status of married women tried to give women more financial powers within the family. Proposed at the beginning of the twentieth century, these efforts had little support. Yet just before the proposals reached Congress, the feminist Elvira López published a document, *El movimiento feminista* [The Feminist Movement], in which she argued that financial restrictions formed only part of women's complaints of inequality. Women of all classes suffered from restrictions placed on married women, and in 1910 Elvira Rawson de Dellepiane drafted the first feminist proposal to revamp the Argentine civil code; the successful 1926 revision of the code incorporated some of her suggestions. Nevertheless, women had to wait until the 1980s for shared parental custody over their children.[1]

In contrast to the letter of the law, mothers contested their presumed powerlessness. Rather than go to court, they used long-standing cultural practices to deal with the burdens and stigmas of motherhood. For example, women unable to control their children's behavior, those who found the economic burdens of frequent pregnancies too onerous, or mothers with children born out of wedlock all turned over their offspring to others during difficult moments. This could be accomplished in three ways. The first involved infant abandonment and usually resulted in separating mothers and children forever, or for years at a time. The second, less draconian, way was through infant circulation practices in which mothers gave children to other family members or strangers in the hope that they could give better care to the child. Finally, mothers could place older children in apprenticeships or let them fend for themselves by working on the streets. Sometimes the threat of maternal abandonment proved sufficient to lead an errant father to declare paternity. If not, the women had few alternatives.

Philanthropic women and feminists tried to stop these practices by supporting campaigns for legal changes that mandated a family wage, enabled women to take men to court for paternity, and provided child care for working women. Philanthropic women opened mothers' canteens where mothers and their children could eat. They also ran most of the orphanages that accepted infants.

Both religious and municipal institutions promoted infant abandonment. From the late colonial period until 1892 a foundling wheel or *turno*, a practice utilized in many European countries by secular and religious institutions, operated at the foundling home in the city of Buenos Aires. Unwanted children, usually newborns but even occasionally dead fetuses discarded by parents, found their way onto this wheel, which gave the donor complete anonymity. The wheel and the practice of abandoning newborns on the doorsteps of the wealthy or politically important figures offered mothers the hope that the child might find a better life and avoid the public scandal of illegitimacy or poverty. These measures of desperation formed a consistent pattern of behavior in eighteenth- and nineteenth-century Catholic countries.

The second method, recirculation, was far more informal and less visible. Parents often asked grandparents, aunts, and even female friends to help with a new child, which meant that female volunteerism operated not only at the institutional level but also within the world of informal child circulation. Under this informal system, an informally adopted child could not become a legitimate sibling within the household. Furthermore, biological parents often requested the return of their children and turned to the courts to demand their parental rights. Adoptive and foster parents thus operated on shaky legal grounds. After political reforms of the 1880s instituted the civil registry of births and deaths, falsification of these registers often served to legitimate the last names given to children adopted in this informal way. After all, children's surnames defined status and community links in Argentina not only for the native born but also for children of immigrants.

Abandoned infants designated as N.N. [*ningún nombre*, or "no name"] became rooted in the politics of names and the society's desire to hide the stigmatic origins of children or eliminate unacceptable families. The history of social policies that led to the welfare state in Argentina began as public and private charity that provided the only protection between life and death through the "kindness of strangers."[2]

In Buenos Aires and throughout Argentina, children deprived of identities ended up in orphanages. Their baptism accorded them two first names but no last name. Some only had matriculation numbers for last names; others appended the surname of their foster parents if so permitted. Those with no last names suffered perpetual embarrassment because the circumstances of their birth were identified in their national identity cards, which were handed to officials upon matriculating in school, serving in the army, getting married, or engaging in any other activity that required state identification. To use as a last name, many chose the term *expósito* [foundling].

The politics of names directly related to patriarchy and any effort to promote a welfare state in Argentina had to deal with this reality. The basic structure of patriarchy, fatherhood, and motherhood, all embedded in the concept of *patria potestas,* or patria potestad [patriarchal control and custody], formed an essential part of European and religious family legal codes. Patria potestad gave all power and responsibility for children to the legal father. Without a legal father, an unmarried mother could exercise these rights and responsibilities unless she was deemed immoral by public authorities. The only absolute authority of mothers over their children resided in the milk that came from their breasts. Thereafter, custody of their children reverted to men. For unmarried mothers, links to their offspring did not provide them with the obligation to recognize their newborns. This legal reality spurred infant abandonment, as did the colonial Spanish laws that permitted adoption for families with no children.[3]

The fluid period between independence in 1810 and the rather tardy passage of the 1869 civil code enabled some Argentine provinces to permit adoption. For example, in 1869 Juan Bernard and Catalina Pirovano adopted a fifteen-day-old infant named María Teresa Lázare. According to María Teresa's biological father Enrique Ansaldo, the existence of the legal document prevented him from claiming his patriarchal rights over the child until 1883. At that time the adoptive couple separated and the father left home, leaving the wife and adopted daughter with few resources. Ansaldo went to court demanding patria potestad and accused the adoptive parents of immoral acts that led to their separation. The nonbiological parents claimed that the adoption had its roots in medieval Spain's legal code, the *Siete partidas* [Seven Parts], which under the Fourth Part allowed for *fijos porfijados* [adopted children]. Ansaldo, hoping to get his child back, preferred to rely on the provisions of the new civil code that did not authorize adoption. The court, however, upheld the adoption, and María Teresa's biological father never regained his patria potestad. The code's author, Dalmacio Vélez

Sarsfeld, ironically justified the absence of adoption laws with the view that Argentines did not practice adoption.

The new Argentine nation-state drew on Germanic, French, Canon, and Roman legal traditions to define the legal family for purposes of inheritance and the maintenance of social order embedded in patriarchy. The civil code, as well as the penal code of 1886 and the commercial code of 1861, regulated legal families. Collectively they reluctantly modernized colonial paternal authority by reducing the age at which children reached majority so that children could enter the workforce at earlier ages. Nevertheless, the law still limited legal protection to legally constituted families, prohibited paternity suits by single mothers, and defined power within the family to be specifically male unless there was no legally recognized father. The earlier commercial code, as well as the subsequent penal code, placed additional restrictions on male patriarchs by allowing married and single women and minor children to engage in commerce, and by adding longer prison sentences to punish relatives who sexually abused children. They did not resolve the question of adoption or that of child abandonment. Only when no male head of household could be identified did the laws consider the legal rights and responsibilities of mothers.[4]

Despite these advances over colonial laws, social realities prevented parents from protecting their children because, well into the twentieth century, many poor families formed without the benefit of marriage. Although Buenos Aires boasted relatively low illegitimacy rates, illegitimacy became the common condition of newborns in the interior provinces. Furthermore the new codes prevented some fathers from exercising their rights as fathers and did not value the role of mothering. Such circumstances led illegitimate and poor infants and older children, many of whom had no last names, to be abandoned in the streets or institutionalized in jails, reformatories, and orphanages.

The consequences of having no last name could be brutal. One such tale comes from the city of La Plata in the province of Buenos Aires in 1926 when the foster mother of a child, "Ana" M., after waiting twenty years for her husband to give the girl the family name, finally wrote to the head of the Society of Beneficence. She asked permission to add her husband's name to that of her daughter so that the girl did not have to face the stigma of having only a matriculation number for her last name. Recognizing the importance of this legal act in the absence of legal adoptions, Magdalena B. de Harilaos, head of the Society, immediately authorized the organization's General

Registry of Children to append the name without direct permission from the foster father. This maneuver, in effect, constituted the only form of adoption at the time outside of falsifying the national civil registry.[5]

A third method of dealing with children, one generally considered a temporary solution, came when a working mother encouraged her youngsters to work or play on the public streets. Sometimes these children chose to return home, but others simply lived on the streets. Predominantly older minors, these highly visible street children might have been deemed capable of fending for themselves. But to many in Argentina, children working and playing on the streets conjured up images of immorality and political danger.

Just what did Argentine law offer to mothers of street children, orphans, and other waifs? Not much. Instead it clarified the duties and privileges of parents and guardians in such a way that excluded most women. For example, the law allowed only adult men to serve as legal guardians, or *tutores*. According to article 398 of the civil code, the blind, the deaf, the mentally unstable, jailed felons, debtors, the clergy, people with residences abroad, *and all women, with the exception of the widowed and grandmothers*, were prohibited from exercising this legal authority.[6]

Only the Ministerio Público de Menores [Public Ministry of Minors], the male-controlled institution that consisted of the municipal defenders of minors, was authorized to provide services for children in need and on the streets. Defenders had the right to assign male tutors and participated in all legal matters that affected any child with a guardian.[7] In reality, this role proved impossible to fulfill given the small number of defenders responsible for the large number of children adrift in Argentine cities. Experts often calculated that ten thousand waifs were adrift in turn-of-the-century Buenos Aires. This problem might have been solved through foster parenting, but few men offered to serve in this role and married women could not offer foster care without the permission of their husbands.

Three choices for helping children became available to Argentine authorities: expand the system of child welfare, allow married women to be guardians, or privatize the problem by permitting adoption. Complete adoption would have given married women more control over adoptive children than their own offspring, thus making it difficult to pass such a law. Adoption challenged inheritance laws and potentially enabled non-biological heirs to inherit the same wealth and status as biological children. The option of expanding child welfare thus proved to be an ideal temporary solution, and in response groups of philanthropic women and male legal

specialists set about to solve the illegality of adoption and the very restricted rights of mothers.

From 1823 onward the state played an active role in promoting child
welfare through philanthropy. In that year the liberal politician Bernadino
Rivadavia took the first step by founding the Society of Beneficence. He
expropriated schools, hospitals, and orphanages from the Catholic Church,
and he created the structure for a group of elite women to operate facilities
dealing with infants and women with government subsidies. By the 1890s,
child welfare groups of all kinds received these funds. The Society of Beneficence thus linked the liberal state to the concept of subsidies as a core
feature of social policy. As José Luis Moreno put it: "When a poor person
receives alms from someone else, . . . this constitutes an individual action.
In contrast, when a group of individuals receives systematic assistance from
an institution created for these ends, whether religious or state supported,
we are confronted by an organization of beneficence. When the organizations of beneficence are incorporated openly into the state bureaucratic
apparatus, aid to the poor is transformed into social politics."[8]

In the early nineteenth century the idea of charity appealed to upper-
class women for many reasons. Particularly significant, group assistance to
the poor gave married middle- and upper-class women a legal leverage that
they did not enjoy in their own families—namely, custody rights over children. Their institutions could serve as guardians to children and protect
them through the court system, even if as individuals the women did not
enjoy this legal right. In this way social policies, particularly from the perspective of children, sprang from the actions of early liberal politicians in
nineteenth-century Argentina.

It was not until the early twentieth century that Argentine family law
initiated reforms to deal with the plight of poor mothers and street children. A more formal set of child welfare policies began to emerge with the
passage of the 1919 Agote law, when the national government signaled its
formal involvement in child welfare by enacting provisions that clearly
redefined patria potestad as a legislated, rather than inherent, right of fathers. The law enabled the national government to assume the custody of
errant children and place them in reformatories.

Early legislative efforts to modify family law included the efforts in 1910
of Deputy Luis Agote from the Partido Autonomista Nacional to give the
national government legal guardianship over all juvenile delinquents and
abandoned children under the age of seventeen. Addressing the issue of
older street children, not infants, Agote argued that from 1905 to 1910 a

total of 1,312 boys had entered national prisons for crimes they committed, and among them 520 were repeat offenders. In addition to these delinquent children, more than 1,000 worked as newspaper boys and even more lived on the streets where they often became part of "anarchist bands." Agote opposed treating juveniles as criminals, and so he suggested that street children be scooped up and placed in an expanded boys' reform school such as the Marcos Paz facility opened in 1899, or in a branch of it that could be habilitated at the former lepers' colony on Martín García Island. He estimated that 10,000 boys could be rehabilitated in such places. Agote, an eminent physician and early leader in the child reform movement, based his legislative proposal on the belief that the state could do a better job than irresponsible paterfamilias. He did not, however, explore the problems of homelessness or the fact that single or abandoned mothers often could not provide for their children.[9] Agote's initially unsuccessful proposition was followed in 1916 by another proposal addressed to the Ministry of Justice and Public Instruction by Eduardo Bullrich and Dr. Roberto Gache. The new plan envisioned the utilization of juvenile courts and mandatory education, rather than work or jail, for abandoned and delinquent children.[10]

A 1910 newspaper article specifically dealt with homelessness by criticizing how throughout the province of Buenos Aires, including its capital city, municipal defenders dealt with abandoned and homeless children by placing them as servants in families. The article specifically argued that the system was inefficient "since few patrons fulfill their responsibilities in a conscientious manner, and the result is that children are left in misery and hunger."[11] Although the article envisioned state protection for both boys and girls as the only salvation for them, it neglected to ask where and under whose legal custody the children would be housed.

Just before Agote's proposal became law in 1919, President Hipólito Yrigoyen of the Radical Party created the Instituto Tutelar de Menores [Tutelary Institute for Minors], which began as a quasi reformatory, more like a dormitory, for boys arrested or found orphaned or abandoned. From the beginning, it provided temporary shelter for approximately two hundred youngsters, who, according to the law, could not remain there for more than twenty days. Gradually the Instituto Tutelar became an organization that served as a coordinating link between the police and the public and private reformatories that began to emerge. The Instituto Tutelar, operated by men who worked for the Ministry of Justice and Public Instruction, with recommendations from judges, sent children to private institutions as well as to public jails and reformatories. Equally important, even after minors had served their prison sentences the organization could hold them for rehabilitation (although they usually remained in the private reformatories). However, the issue of patria potestad remained unresolved, and parents could protest any state actions regarding their minor children.[12]

After Luis Agote's efforts to resubmit his proposal failed again in June 1918, President Yrigoyen continued to make child rights reforms a high priority. He sent a message to Congress on January 20 supporting congressional efforts to draft new legislation to form a new welfare association for minors. This organization, the Patronato Nacional de Menores [National Child Protection Association], was to have a governing board of juvenile delinquency specialists. As Yrigoyen put it, he "recognized the urgency that exists to provide the nation with a law that contemplates . . . the problem of the destitute child, and presents comprehensive solutions for the diverse situations in which the children encounter the hazards of life so that the child will be steered away from the path of evil . . . and converted into a useful person to himself and to society."[13] Yrigoyen's speech built support among fellow Radical Party politicians, and in 1919 a revised version of Agote's bill was finally enacted as Law 10.903. During the debates Carlos Melo, a Radical Party member, argued that there were twelve thousand abandoned children in Buenos Aires. For this reason he wanted "the welfare organization of the Argentine state from this day forward to aid minors who are abandoned or delinquent, and will give them the protection, the direction, and the support they have lacked. In this way they will be able to learn how to work and form their sense of morality."[14] In other words, he advocated state patriarchy to replace errant fathers. Yrigoyen successfully founded the Patronato Nacional, and Congress passed the Agote law in 1919. However, Congress allocated no funds for the Patronato Nacional, and authorized no juvenile courts.[15] For the time being, provincial and municipal authorities had to wrestle with the realities of child rescue— along with the philanthropic organizations.

The Agote law clearly addressed patria potestad and justified state custody of delinquent and abandoned children. Its first article removed Article 264 from the civil code. Rather than patria potestad limited only to legally recognized male heads of households, a new article conferred patria potestad to the mother if the father died or lost his right to exercise patria potestad. Furthermore, it specifically gave patria potestad to a single mother, or to parents who formally recognized their *hijos naturales* [offspring of unmarried couples who had no legal impediment to marriage]. Another article totally revamped articles 307–310 and explicitly removed patria potestad in cases involving child abuse and child abandonment, and those in which bad advice was offered that led children to be at risk "materially or morally." Convicted criminals lost their patria potestad, along with those parents who abandoned their homes or were alcoholics, and the suspension could last for one month or more, or until the child reached the age of majority. The new law also clarified the earlier codes and gave child welfare and penal institutions patria potestad over children in its care, even those with known parents.[16]

Although these revisions modernized the civil code, limited male patriarchy, and supported single mothers' claims to child custody, they did little to help married women obtain legal rights over their children. The new provisions only allowed mothers the equal right to commit unruly children to reform schools. However, the presence of female philanthropists operating reform schools meant that the new law empowered these facilities. In fact, when juvenile courts were first established in 1922, the education specialist Ernesto Nelson reminded court delegates that the law not only authorized parents to voluntarily surrender children to the state but also mandated that the children be placed under the "definitive tutelage" of the director of the institution. Nelson's wording presumed that the director would be a female.[17]

Reforming the Civil Code

Beginning in the early twentieth century, feminists, both male and female, advocated reforms to enable women, particularly married women, to enjoy greater economic and legal rights. Furthermore, feminists demanded married women's equal custody rights over their children. Generally speaking in the Argentine case, male members of the Socialist Party who backed this legislation in Congress often heeded the advice of feminist allies. Radical Party legislators soon joined them and offered their own legislative proposals. Although legislators in 1926 granted married women the right to choose their own professions and keep their salaries, it soon became clear that it would be easier to provide women access to the workplace than to revise male control over patria potestad except in the case of delinquent children.

Despite the resistance to drastically limiting male patria potestad, the resulting 1926 law offered new protections and responsibilities for single and widowed mothers. It explicitly reaffirmed single mothers' patria potestad over all of their children, not just delinquent ones, and mothers over the age of twenty-one could also obtain custody of their children from another marriage.[18] The reform enhanced the ability of single mothers to govern and protect their children. We shall see, however, that judges rarely concurred with this provision if anyone questioned the morality of a single mother. Not until the Peronist years (1946–1955) did Argentina make additional major changes to the civil code regarding issues of adoption, patria potestad, and the rights of married mothers. A parliamentary commission tried to do so, and in 1936 it drafted new provisions that added keeping house and performing domestic chores in the definition of mothering. The commission also advocated absolute divorce and the ability of parents to recognize offspring of adulterous or incestuous relationships. The first presidency of Perón resolved most of these issues, at least temporarily, although the final issue of granting shared patria potestad did not occur until after the Dirty War in 1985.[19]

Family Law and Child Custody

Although extreme criminal cases of parental misconduct came to the attention of municipal and provincial officials, families often solved problems on their own. When they were not able to do so, the civil courts decided where children would live as well as with whom. For generations family law determined which children would be recognized and who would be discarded. Yet this patriarchy-derived tradition eventually conflicted with the needs of a modern nation-state that identified future citizens based upon all individuals born within its geographic boundaries. The legal fate of children with no patriarchs or with dysfunctional fathers remained unresolved. Furthermore, the tension between the rights of fathers and the needs of the nation became more intense. If fathers left minors on the streets and in danger, it threatened the nation's need to ensure that all children born within its territories lived to become useful citizens. The national government had to become an advocate for child rescue. For Argentines, this meant that the government provided aid for poor families and protected children from the vagaries of patriarchal family politics.

Both before and after child-focused social policies emerged in Argentina, judges only reluctantly enforced any part of the law that empowered women to be guardians of their children. Furthermore, issues not discussed in the laws, such as the relative merits of specific fathers, mothers, or relatives, often proved central to the disputes. For this reason, the politics of making legal decisions about child custody pragmatically evolved in two directions. The first avoided the courts altogether: families simply made informal arrangements that included falsifying records to claim that a child was a biological relative, sending children into foster care or an orphanage, and even stealing children. This process bolstered the informal networks of child circulation and welfare.

If these strategies did not work, the second choice enabled families to work out their grievances in court. Even in the 1970s efforts to determine the paternity of children kidnapped by the police or the military and given to new families utilized the same procedures that were followed in the 1880s. By 1970 DNA blood samples determined paternity, but as in the past only the courts could provide closure for disputed cases. Thus the courts provided continuity rather than facilitating change in the transition from a system of subsidized philanthropy to the Peronist welfare state.

The difficulties confronting parents who wanted their children returned lasted a century and the names and places differed, but the pain experienced by families made these cases poignant. I begin the story of judicial tensions and family realities in 1886 when Pedro Adamo went to court in Buenos Aires to secure the guardianship of his eight-month-old nephew Antonio. Several months earlier Pedro's sister had died, leaving the infant in the hands of his father and a wet nurse. Pedro feared for little Antonio's future because his father was a notorious alcoholic. As Pedro put it, "I am the blood uncle of this child and I feel true affection for the only offspring of my sister Carmen. I cannot remain indifferent to the dangers confronting the child."[20] In order to obtain custody of Antonio, Pedro asked that his brother-in-law be deprived of his fatherly rights. Since both the defender of minors and the child's legal guardian concurred, the uncle, who was unable to sign his name, obtained guardianship [tutela] of the infant.

In 1921 Santiago Ferrero tried to limit someone else's patria potestad in the nearby city of La Plata. He accused his neighbor Tomás St. John of waiting for ten years to recognize his daughter Aguëda Delia Nuñez, and of doing so only to take advantage of the girl's ability to earn money as a domestic servant. Santiago had raised Aguëda Delia until Tomás demanded his paternal right to govern his child. As Santiago's lawyer put it, "In legal terms, the question is rooted . . . in the fundamental differences between legitimate paternity and biological paternity." He argued that Santiago was the real father because he had given affection, food, and clothing to the child, and had not forced her to work as the family's servant. The court did not agree, and Agüeda Delia went to live with her biological father. In this case, blood relations became more important than the father's parenting record.[21]

A Tucumán case showed what might happen to children caught up in custody battles involving living parents. In 1938 "Elisa Borgano," a single mother, petitioned the court for the return of her eight-year-old daughter who had been kidnapped by her paternal uncle.[22] The father had never recognized the child, and Elisa had sued him in court in 1934 to pay for feeding her daughter. As Elisa put it, her sick daughter "required the care that only a mother can provide."[23]

The father, a railroad employee, argued that his poverty necessitated a public defender. At the same time he claimed to be in a better moral position to care for his daughter. The child's mother lived with another common-law husband. Further, the biological father had recognized this daughter and she could now live with him. While the parents and attorneys bickered, the young girl languished in the women's jail for seven years, a victim of custody battles. The case dragged on until June 23, 1941, when the judge decided in favor of the biological father, principally because of the mother's sexual history. Her history, according to the judge, merited the suspension of the mother's patria potestad, although she could still visit her daughter once a week. The passage of years between the first case and the second did not translate into a more enlightened vision of children's needs and mothers' rights.

On specific occasions, Argentine law dealt with fathers equally harshly because, according to the law, some biological fathers and mothers had no legal right to "father." This applied to fathers and mothers of children born of adulterous, incestuous, or sacrilegious relationships. Blanca Gontrán and her former lover Miguel Lani discovered this unpleasant truth in 1897 when Blanca went to court to get custody of their daughter, Julia Artemisa. Blanca claimed she never knew of Miguel's married status; not only had he tricked her, but he had also taken Julia Artemisa when she was less than five, an age when mothers almost always had custody. Miguel saw the situation very differently. He insisted that he had been open about his marriage, and he defended himself by claiming that "a caring and affectionate father [un padre cariñoso y afectuoso] can not snatch a child to hand it over to a mother who never showed any affection and, on the contrary, mistreated the child from the first day. . . . A father with an unblemished reputation and who possesses the necessary means to take care of his daughter, to whom he has given his name and for whom he works to give her an easy life, will never hand over his daughter."[24]

In this plaintive statement Miguel placed as much emphasis on his emotional attachment to his daughter and his standing in the community as in his ability to provide for her. Unfortunately for the child, the courts frowned on the adulterous relationship. The attorney for the Ministerio de Menores argued that neither parent could exercise patria potestad over this unfortunate child. Thus on August 12, 1899, the judge awarded custody of Julia Artemisa to a nonrelative.[25]

Mothers in a marriage gone awry had an even harder time protecting their children. In 1886, five years after Margarita Suffern de Smith received an ecclesiastical divorce, she asked for patria potestad over her son. From the time of her separation, her husband Carlos had neither shown interest in his son nor provided for him. Margarita offered a letter from James P. Kavanaugh of the Holy Cross School testifying that she had been the sole supporter of her child. Carlos never responded to these charges. Despite all evidence pointing to Margarita's dedication to her child, the court determined that Carlos's failure to respond to the court's inquiry offered insufficient proof that he had no interest in his son. All that Margarita could obtain from the courts was the right to keep the child in her custody.[26]

Although mothers were supposed to care for their babies, particularly those who had not been weaned, some fathers insisted upon taking the child away. In 1925, Casilda Freire de Basilia, then eighteen years old, went to court in Santa Rosa, La Pampa, to insist that her husband return her unweaned one-and-a-half-year-old daughter Nafla. Salvador, a twenty-five-year-old "Arab" merchant with fourteen years of residence in Argentina, complained that Casilda had abandoned their home and that he intended to maintain custody of the child unless he were forced to surrender it. Unlike the Buenos Aires defenders of minors who usually sided with the mother of an unweaned child, the appointed official in La Pampa declared that only the husband had patria potestad.[27]

While patriarchal privileges abounded in Argentine legal codes, thorny questions remained. Could men truly govern their biological children? Was this a "natural" right or contingent upon legal statute? Could fathers ignore these rights if they wanted to? What rights did mothers enjoy? In other words, how absolute was the concept of patriarchy? To the dismay of jurists and fathers, Argentine law never completely defined the extent of men's authority over their families. From the outset, the civil code indicated that the Argentine government could remove a man's right to govern his children if he abused or abandoned the family, or showed a lack of moral authority. Delineated in a general way, the state's right to interfere in patria potestad became clearer in the 1919 Agote law in order to deal with juvenile delinquency. Nevertheless, the state officials and specialists opposed the strong language that permeated the code and insisted that men govern their family.

As late as 1993, Julio J. López del Carril, a distinguished conservative Argentine law professor, emphatically stated that patria potestad existed as a natural, not legislated, right. "Patria Potestad, whatever might be its origins and concepts, precedes the existence of the law. Even if men had not elaborated the law, it was understood that they could and should govern and direct the lives of their children until they became men and women."[28] Although López del Carril held his views firmly, the issue is not so easily resolved. In stating that fathers and single mothers (and by 1985 all mothers) had the right to make key decisions for their children, he ignored the role of mothers as well as the issue of how adopted parents obtained rights to parent their children and how the Argentine state consistently contested the parental rights of men and women whom the courts considered inappropriate fathers and mothers.

If parents could not be the legal guardians of their children or, as in some cases, became ineligible to do so, who would care for them? Argentina adhered to a concept rooted in early-nineteenth-century French Napoleonic codes that prohibited the formal adoption of minor children. Children could be made legal wards or informally adopted, but both relationships prevented them from being considered relatives of the family with whom they lived. This prohibition existed for two reasons. First, the laws were intended to protect minors from entering into contracts. Second, and more important, Napoleonic and Latin American civil codes protected biological children from losing their inheritance to nonblood family members. The codes also protected the legal and biological basis of patria potestad. Once again inheritance, property rights, and patriarchy took precedence over all other issues; mothers had few rights, and children who were taken in by virtue of the kindness of strangers were poorly protected by the law. The battles over adoption therefore transcended debates about how infertile middle-class people could obtain babies. Indeed, the debates struck at the heart of family and property law and explained the need for philanthropic organizations to provide child welfare for unwanted or orphaned children.

Adoption Law Politics

The battle to enact adoption legislation comprises one of many child rights issues that are rarely discussed in the political history of Argentina. Yet among its early advocates was the first modern Argentine political party, the Partido Autonomista Nacional. As a nineteenth-century liberal political party later identified as politically conservative, the PAN advocated free trade and limited government intervention in society. In their concern with what they perceived to be the breakdown of the family due to immigration, many progressive nineteenth-century liberals supported the Patronato de la Infancia [Child Protection Agency], founded in 1892 by the municipality of Buenos Aires to help educate and care for poor young children. In some cases, wives of PAN politicians were involved in similar charitable works in their service as members of the Society of Beneficence.

In Congress, the PAN liberals viewed older wayward children as potential criminals. To reform the children, they advocated subsidies to religious and other private institutions. After many liberals began to doubt the cost and efficacy of orphanages and reform schools, they suggested that wayward children and abandoned infants be placed with other parents. In so doing they supported adoption, but only for abandoned children or barren couples. For these reasons, the group known in the twentieth century as conservatives became staunch supporters of child rights legislation, usually associated with liberal groups.

Adoption was rarely discussed by the Socialist Party, a non-Marxist reformist workers' party that was formed in the 1890s and led by middle-class public health physicians and lawyers. In line with feminist thinking, socialists focused on providing basic government, health, and educational rights for poor children so that upper-class charities could be closed. Socialists thus advocated state-subsidized mothers' pensions, school lunch programs, and better housing for the poor. They also advocated granting equal social status to illegitimate children. Their beliefs generally placed the burden of social welfare on an alliance between the state and the private family rather than on residential orphanages or adoption. The recognition of illegitimate children also placed the burden of social justice on men who fathered children out of wedlock.[29]

Two other major political parties developed policies that addressed the problem of abandoned, orphaned, and wayward children. The Unión Cívica Radical [Radical Party] also advocated for children's issues and created new agencies to reform older children and help newborns. The party did not, however, advocate unrestricted adoption during its early years, most likely because adoption legislation came from the PAN. Yet Radical Party members so prided themselves on their efforts to promote child welfare that during Hipólito Yrigoyen's second presidential campaign in 1928 the party produced a documentary that praised its record on social welfare. Included in this praise was the information that, during Yrigoyen's tenure as president, he had donated his entire salary to the Society of Beneficence.[30]

After Yrigoyen's death, other Radical Party members took up the banner of child welfare. Eventually the Radical Party, like the PAN, defined adoption as a process designed to solve social problems, and it allowed as many barren couples as possible to adopt as many children as they wanted. This process, however, dragged on at a glacial pace. Not even the impact of the world depression in Argentina could foster consensus. The eventual catalyst for adoption laws finally came from a devastating earthquake in 1944 in the province and capital city of San Juan.

The reluctance to enact adoption measures indicated strong support of the supremacy of the biological family. At the same time, however, Argentine public authorities did not have the financial resources to establish enough orphanages for those unprotected by their kin. They certainly lacked the means to solve the problems of difficult adolescents. The plight of abandoned or orphaned children became both a public and a private problem to be solved both by government authorities and private philanthropies. After all, children often lived in inappropriate environments. Not only did the courts prevent some parents from assuming their responsibilities but many parents simply did not have the means to do so. Their problems, ranging from illness in the family to poverty and spousal abandonment, became principal causes of infant and child abandonment in Argentina. The Society of Beneficence, the municipal defenders of minors, and the various agencies set up over the years to protect children took over when parental and kin networks collapsed. Among them, organizations led by women provided the basic framework for infant care. In the case of older children, men's organizations operated institutions for boys, while women ran those dedicated to girls.

As the largest state-subsidized child welfare organization, the Society of Beneficence operated orphanages for both boys and girls. These facilities often housed children abandoned by dysfunctional families that had few ties to other community-based organizations. Both mothers and fathers asked for help, as illustrated in the case of "Ronaldo H. Pantelo." Born in 1930, his father was ill and his mother was a servant with five children. The mother turned over Ronaldo, the youngest, to a wet nurse, and in 1934 he entered the foundling home. Because his parents never responded to queries from the Society of Beneficence, Ronaldo was moved from institution to institution as he grew up.

Ronaldo spent his entire childhood in orphanages because he had living parents. Yet it was not until 1952 that Ronaldo's mother made contact with the Society. She claimed to have lost her papers proving her maternity. In September 1952 Ronaldo recounted the bitter experience of meeting his mother, at which time he discovered that she had never loved him and only wanted him back if he could contribute his income to the family. He felt as if "for a second time I have become an orphan as before," and he stated that he preferred to return to the orphanage where he might be happier. Shortly thereafter, orphanage officials asked Ronaldo to leave.[31]

"Mirta Luisa" had better luck with her mother. In 1933 the eight-year-old girl arrived at the Society of Beneficence. Her mother, a domestic servant, abandoned her after her father supposedly died of pneumonia. For the next two years, the child was shuffled from institution to institution until she arrived at the girls' orphanage. During this time, her mother visited her constantly until 1942, when the woman won the Society's Virtue Prize [Premio a la Virtud]. Evidently the prize money, four hundred pesos, was intended to enable the mother to request the child's return. Mirta Luisa's stay was extended, however, because the damas discovered that not only had the husband not died but the mother had remarried in Montevideo. Nevertheless, the mother persevered, and in 1943 Mirta Luisa went home to her mother; they seemed to have a happy ending when Mirta Luisa went to work alongside her mother in a factory.[32]

Turning to kin did not always solve child custody problems, and the Society of Beneficence provided the only other alternative. A grandmother with several children lived in a hut in "great poverty and neglect." In addition to her own offspring, she cared for two grandchildren, ages eight and five. Their father cared for two older children while his wife was hospitalized for mental illness. In 1938 the grandmother requested that the eight-year-old granddaughter "Irena" be admitted by the Society of Beneficence, but she was not given a place until the following year. At that time she went to the Saturnino Unzué Asylum, but found little happiness there. In 1943 Irena wrote to her mother about her attempted escape. Finally her mother appeared seven years later in 1945 to retrieve the teenager.[33]

Sometimes parents needed to institutionalize all of their children. The director of the Cotolengo hospital informed the Society of Beneficence in

1939 that a mother of four had been hospitalized for a chronic illness and the mentally disturbed father had disappeared. The Society first admitted the youngest son, and then allowed the rest of the children to enter after the officials verified the situation. The parents did not keep in contact with their offspring, even though the youngest wrote frequently to his older brother who ended up in the army. The youngest boy, after a short stint in the military band of the Colegio Militar [Military High School], stayed institutionalized until he reached the age of majority.[34]

There are thousands of stories like these in the archives of the Society of Beneficence, in the Consejo Nacional de Niñez, Adolescencia y Familia (CNNAF), and in civil courts throughout the country. No statistics offer an accurate picture of what happened to the individuals involved. Each case tells of specifics, and the group portrait that emerges is one of families in rapidly growing cities with high rates of poverty and family dislocation in both the city and the countryside. For immigrants, there were few kin capable of caring for the minor children of their relatives, and, particularly from the 1930s onward, families and individual children migrating from other provinces to Buenos Aires in search of work encountered the same problem. For all of these people, the civil code and its emphasis on patri-archy and inheritance rights meant little. When possible, the poor turned to the many organizations sponsored by philanthropic groups and the emerging welfare state.

Since basic relationships between children and inherited property mili-tated against an early decision to support adoption laws, abandoned and orphaned children remained in the hands of state and private orphanages, as well as in the informal exchanges of children through midwives, strang-ers, and friends of the family. This placed female associations for child welfare in an ideal position to not only protect children but also shape child welfare policies. For example, in 1912, the damas of the Society of Benefi-cence watched closely as a custody case worked its way through the judicial system. This particular case is important in terms of the words that the women used to express their opinions regarding the case. For the damas, the legal fate of children in foster care, as well as the status of parents who had abandoned them, had become a critical issue. As stated in the minutes of their meetings, the women favored legal procedures that would "give rights to people who care for orphans in order to protect them against the demands of parents who had once abandoned them, or who are not in evident conditions of morality to guarantee the future of the child."[35] Yet few private groups other than the Society mentioned this issue until the

1930s. Instead, politicians first broached the problem of patriarchal authority in the context of juvenile delinquency.

The Struggle for Juvenile Delinquency Laws

Juvenile delinquency, in comparison to adoption, became the target of polemical discussions in the Argentine Congress until the 1940s. For many years, child rights advocates argued for penal code reforms to distinguish the crimes of minors from those of adults and to create special juvenile courts patterned after the U.S. model pioneered in Chicago in 1899.[36] From the outset, legislators and specialists recognized a fundamental problem rooted in the Argentine civil code: fathers' rights superseded those of single and married mothers in matters of patria potestad over children. What if parents did not watch out for their children or set bad examples for them? Specialists believed that a clear-cut law could give the government the right to rescind child custody from biological parents or guardians so that a child could be incarcerated for more than one month.

As early as 1894 child rights advocates targeted patria potestad as an outmoded principle. They insisted that the state protect children from bad parents. The noted public health physician and reformer Dr. Benjamín Dupont even argued that patria potestad was "a feudal right." Fathers should enjoy these powers so long as they were good. Unfit parents should hand over their parental rights. Within this category he identified two groups: "the indifferent and the criminal."[37]

After the passage of the 1919 Agote law, reform schools operated by religious and private philanthropists began to crop up all over the country, and their record keeping made the problem of street children even more visible. The situation in the Argentine territories, however, had not changed, and the 1932 annual report of the prisons claimed that for all intents and purposes the Agote law did not exist in these regions.[38] Furthermore, specialists criticized the Agote law from the outset. One judge blamed the law for increasing the number of children imprisoned without guaranteeing their rehabilitation.[39] Carlos Brodeur, who served on the committee that in 1924 reformed the government-operated Marcos Paz facility, issued his own criticisms in 1937.[40] He argued that the law focused too much on judicial matters and too little on the social aspects of child rescue. And, without funding, its impact had been limited.[41]

Despite the absence of funding, the Agote law along with the Instituto Tutelar de Menores provided the legal and philosophical underpinning for a comprehensive system of juvenile delinquency programs that until the 1930s remained focused on boys, whether delinquent or homeless. The law limited the rights of defenders of minors to find work or homes for street children. Henceforth the national government was mandated either to send children to private institutions or to create the reform institutions for boys while charitable institutions and the Society of Beneficence had the principal responsibilities for girls.

In 1924 the Instituto took over the state-operated Marcos Paz reform school after a boy living there ran away and then tried to commit suicide because of the harsh conditions at the school. Once an investigation took place, it became clear that the warden used corporal punishment far too often, and inmates often ended up hospitalized. President Marcelo T. Alvear named a new supervisory group made up of the child welfare specialists Jorge E. Coll, Judge Carlos de Arenaza, Ernesto Nelson, and José María Paz, the head of the Patronato de la Infancia.[42] This marked the first time that specialists could participate in the reform school movement, and the Instituto became a sounding board for progressive policies. Alvear demonstrated his support for the group by subsidizing their new construction efforts through a decree enacted on December 29, 1924.[43]

In 1921 a newly reformed penal code revised notions of juvenile delinquency that had been operating since the 1880s. The new law not only protected children but also gave the state more rights over children accused of crimes. For the first time, a law forbade punishment of all children under the age of fourteen. In appropriate cases, offenders could be committed to institutions until they turned eighteen, although this happened infrequently. Nonetheless, the code ignored those male juveniles incarcerated because of homelessness, and all girls on the streets. These children either languished in jail or ended up in reform institutions, often operated by religious orders or philanthropists.[44]

Feminism and Child Welfare Movements

Although feminists did not operate the child rescue organizations, they did promote public awareness of the dangers faced by children and their mothers. Their concerns served as the catalyst for a hemispheric child welfare movement. The Liga para los Derechos de la Mujer y del Niño [Rights of Women and Children's League] and its president Dr. Julieta Lantieri organized the first Argentine Child Congress in 1913. The women invited distinguished Argentine child specialists such as Carlos Octavio

Bunge, Dr. Antonio Vidal, Dr. Horacio Piñero, and Dr. Gregorio Aráoz Alfaro to head, respectively, the sections on law, hygiene, infant psychology, and assistance and protection for mothers. Other specialists dealt with education, another feminist concern.[45]

A second meeting, one with greater international significance, took place in 1916. This meeting, the first of many Pan American Child Congresses, openly displayed the gendered tensions of child welfare. When men felt that women demanded too much, they acknowledged their dissent and sometimes undermined progress on issues regarding private and public funding. Feminists opposed private orphanages and child care institutions, while their male counterparts supported them. The vice president of the congress, Dr. Francisco Súnico, for example, only gave his conditional support to the hygiene groups' recommendation that American nations aid weak children [niños débiles] by trying to help them in school as well as providing them summer camps, medical treatment, and proper food. Súnico believed that most of the social activities should be handled by private, not public, organizations.[46] Other areas of dispute included the desires by feminists to include sex education in the public schools as well as to close down large orphanages and place children in family-type settings. Feminist women tended to support state intervention and smaller organizations, while nonfeminist women and male professionals supported the larger private orphanages.[47]

After the 1916 congress the Pan American child meetings became dominated by male Latin American child welfare specialists. Although the meetings generally were held in the national capitals of many Latin American countries, in 1942 the United States sponsored a congress in Washington. The meetings introduced new political concepts: the need for governments to care for children and prove their modernity by lowering infant mortality statistics and helping poor women. They also supported laws enabling women to force men to acknowledge paternity through court cases.

The significance of these meetings for Argentine child welfare politics was critical. Despite the uneasiness about adoption, concern about the plight of abandoned children and street children continued. After the first Pan American Child Congress in 1916, subsequent meetings supported child welfare legislation advocated by either feminists or female philanthropists. These two groups of women rarely agreed with each other. Nevertheless, the Pan American child meetings legitimated the child welfare demands of feminists and female philanthropists and by the 1930s they both commenced major campaigns in favor of child welfare.

What began as the politics of names based solely on the patriarchal codes enshrined in the civil codes soon blossomed into more complex issues of whether mothers could protect their children; how parents could retrieve children given to others for care; and who would take care of children unwanted, abandoned, or orphaned. Although the rigidity of the codes did not cause all these issues, it certainly made them harder to resolve. Consequently, diverse groups of women began to address child welfare problems in a variety of ways including supporting the operation of large institutions like orphanages, opposing such institutions, proposing more public education, and expanding the rights of both single mothers and married women.

In the meantime, abandoned children and street children who had no place to live ended up in jails. The results of incarceration often led to the children's stigmatization and the loss of their social identities, and thus made their difficult situations worse rather than better. Feminists and nonfeminist women devised their own solutions to the various problems confronting both mothers and children in Argentina. The campaigns to help children began first and foremost with philanthropic women addressing the problems of infant abandonment and the high rates of illegitimacy and infant mortality. The resolution of other issues had to wait for more organized private and public strategies to encourage better mothers, the legal recognition of illegitimate children, and improved infant health care.

Mothers became an integral part of the solution and feminists banded together with male legislators who believed in the cause. Together they demanded expanding parental rights for married women. Their victories came about slowly, but the process kept at the forefront of social policy the issues of mothers and child welfare—concerns that were increasingly addressed by governmental social policies.

CHAPTER 2

Benevolence and Female Volunteerism

The nineteenth-century European diaspora contributed to the great demand for child welfare in Argentina. From 1857 to 1914 more than 4.5 million immigrants entered the nation. This influx created numerous and extremely visible newcomer communities, particularly in the national capital.
The two principal immigrant groups were the Italians (2,283,882) and the
Spaniards (1,472,579). By 1895, four out of every five adults in the capital had
been born abroad. Not everyone remained in Buenos Aires or in Argentina,
however. Indeed, a constant floating population entered the country and
then departed for the provinces, crossed the Río de la Plata, or returned to
Europe. This situation continued after the turn of the century, and Argentina periodically experienced immigration spurts and floating populations
before and after the two world wars.

Prior to 1914, male migrant farmers formed the great majority of immigrants who annually traveled to Argentina seeking well-paid harvest labor.
Others looked for work and wealth in Buenos Aires. The urban poor included internal migrants, local inhabitants, single women in search of work,
and entire families with inadequate means. Given the high cost of decent
housing, families could rarely afford to live on just one salary, and single
mothers barely eked out a living. In search of work, some families made
their way to smaller cities or to farms and ranches outside Buenos Aires.[1]

Gradually the lure of comparatively high wages in seasonal labor, as well
as the possibility of turning family-based workshops into larger manufac-
turing establishments, encouraged immigrants and migrants to stay in Argentina. After deciding to settle, immigrants urged family members and
fellow villagers to join them. Most lived in the crowded tenements called
conventillos, which consisted of old single-family dwellings partitioned off
into many rooms surrounding a patio, with each room housing an entire
family or a group of single people. Those who chose to view the city's

rapidly growing architectural splendor of public buildings and theaters rarely commented on this Buenos Aires of the poor.

After 1900 life in the conventillos became a typical fate of immigrants, as recounted by James Scobie.[2] That reality changed little in the first half of the twentieth century: as late as 1946, despite all the wealth created by the export economy, the conventillos in the heart of the city still housed the poor. A social worker's 1946 report on a child about to be evicted from a tenement house observed that "the municipality of Buenos Aires demanded the eviction of all the conventillo's tenants because the building had been declared uninhabitable. They should have left by last April 30, and possibly a later date will be authorized, because none of the neighbors have been able to find lodging. The house comprises thirty-four rooms with an average of five people per room, or a total of 170 lodgers. The inhabitants are of different nationalities and social levels, there are workers without vices and vicious ones without work, drunks, prostitutes, and even a thief in room 14. . . . The woman who wants to intern her son, her mother-in-law, and five children occupy a tiny room and they only have two beds." The continued presence of conventillos testified to a long-standing situation of inhospitable lodging, high rents, and too many children lodging in unsuitable environments.

Personal Responses to Immigration and Poverty

Mothers were among those most immediately faced with the problem of expensive and limited housing. Their survival strategies deeply concerned medical specialists, community leaders, and welfare providers, who were especially alarmed by the high level of infant mortality. They were also troubled by the rates of illegitimate births, which in late-nineteenth-century Buenos Aires hovered between 12 and 14 percent. These rates were similar to those of German cities such as Berlin or Hamburg, which had rates of 14.9 and 12.1 percent, respectively. Like its European counterparts, the problems faced by Buenos Aires were compounded by religious values and rapid urbanization, as well as by the influx of immigrants who came from European countries where child abandonment and the abandonment of babies frequently occurred: in Paris in 1891, for example, 28.6 percent of all live births were registered as illegitimate.[3] In the interior provinces, illegitimacy rates even in the twentieth century could exceed 40 percent.[4]

Infant mortality rates also perplexed public health officials. The deaths of these future citizens rapidly endangered the growth of a nation in which citizenship depended almost entirely upon the birthrate rather than upon the naturalization of immigrants. Argentina's 1853 constitution welcomed immigrants with many rights, yet the political system discouraged naturalization. A study in 1892 of poor children in Buenos Aires somberly noted that "during a period of sixteen years, 36,568 infants under one year of age died in the city of Buenos Aires." Also during this period 8,632 infants died at birth, along with the deaths of 16,653 babies between the ages of one and two years old. As a result, of 212,768 live births only 159,547 infants survived to the age of two.[5]

How did parents devise strategies to deal with these conditions? Physicians and other public officials linked infant mortality to infant abandonment. Latin American rural poor families, in contrast to Protestant urban models, tended to keep older children, if possible, and give infants and sometimes youngsters to other families rather than abandoning them.[6] Since foundling wheels were woefully scarce outside Buenos Aires, increased urbanization, even in the provinces, led to infant abandonment in alleys, on doorsteps, or outside the houses of wet nurses. This behavior challenged Creole or native-born practices, and it produced the need for a new, more comprehensive public response.

When poor families avoided the scrutiny of public authorities their success stories remained untold, while their failures or problems often led to the courts. Abortion and infanticide occurred throughout Argentina, as in other countries. Kristen Ruggiero's study of late-nineteenth-century Buenos Aires noted that infanticide, often committed by immigrant domestic servants, left dead newborns in latrines or in the more modern toilets in the homes of their employers. María Celia Bravo and Vanesa Teitelbaum reaffirmed this phenomenon in late-nineteenth-century Tucumán in northwestern Argentina. They hypothesized that the rate of abortion and infanticide there related to the absence of a foundling home in the province.[7]

When the Buenos Aires foundling wheel closed under political pressure in 1892, many believed that infanticide rates would increase. Both infanticide and abortion continued, but they became difficult to enumerate and to prosecute. In 1922 Angel Giménez, a socialist legislator and supporter of progressive social reforms, published a study of abortions and infanticides during the period of 1901 to 1921. The statistics, based on police information for the city of Buenos Aires, showed that far more infant deaths occurred than did infanticides or abortions, thus emphasizing the need to address the general causes of infant mortality.[8]

Enrique Bordot's report on pregnant women and women with new-borns, which was based on statistics from one dispensary, provided additional information on abortion. The report indicated that between 1910 and 1921, the 7,900 women studied had averaged somewhat more than three pregnancies each and aborted 2,825, or 12 percent. Bordot did not offer any information on infanticides. From the perspective of these cases, abortion rather than child abandonment had replaced illegitimacy.[9]

Child abandonment escalated during moments of increased immigration. After 1883, Buenos Aires recorded for the first time more than 500 infants abandoned at the foundling home. Six years later the number had doubled. Specialists often linked child abandonment rates to illegitimate births; nevertheless, the number of illegitimate births began to exceed one thousand per year in 1879, and by 1889 it had reached 2,798 or 12.6 percent of all births, far more than the number of abandoned babies. After 1900 the rate of illegitimate births rose to 15 percent for a total of 4,987, which was far more than the number of children entering state orphanages.[10] Finally in the 1920s the rate of illegitimate births in Buenos Aires began to decline—from 12.9 percent in 1921 to a low of 10.59 percent in 1929. This rate would, however, rise to 12.22 percent in 1940 and again to over 13 percent after 1943, precisely at the time that Juan Perón began his ascent to the presidency. These figures did not parallel the decrease in the number of infants abandoned at the Society of Beneficence after World War I. Thus, although illegitimacy had a weak correlation to infant abandonment, the existence of large numbers of abandoned babies linked together the two issues, and both served to preoccupy public officials.[11]

Many babies or children whose caretakers did not have the good fortune to have contacts with mutual aid societies or women's charitable organizations first passed through the informal fostering system. Left in the care of relatives, godparents, legal guardians, or wet nurses, these infants had no secure future. Although parents hoped that kin would provide for these children and that the children would consider these surrogates as parents, this outcome did not always occur.

Other parents dropped off children somewhere relatively safe and left infants to the kindness of strangers. Most of these stories did not have happy endings. The question became how and when to leave children in the care of others. Even more important, parents had to decide whether family or ethnic ties would resolve the problem before they had to resort to the Society of Beneficence or simply abandon children in the streets.

Sometimes parents abandoned children with specific instructions for the new caretakers. In 1883 the Society damas found a child on the foundling wheel with the following letter: "This child ain't Christian and was born on February 1, 1883." This information ensured that the child would be baptized. More often, however, parents included no information with the infant. Another child, an eight-day-old boy, was turned into the foundling home after being found abandoned in a ditch alongside a house on San Juan Street. In another case seven years later in the city of La Plata, capital of the province of Buenos Aires, a mother left an infant baby boy with a woman named Clementina N., presumably a wet nurse. After caring for him for nine months without remuneration, she turned him over to the local defender of minors who, in turn, asked the Society of Beneficence in the capital city to care for the child.[12] In February 1909, Eugenia D. de Badano claimed that a man stepped down from his carriage in Buenos Aires, knocked on her door, and gave her a baby girl only a few hours old. He asked her to look after it while he went to the hospital. He never returned and Eugenia turned the baby over to the police, who sent it to the foundling home.[13]

Sometimes the strategies of mothers who left offspring with wet nurses worked because many bonded with their wards. If they did so, however, they got little monetary recompense for their efforts. In 1883, Bartola Tabares, a former wet nurse, took Manuela Nadal to court in Buenos Aires hoping to be paid for her altruism. In 1859 Bartola had accepted Manuela's son as a client, with the promise that the mother would pay her for her services. Bartola nursed the child and raised and educated him until he turned eighteen; she presented him to her family as her own child because his biological mother never compensated her. Without any chance of success, Bartola much belatedly tried to get paid for her services. The judge threw her petition out of court on technicalities. Nevertheless, the story reveals how a single mother might abandon her newborn child and later be held accountable by a wet nurse who refused to give up on the child.[14]

Among the few successful cases of wet nurses gaining permanent custody involved a woman, "María Teresa," who was hired in 1937 as a wet nurse for a child named Oscar. His mother, a single domestic servant, never paid any attention to him or his twin brother. Finally, in 1943, Oscar became a foster child in María Teresa's family. Although the family already had four biological children, the parents soon took in Oscar along with his twin brother. According to social workers' reports, they lived in a caring household.[15]

After 1892, people wishing to leave children with the Society of Beneficence had to go to a special office instead of abandoning them on a found-ling wheel. A birth registry later opened in 1925, and parents had to answer the questions of social workers. The stories of abandonment continued throughout the period under study and long after the foundling wheel closed, but the numbers decreased significantly by the 1920s, probably due to social workers' efforts to encourage parents to keep their children.

Thousands of unopened envelopes from the Society of Beneficence be-fore 1892 contain bits of ribbon or medallions that might identify an aban-doned infant. The fact that they remain unopened today means that neither parents nor relatives ever claimed the babies. This left abandoned children with many questions about their origins.

The archives of the Society of Beneficence rarely revealed actions of minority mothers. One of the very few Afro-Argentines identified by the Society of Beneficence had been left by his mother and placed in the care of a wet nurse. He grew up in the orphanages of the Society and eventually ended up in the Ricardo Gutiérrez facility because of bad conduct. There in 1950 he wrote a composition as part of a test of his language ability. It is unclear if the composition is his or if he simply copied it: "I am in the establishment because of an accident of life. In this locality I work polishing furniture. When I leave I hope to work and maintain my future home where I will live with all my happiness." That same year the damas finally identi-fied his mother, but she refused to recognize him. He lived off and on with several families as a servant until he reached the age of majority and went into the army.[16]

Fathers also abandoned their children. "Marta Lara," a fifteen-year-old girl, wrote to her father in 1949 from the girls' orphanage operated by the Society. An inmate since 1935, she begrudged her father for not taking her to Spain with him. She had been raised without nurture or a family, and she only asked for some love; as she put it, "I have been truly an orphan without kindness." When a social worker subsequently interviewed the woman who rented rooms to Marta Lara's father, the landlady claimed that he planned to move without telling the daughter because "if he saw her under the wheels of a vehicle he wouldn't lift a finger to help her."[17]

A Buenos Aires defender of minors proclaimed that the situation of children with parents was even more wrenching than that of orphans. The orphans he could perhaps help. But when parents showed up at this office with several children and claimed absolute poverty, the defenders had few solutions. They often tried to send babies to the Society's foundling home, but the damas had no obligation to accept them if no vacancies existed. As the defender noted: "According to what can be judged by the appearance of the petitioners, what they say is true. But with all the pain in my soul I have to close my door to them, because I have nowhere to place them."[18] Children required housing and care, both of which were scarce resources in nineteenth-century and early-twentieth-century Argentina, and many children were left to the streets and then later ended up in jail. The reluctance of the damas to take in all children was realistic owing to the lack of space, but it often provided the fodder for criticism.

At the same time, the damas frequently went beyond the call of duty. María Cilan ended up in the girls' orphanage operated by the Society after a court decision determined that her guardian did not have the means to feed and educate her.[19] Sara M. de Venn left her daughter (named for her) at the girls' orphanage, at that time called the Colegio de la Merced, because her British husband had abandoned her and their three children for, she stated, a life of drunkenness and debauchery. Her daughter had been accepted as an orphan, even though she had both living parents.[20] Most often the decisions made by the damas rested on the availability of beds in the orphanages, rather than on the existence of parents.

Municipal Responses

The individual actions of mothers and fathers often provoked the scrutiny of public authorities as well as benevolent groups. In the case of Buenos Aires, municipal public health programs developed rapidly. The University of Buenos Aires had a medical school that reopened with the fall of the dictator Juan Manuel de Rosas in 1852. After the yellow fever epidemic decimated Buenos Aires in 1871, Guillermo Rawson, a noted public health physician, became the first chair in public health at the school. He trained a new generation of physicians according to the latest European health ideas. Imbued with an understanding of positivism that promised practical solutions to social problems, many of his students not only served as physicians in Buenos Aires, but also helped shape public health legislation for the municipality and for the nation.[21]

Buenos Aires became the role model for other municipalities as well as for the national government. Since the time of Rivadavia and even during the colonial period, there had been defenders of minors to care for orphans. After the national government federalized the city in 1880 the new mayor, Torcuato de Alvear, began to organize the defenders, as well as many hospitals, asylums, and charitable facilities, into a more rationalized system, which was based upon the French model of public assistance. In August 1882, the city created the Asistencia Pública [Public Assistance] to centralize and expand medical treatment and to offer free services to the urban poor who registered as indigents.[22]

The national political and economic crisis of 1890 added to the suffering of the poor and increased infant mortality. The mayor of Buenos Aires, Francisco Bollini, attributed infant mortality increases to the practice of abandoning infants, and he resolved to address the problem because he believed that "one of the most important responsibilities of municipal authority is to contribute, within its jurisdiction, to the assistance and protection of childhood according to the principles of modern science."[23] The mayor's concerns led to an extensive report, released in 1892, that analyzed the problems of infants, children, and mothers and proposed a series of solutions. Rather than close down existing charities and start over, specialists offered these groups strategies for expanding their efforts and even proposed the Patronato de la Infancia. The Patronato had links to public assistance medical services but it was privately run by distinguished men of the community. The 1892 report suggested a wide range of child welfare programs, such as helping children in tenement houses; creating a centralized society to protect children, establishing day-care centers and homes for parturient women; closing the foundling wheel to prevent anonymous child abandonment; checking on the services of wet nurses; reforming existing child welfare institutions; and authorizing the state to become the legal guardian for children mistreated or in moral danger. In many ways, the report became the blueprint not only for municipal assistance to children but also for the national welfare state. Given the economic crisis, the municipality could not possibly implement all of the programs suggested by the special committee. Nevertheless, their efforts outlined government assistance to philanthropies that promoted child welfare.

The Patronato de la Infancia became the most ambitious charity outside of the Society of Beneficence. Although it proudly identified itself as a privately endowed institution, the Patronato accepted municipal subsidies to implement its programs. Until 1967, a series of highly distinguished elite men served as presidents, most of whom were not averse to accepting public donations. In 1892 the mayor allowed the Patronato to use the old Hospital for Chronic Patients to offer emergency care to more families. The following year the organization opened its first infant day-care center by asking patrons to contribute enough money to purchase a bed. Private subscriptions proved to be insufficient and the Patronato members drew up plans to ask for a share of public lotteries already a source for the Society of Beneficence. In addition to seeking public funds, the Patronato also sought to promote new laws through major campaigns that defined congressional and municipal concerns from the 1890s through the 1930s. The Patronato advocated anti-vagrancy laws as well as legislation to remove patria potestad from irresponsible parents, provide state guardianship, and promote child protection laws.[24]

Although men led the Patronato, women became its principal employees and volunteers. In 1895 a women's commission was created that paralleled and often overlapped with the women serving the Society of Beneficence. Indeed, a number of presidents of the Society became founding members of the Patronato's women's commission. Furthermore, the men openly encouraged upper-class women to volunteer with the organization. With its relatively low overhead, the Patronato managed to expand beyond day-care centers to manual trade schools for urban children and agricultural schools for urban and rural boys.

In 1921 the Patronato also created a school for mothers. Designed to teach mothers how to take care of their children "according to the most modern concepts of scientific child raising [*puericultura*]," the school claimed that its objective was to ensure the health of young children. But other agendas guided their efforts, most obviously the transmission of upper-class normative values about mothering to the working classes. Furthermore, the school served as a means of obtaining inexpensive wet nurses for infants left in the care of the Patronato. Mothers who attended the school received room and board, classes, and a small salary in return for breastfeeding another child along with their own. The mothers were allowed to leave the institution only once a month for three hours, unless they obtained a job.[25]

The great difference between the women who worked for the Patronato and those in the Society of Beneficence involved subordination to men. Patronato women could not set their own policies, and they found themselves completely subordinated to the all-male executive council. In many ways the Patronato's organization exemplified the gender structure that men could never achieve with the Society of Beneficence. And to avoid the impression of competing with the Society, the Patronato focused on rehabilitating older children and promoting juvenile delinquency law reforms, which were not strong concerns of the Society of Beneficence. Elite women benefited from this situation. The existence of women's auxiliaries to male child welfare groups provided powerful male elite allies when female philanthropies were criticized by politicians.

The Growth of the Society of Beneficence

Elite men created their own child welfare programs, but that did not deter the damas of the Society who enjoyed the greatest public subsidies from national, provincial, and municipal governments. From 1900 to 1940, the Society of Beneficence, which always called itself the Society of Beneficence of the Capital, expanded beyond the borders of the city as bequests and public funding facilitated the opening of all kinds of establishments for children and women. A few examples here will provide a clear picture of that expansion. In 1901 The Society opened the Mercedes Asylum in the province of Buenos Aires for boys aged five to eight. After 1915, the damas renamed the asylum the Asilo General Martín Rodríguez after the governor who had appointed Bernadino Rivadavia minister of government, thereby leading to the creation of the Society. By 1942 the establishment housed seven hundred boys supervised by the nuns of the Congregación de Nuestra Señora del Huerto. There the children learned rural farming tasks and carpentry while attending primary school. In 1928 María Unzué de Alvear left a legacy that enabled the damas to set up another agricultural school in Luján in the province of Buenos Aires.

For girls, a large legacy led to the establishment of an industrial school named after the donor's husband, José María Pizarro y Monje. It opened in 1925 and offered housing and sewing classes for girls and industrial workshops for nonboarding boys. The girls learned domestic skills and the staff sold the girls' production to hospitals and to the public. Similarly, an asylum in San Fernando, province of Buenos Aires, opened in 1916. Eventually it housed sixty girls. In the province of Córdoba, the damas opened the Casa San Sebastian for fifty girls at risk for (but not ill from) tuberculosis. They also sent twenty-five orphan girls there each summer. At the San Sebastian House the girls labored in workshops that taught them how to be good housewives or maids.

For poor children who lived with parents the Society opened the Asilo Manuel Rocca, a day school for four hundred children between the ages of five and fourteen. The students stayed at school for the entire day at no cost to parents. And in 1927 the Society built the Instituto de Maternidad [Mothers' Institute], where poor or expectant mothers could give birth, learn domestic skills, and find wet nurses for their babies if necessary. Funded by the national government, the facility offered the mothers "medical protection, moral and material aid, thereby assuring them absolute secrecy if necessary."[26]

training to be housekeepers — bec. it's skilled that produces individuals/citizens / work

The Instituto de Maternidad identified its goals as "protecting mothers medically and socially during all of their 'genital' [reproductive] lives." It also protected infants, at least until the age of eighteen months. The Institute offered shelter for poor, homeless parturient women as well as for those with newborns, and wet nurses were available for orphans and for children whose mothers could not nurse. The Instituto de Maternidad also offered a legal office to defend the rights of the mothers and to facilitate efforts to legitimate children and marriages. Clearly the organization targeted single mothers who might abandon their children.[27]

In a world dominated by men, the damas of the Society initially struggled to command respect. The gendered nature of social knowledge placed different emphases on how to deal with female clients more often considered targets of moral reform than candidates for medical treatment. This did not, however, deter physicians from challenging the power of female philanthropists. Public health physicians who did not have direct access to the female-controlled institutions of the Society of Beneficence frequently criticized the damas and the foundling home. Male doctors often attributed insalubrious orphanage conditions to the damas' lack of management skills and medical knowledge, even though physicians with excellent training worked for the Society of Beneficence. In response, the damas responded to these attacks by gathering the necessary medical data from their own doctors and then challenging others to do better.

A perfect example of this endeavor was the damas' answer in 1891 to efforts to close the foundling wheel. In response, the Society's president argued that incorrect information was in circulation about conditions at the foundling home. The cause of problems related to the fact that the home was understaffed and underfunded. The damas first offered to either close the foundling home temporarily or turn over its management to public officials. Then, to make their point, the damas resigned from managing the home. The national government and the public health physicians thus had the unique opportunity to take over the foundling home, but the country struggled amid a political and economic crisis. President Pellegrini refused the resignation by the damas, and then he invited them to propose suggestions for reorganizing the operations of the home. The foundling wheel closed in 1892, but other reforms proceeded according to the damas' wishes.

Eight years later, Dr. Eduardo Wilde wrote a scathing letter to the Society of Beneficence, citing horrendous levels of infant mortality in Buenos Aires and poor pay for wet nurses. Now that the damas knew that the state had no intention of replacing them, they responded assertively. They refuted point by point many of the incorrect claims that Wilde had made (after verifying conditions in the foundling home with their physicians and inspectors). At the same time they recognized that the situation would improve with more funding. Even when male physicians complained, until 1946 Argentine presidents refused to close down the institution linked to the liberal state. It would have been too expensive to replace the female society that worked for free but demanded respect.[28]

Wilde blamed the Society for the high infant mortality rate because he equated infant abandonment and infant mortality in Buenos Aires to the situation in the foundling home. Yet most specialists admitted that such figures were imprecise because parents abandoned infants in many ways and children died for many reasons. Furthermore these figures included neither older children living in other orphanages nor those sent to the foundling home by local chapters of the Society in other provinces.[29] New orphanages not operated by the Society opened up, and newborns died in their own homes as well as in orphanages.

No matter how displeased public health physicians were about the foundling home, the home initially constituted the only facility for babies under the age of six months. At the home the damas hired both internal and external wet nurses [nodrizas or amas de leche]. After 1900, other orphanages and day-care centers offered similar services, but the foundling home remained the principal destination for abandoned and orphaned infants in the nineteenth and twentieth centuries.

Doctors openly opposed wet nurses and campaigned for the right to monitor and replace them with lactaria [offices where these women could initially be observed and then have their milk extracted and tested by physicians]. Buenos Aires physicians obtained the right to inspect and register wet nurses in 1875 as part of a municipal domestic service ordinance, but physical inspection did not begin until 1888. Gradually the public accepted the idea of inspection as well using impersonal breast milk extractors. By the 1930s, women, whether wet nurses or not, with excess breast milk went to breast milking stations where machines attached to their nipples extracted milk. The milk then went to laboratories to ensure quality and hygiene. Under this system there would be no mothering involved in the production of breast milk by wet nurses who sold their services or donated excess milk. The damas successfully opposed and resisted these policies within their own institutions.[30]

The Society of Beneficence thrived not only because of the damas' excellent political skills as negotiators but also because the institution functioned as an important catalyst linking the liberal state with the Catholic Church by hiring nuns to operate their establishments. Significantly, as a government agency from 1880 until 1943 it reported to the Ministerio de Relaciones Exteriores y Culto [Ministry of Foreign Relations and Religion]. All of this happened while the damas maintained deep loyalty to the memory of the liberal Rivadavia and each year publicly celebrated the hero of liberalism with the orphans. This potentially conflictive dual identity protected the damas from political interference for many years.

Collective Benevolence

In Buenos Aires and across the country all kinds of private institutions, usually funded by *colectividades* [collectivities] of immigrants, religious organizations, and laborers, opened their doors after 1880. Alberto Meyer Arana's philanthropy essay in the city's 1909 census noted that new orphanages had opened in the 1890s to house children of deceased military men and orphans of naval personnel. The military orphanage was established in 1891 by Sra. Carmen Eguiluz de Ayala, and the naval orphanage took shape under the initial patronage of Sra. Angélica García de García but subsequently was funded by a group of elite men and the prestigious Jockey Club. In 1897 María Larroque de Fonrouge, after suffering through her three children's diphtheria attacks, organized a committee called "Argentine Mothers." This group, made up of elite women, distributed free supplies of vaccine to poor mothers until adequate supplies could be obtained by the Asistencia Pública of the municipality of Buenos Aires. Subsequently, the women focused on distributing clothing to poor children, and they set up sewing workshops. The following year women from the Italian community established an infant day-care center for poor women in their community.[31] Meyer Arana's philanthropy essay listed many more organizations that aided poor women and children.

Immigrant community organizations also provided more general welfare assistance. José Moya has argued that the Spanish community in Buenos Aires joined a huge number of mutual associations that provided all kinds of subsidies, health care, and burial programs.[32] They were not alone. In 1904, for example, Italians had established sixty-two mutual aid societies, while the Spanish had seven and the French had five. By 1914 the Spanish had sixteen such societies. By this time mutual aid societies had been established in most provinces and territories, where 1,202 organizations operated with more than 500,000 members in a nation of 7.8 million inhabitants. Prior to 1937, mutual aid societies helped working-class families purchase medicine and seek help for their children, but in 1927 there were only ninety-two mutual aid societies in the city of Buenos Aires.[33] Although these organizations could not always prevent child abandonment, many associates most likely relied upon them during lean times so that families could stay together, and philanthropic societies carried out this mission in a very effective fashion.

Although mutual aid societies flourished and became an object of scrutiny, the organizations administered and financed by women remained outside the category of mutual aid organizations. They operated on contributions rather than dues, but it was precisely these groups that targeted poor women and children. For this reason philanthropic women became invisible to those interested in the ways that the immigrant communities organized. In these various reports on mutual aid organizations, the entities identified varied considerably from report to report—a reflection either of the distinct ways of identifying such associations or of their rise and fall.

Without a doubt, in addition to formal mutual aid societies, women organized immigrant and religious-based charities throughout the years of massive immigration and even afterward. The Jewish community's philanthropic institutions provide an example of collective benevolence. Although the Argentine Jewish community was very small in comparison to other groups, its identity as a religious minority, as well as its tradition of acting as a community, or *kehilla*, prompted leaders to develop a series of organizations to help fellow Jews. Among other charitable works, by the 1920s they had established the Chevrah Keduscha, the burial society that eventually became the AMIA or Asociación Mutual Israelita Argentina, the Hospital Israelita, and an orphanage for boys and one for girls. The records of the children who entered the Jewish boys' orphanage, the Asilo Israelita Argentino de Niños, demonstrate that children arrived there from locations all over Argentina, including the Jewish agricultural colonies. Many, such as "child No. 148," a five-year-old boy, entered the institution through "the efforts of the Alianza Mutual de Barracas [Mutual Aid Society of Barracas]." Another child, No. 329, was sent by the Asociación Israelita de Mendoza, while No. 379 entered the institution through the efforts of the Asociación Alianza de Socorro Mútuos de Salta [Mutual Aid Alliance of Salta], and No. 406 arrived with a recommendation from the Sociedad Unión Israelita de Tres Arroyos [Israelite Union of Tres Arroyos Society]. Local committees from Carlos Casares, Córdoba, the Chevra Keduscha, the Subcomisión de

Moisesville, and the representative of the orphanage in the Colonia Monte-fiore also forwarded children to the orphanage. These orphans might have had no parents, but they were still recognized as part of a community.[34]

The first Jewish orphanage for boys opened in 1918 as an adjunct to an old age home. The following year the Jewish girls' orphanage began opera-tions and became the special responsibility of the Sociedad de Socorros de Damas Israelitas [Rescue Society of Israelite Ladies], which in 1927 re-named itself the Sociedad de Damas Israelitas de Beneficencia [Beneficent Society of Israelite Ladies]. The girls' asylum filled another important need within the community, and shortly after its opening it became clear that the dormitory space was insufficient. In response to this problem the Chevra Keduscha Ashkenazi Society donated 5,000 pesos, and the Buenos Aires Municipal Council offered an additional 5,000 peso subsidy to deal with the large number of children seeking entry. By 1923, the Argentine government began to subsidize the orphanage with a yearly stipend of 1,800 pesos, a sum that eventually increased to 10,000 pesos annually.[35] In this way the Jewish girls' orphanage joined the long, and growing, list of government-subsidized welfare organizations.

The orphanages also fulfilled another important function for the Jewish community. The risks of relying on the orphanages controlled by the So-ciety of Beneficence were high because the Society baptized all infants who did not enter the home with proof of baptism. A 1914 article in the publica-tion of the Jewish *Ezrah* society clearly noted this problem:

> Our collectivity, whose advancement can be tracked year by year and which already has resulted in mutual associations . . . still completely lacks an asylum that collects and cares for our orphaned or abandoned children.
>
> Perhaps we justify this omission because there already are many asy-lums in the country. But we must keep in mind that these charitable institutions pose a grave risk for the continued independence of certain religious traditions because far from being lay associations, on the con-trary, they are eminently Catholic, run by nuns who are strongly influ-enced by a proselytizing mission. And already there have been cases of baptized Jewish children.[36]

Equally disturbing to the Jewish community was the fact that when moth-ers had to choose between baptism and misery that could lead to death, maternal instinct to keep their babies alive led to baptism.

The Jewish community was not the only religiously based group of women to respond to the needs of child welfare. The Damas de Caridad [Charitable Ladies] operated orphanages and child facilities in Buenos Aires and in the interior. In 1870 in the river port city of Rosario in the province of Santa Fe, for example, they opened an orphanage in the home of Blanca M. de Villegas. Associated with the provincial Society of Beneficence, the Charitable Ladies placed the children in the care of the religious order of the Sisters of the Garden. Soon they had the backing of many representatives of the foreign community and along with provincial subsidies they built an orphanage in 1879.[37]

From the 1890s onward, more overtly Catholic charities like the Conferencias de Señoras de San Vicente de Paul [Conferences of Women of Saint Vincent de Paul] also promoted child welfare. Founded in 1889 as an organization separate from other devotees of Saint Vincent and similar to the Charitable Ladies, it soon had chapters all over the country. In 1889 the women opened an asylum for orphans and beggars in Corrientes, and in 1893 they opened a boys' orphanage there and a mothers' asylum in Córdoba. Subsequently, women founded Conferencias in Córdoba, Paraná, Catamarca, Santiago del Estero, Mendoza, San Juan, and many smaller communities within Buenos Aires and other provinces.[38] Devoted to reducing class animosity, the women encouraged the construction of moderate housing, visited the working poor, and established the Casa de Santa Felicitus for working girls.[39]

The home visitations of Conferencia women had special meaning. As Katherine Lynch pointed out in the case of the St. Vincent de Paul Society in nineteenth-century France, "The home visit constituted the ritual that served symbolically to dissolve the estrangement between bourgeoisie and workers."[40] While helping to soothe class conflict, the Argentine Conferencia women wanted to help poor working women and mothers. The organization reached its most influential moments before 1916, after which the women's activities began to be challenged by the male church hierarchy.[41]

The Politics of Subsidies

Many of these church groups received municipal, provincial, and national subsidies. In 1913 the province of Córdoba authorized subsidies not only for provincial and municipal hospitals, orphanages, and poor houses but also partially funded twenty-six organizations providing shelter and food for the poor, many founded by religious organizations. Furthermore, religious schools also benefited from public support.[42] In the territory of La Pampa in 1928, the Sociedad de Hermanas de los Pobres [Society of the Sisters of the Poor] received 23.2 percent of its income from municipal and national subsidies. The organization operated a maternity ward, one of the few in the area. Subsidies on a provincial level often led to national support.[43]

The city of Buenos Aires became particularly well endowed with child welfare institutions that received subsidies. Emilio R. Coni's 1918 study of Buenos Aires listed more than one hundred institutions, public and private, dedicated to helping single mothers and poor or orphaned children. Most had been founded by private individuals, often women who solicited the help of the Catholic Church, but increasingly the municipal government of Buenos Aires, along with secular elite groups, also offered their services to needy families. Furthermore, different religious organizations, national groups such as the British, Irish, Spanish, and French, and the Freemasons founded their own orphanages.

Besides the municipal hospitals and clinics, more than ninety existing organizations received either municipal or national subventions, and nineteen received both. They included such diverse organizations as the Salvation Army's night shelters, the Patronato Asistencia de la Infancia, the Sociedad Protectora de Niños Pobres de General Urquiza [General Urquiza Society for the Protection of Poor Children], the Colegio Taller de Santa Filomena [Saint Filomena School Workshop], and the Casa del Niño [Children's Home], founded by an elite philanthropist woman. The municipality itself received national subsidies, which were then redistributed to local child welfare associations. New entities were added to the swelling list while some closed, making it even more apparent how funding was uneven and politically motivated. As Coni angrily observed: "A simple glance at the figures makes it immediately clear that the distribution of subsidies to charities has no method and owes only to the influential action of institutions with the parliament and the municipal council."[44]

In 1917 Coni offered his own proposal to rationalize the welfare regime of subsidized charities. It involved the nationalization of all of hospitals of the Society of Beneficence, which would be placed under the Departamento Nacional de Higiene [National Department of Hygiene] while the Society itself retained existing and future orphanages. A new agency, Asistencia Pública Nacional [National Public Assistance Agency], would manage regional hospitals and asylums, which Coni claimed totaled 170 hospitals and

170 asylums of all kinds. He believed that the new organization would make clear to the national Congress the inequitable distribution of subsidies.[45]

In 1926 legislators unsuccessfully attempted to create a Consejo Nacional de Beneficencia [National Beneficence Board] to centralize charities. Coni's own dreams of a coordinated welfare state only began to develop in the 1930s. In 1933 the newly organized Patronato Nacional de Menores [National Child Protection Association] attempted to conduct a survey of child welfare institutions in an effort to work out a "general plan of construction and organization of child welfare establishments in the capital city, provinces and territories," but the Society of Beneficence never cooperated. The resulting report provided only a partial picture of philanthropy in Buenos Aires. The Patronato Nacional survey discovered that among the children found in the institutions of the national capital that responded, most had only one parent. Slightly more than a half of the children were Argentine, and approximately half of the remaining children were either of Spanish or Italian origin. More institutions existed for girls than for boys, which was probably due to the lack of state facilities for girls.[46]

The city police operated five institutions, while the Asociación Protectora de Hijos de Agentes de Policía y Bomberos de la Capital [Protective Association of Sons of Police and Firemen of the Capital] subsidized a small home for eighty boys. By this time the Sociedad Damas de Caridad de San Vicente de Paul [Charity Ladies of St. Vincent de Paul] maintained five homes for parturient women along with the San José orphanage. The Patronato de la Infancia had a series of colonies and schools for retarded children, as well as the San Martín orphanage. The Argentine Navy operated a home for boys and girls, while a series of additional religious institutions had been founded. Almost all of these organizations received either national or provincial subsidies ranging from 784,270 pesos for the Comisión Asesora de Asilos y Hospitales Regionales [Advisory Commission on Asylums and Regional Hospitals] to 120,000 pesos for the Patronato de la Infancia and 1,900 pesos for the Sociedad Hijas del Divino Salvador [Society of Daughters of the Divine Savior], who still operated a religious retreat and quasi jail for women called the Casa de Ejercicios [House of Spiritual Exercises]. In the 1930s as in the 1920s it remained clear that any government that desired to replace or operate these facilities would need extraordinary financial resources and a strong political will. And, curiously enough, the demands by feminists for equal access to advanced education for women ultimately reduced the pool of women who traditionally served as volunteer philanthropists.[47]

Quantifying Subsidies for Private Child Welfare Charities

Although politicians and philanthropists made no effort to conceal the annual scramble for national, provincial, and municipal subsidies, the specifics of financial packages rarely became public knowledge. As in any other political system where special interests receive subsidies, the nature and extent of the monies allocated have been scattered throughout extensive budgets, and the appendices changed names and defined allocations differently over time. Emilio Coni's efforts to quantify subsidies in 1918 only related to the city of Buenos Aires, and the effort in 1933 by the Patronato Nacional de Menores depended on the willingness of groups to provide information rather than searching through printed budgets. Furthermore, provincial and municipal governments received national subsidies for welfare activities, which they redistributed to local groups. Thus it is impossible to develop a consistent series on subsidies at any level, and all evidence is partial.

An examination of several early-twentieth-century budgets for the municipality of Buenos Aires indicated how directly the city responded to the demands by welfare and immigrant groups. In 1908 it accorded the Patronato de la Infancia 42,000 pesos, but it also gave subsidies to the Casa del Niño (10,000 pesos), the Escuelas Evangélicas Argentina [Argentine Evangelical Schools] (8,000 pesos), the Sociedad Escuelas y Patronatos [Society for Schools and Protection] (2,000 pesos), and the Sociedad Protectora del Colegio Sirio Argentino [Protective Society of the Syrian-Argentine High School] (115 pesos). That same year the victims of an earthquake in Italy received a massive donation of 20,000 pesos, while funerals for municipal employees were accorded 10,000 pesos. Furthermore a series of neighborhood organizations, including those that handed out food and clothing to the poor, received direct subsidies, while others benefited from tax free status in lieu of subsidy.[48]

The province of Tucumán, a poorer community but one endowed with income from the sugarcane industry, offered provincial subsidies to welfare organizations. Between 1900 and 1939, the costs of maintaining the police increased from 415,788 pesos to 3,162,080, while welfare subsidies increased at about the same rate—from 21,280 pesos to 158,200. These subventions were awarded to a variety of recipients including a provincial Society of Beneficence, the Children's Hospital as well as local hospitals outside the capital city, the Conferencias de San Vincente de Paul and other religious groups, a school milk program [Gotas de Leche], and the women's jail (run by a religious order). Interestingly, despite the growth of the large Jewish and Arabic-speaking communities, unlike in Buenos Aires municipality Tucumán awarded no provincial subsidies for non-Catholic welfare groups. Nevertheless, immigrant mutual aid societies such as the Societá Italiana di Unione e Mututo Socorro [Italian Society of Union and Mutual Aid] and the Sociedad Española de S. M. de Concepción [Spanish Society of Our Lady of Concepción] along with other groups sought legal recognition but no subsidies.[49]

On the national level, the landscape was quite different from that of Tucumán. In 1910, for example, over one hundred groups from all over the country sent requests for subsidies to the national government. Although many religious groups petitioned for help, other entities such as the Escuelas Gratuitas para Obreros [Free Schools for Laborers], the Patronato de la Infancia of Salta, and the Sociedad Nacional del Kindergarten [National Society of Kindergarten] asked for government aid. On the official list that year, in addition to schools and hospitals, were fifty-seven asylums, mostly for women and children; ninety groups, many of whom provided child welfare such as the Asociación Protectora de Niños Desválidos de la Sección 19 de Policía [Protective Association of Destitute Children of Police Section 19] (Buenos Aires); the Patronato de la Infancia de Flores (a Buenos Aires neighborhood), a building for the Sociedad Damas Protectoras de la Infancia del Río Cuarto (Córdoba) [Ladies' Society for Child Protection of Río Cuarto], and the Sociedad Madres Cristianas de Tucumán [Christian Mothers of Tucumán]. Many of these allocations were noted as *al año*, or predetermined yearly subsidies, mostly to pay for salaries and fixed costs.[50]

By 1920 the organization of the national budget had changed and subsidies to welfare groups became part of Annex M. The new format made it clear that the Society of Beneficence had become the principal recipient of subsidies with an allocation of more than 5 million pesos. Nevertheless, aid provided throughout the country in the category of "Beneficence" was divided between the national capital and territories and individual provinces. Within the first category, institutions as diverse as the Masonic Orphanage, the House of Jesus, and various children's homes, all got a portion of 776,300 pesos. This did not include hospitals or schools, which were usually listed separately. Meanwhile, welfare institutions in the province of Buenos Aires received more than 90,000 pesos, and institutions in the province of Corrientes got even more—93,100 pesos—because provincial hospitals were included in this category. The national government awarded a grand total of more than 12 million pesos to "Beneficence," including the 5 million pesos for the Society of Beneficence. The unevenness of these allocations that had enraged Emilio Coni several years earlier still prevailed.[51]

In 1930 Congress did not publish a budget, and the next glimpse of subsidies came in 1933 after General Agustín P. Justo assumed government under an alliance of independent socialists, Anti-Yrigoyen radicals, and old-time liberals who supported the formation of a welfare state. That year a wide range of welfare institutions received new subsidies under Annex L, "Trabajos Públicos," or Public Works. These funds underwrote the construction of new facilities or the repair of existing ones such as a home of *niños débiles* [physically or mentally weak children], several grants to local Societies of Beneficence for maternity hospitals, and lactaria. Philanthropic groups such as the Sociedad Damas de Misericordia [Society of Ladies of Mercy] of Mercedes, the province of San Luis, and the Patronato de Menores of Santa Rosa in La Pampa also received government aid in the form of a lump sum for general purposes.

At this time, however, Congress divided the subsidies in a new way: private social assistance received just over 8 million pesos, and social assistance under government control totaled more than 17 million pesos. In the category of private social assistance, the national capital and territories got 2.7 million pesos out of the 8.3 million pesos given to groups throughout the country. The Society of Beneficence came under the other category, and all annual subsidies remained unreported. Instead the budget announced only new or extraordinary subsidies.[52]

After the Concordancia arranged the election of General Agustín Justo, the system of collective benevolence began to change in fundamental ways. The national government became a more vigorous actor and sought to rationalize scattered welfare subventions and develop clearer national policies. Until that time, however, the politics of benevolence and the critical role of the Society of Beneficence, the Patronato de la Infancia, and collective benevolence still held sway. Throughout Argentina, women banded together to provide the social assistance ignored both by the state and by mutual aid societies.

As women joined charities, philanthropic activities not only came under the scrutiny of the local, provincial, and national authorities but they also received funding that ranged from a token amount to a substantial portion of their institutions' operating budgets. In this way female-headed child philanthropies became a keystone of evolving social policies. Just as feminists had become principal actors in the demand for equal civil, legal, and social process, the petitions of philanthropic women became central to the process of promoting social policies at the national level. At the same time, local communities recognized philanthropic women as important to the cohesiveness of the groups. Until these social values became less important to educated women, or national government began to take over child welfare, the social status for philanthropic women continued to improve through the performance of charity.

CHAPTER 3

Performing Child Welfare

PHILANTHROPY AND FEMINISM FROM

THE DAMAS TO EVA PERÓN

Philanthropy in Argentina provided important benefits to both patrons and clients. As Natalie Zemon Davis has pointed out in the case of female philanthropists in early-twentieth-century Islamic countries, the act of charity had both political and social implications. Both donors and patrons could obtain prestige for themselves and their communities, and "charitable institutions also created and consolidated ties between patrons and clients, in the neighborhood and further afield." Moreover, such institutions performed an important role by "defining boundaries of community and gender and in controlling and classifying populations."[1] Such acts became ritualized in a series of performances. In Argentina, the performance of female philanthropy began with the damas of the Society of Beneficence, but they were not the only women aiding street children, orphans, and mothers. Women had many reasons to become involved in welfare and their concepts of benevolence varied tremendously. When analyzed as a group, their combined activities provided a blueprint of social policies for the subsequent formation of a Peronist welfare state based upon concerns for children and mothers.

Take for example the unknown and unheralded Damas del Socorro [Ladies of Aid]. Founded in 1880 during the revolution that led to the federalization of Buenos Aires and the nationalization of the Society of Beneficence, women banded together to help the families of wounded National Guardsmen. Directed by Julia N. de Huerto and Eloisa P. de Wehely, the group initially consisted of 526 prominent women who paid fifty pesos per month for the privilege of helping the wounded. They divided themselves initially into four committees to cover the city of Buenos Aires. When their own funds ran out, they ran raffles and went to their friends to cover the remaining expenses including medical costs for the wounded and food and clothing for the families of the patriots. All of this occurred in the midst of revolution, and the women went to the trenches to provide aid and sustenance to the troops. In the following weeks the women provided aid to more than one thousand families according to need. As one representative noted: "Aid was not distributed equally as we sometimes encountered misery in its most extreme forms. It was not unusual to find a family with two or three adults and seven or eight children of all ages in one single room, humid and murky; often made of wood with a zinc roof, without furniture, beds and some even without sufficient clothing to cover them."[2] Philanthropists became particularly concerned by the sight of women and young children who had not eaten in days because their husbands or fathers were wounded or dead. Elite women gave out sewing machines to poor women. Once they completed their task, the Ladies of Aid published their records noting who had received aid and how much. Mothers and widows had been the principal recipients.

The Ladies banded together initially because of patriotic sentiments. But as they became more involved with the people they helped, poverty and the needs of poor mothers and children quickly informed their understandings of patriotism—typical experiences of upper-class philanthropic women who did not work outside the home and who began their philanthropy amid emergency situations, often prompted by religious sentiments; by family connections that led to their invitation to participate in philanthropic groups; or by their own desire to help solve public problems in a socially acceptable fashion. Their clients, who were often much poorer and less socially acceptable than themselves, engendered few feelings of class solidarity. This was seen in the public ceremonies used to convey the spectacle of charity. The cinematographer Max Glücksmann's early silent documentary of the women's committee of the Patronato de la Infancia giving out clothing to poor children in 1913 shows how these stern women, in the midst of philanthropic spectacle, could bully young boys who did not wait patiently in line for their modest portion of clothing. In other documentaries filmed by Glücksmann, performance involved female philanthropists bravely trekking to the muddy suburbs where poor mothers and children awaited a hot meal.

Still photographs reveal other facets of class tension: picturing, for example, poor children with uniforms to show their status as orphans, or scenes of charity campaigns when well-dressed women took to the streets to solicit contributions. In these Victorian- and Edwardian-style pictures, elite women were never photographed embracing a poor child or displaying emotions of caring. Such a spectacle eventually became a hallmark of photos of Eva Perón, the wife of President Juan Perón.[3]

Most of the pictures preserved of children aided by upper-class charities, regardless of religious or collective sponsorship, are bereft of markers of individual identities.[4] These wards usually dressed in uniforms and lived in large dormitories where each child received the same amount of space, bedding, and clothing. In public, the children looked like a miniature army of uniformed waifs. The orphans performed charity in their own way by going out into the streets of Buenos Aires and other cities collecting funds in *alcancías*, or piggy banks. Often these alcancías had distinctive shapes to inform the public as to which charity was soliciting funds.

In a book entitled *Cien Años de Amor* [One Hundred Years of Love (1993)] celebrating the hundredth anniversary of the founding of the Patronato de la Infancia, the only children who do not appear in uniform are waifs awaiting admission. This was done to show the differences before and after admission. Employees and individuals associated with the Patronato undoubtedly showed some love and caring to individual children, but the public portrait presented order and uniformity.[5]

Until the 1950s the files of the children entering the Society of Beneficence rarely included pictures. After fingerprinting was developed in Argentina, almost all documents of children admitted by either the Society of Beneficence or any of the schools or reformatories administered by Argentine government agencies included a fingerprint for identification purposes. Additionally, while under the supervision of the Society, children wore identification medallions with their matriculation numbers. Although these items clearly identified the individual, they reveal far less than a photograph and offer a stark contrast to the typical sentimental family portraits of children of the middle and upper classes, including the offspring of feminists. In this manner, orphans performed their lack of identity.[6]

Catholic Damas

Despite the political inroads of liberalism, the Catholic Church sponsored or became affiliated with most but not all orphanages and homes for street children and orphans. Since the majority of Argentines and immigrants were Catholic, the presence of Catholic women and their child welfare

philanthropies does not seem unusual, although the Argentine liberal state had taken great pains to secularize the country. The growth of urban labor movements inspired by anarchism, socialism, and, after 1918, communism produced fears of class conflicts. In 1906 socially concerned Catholics attended the Congreso Católico Argentino-Uruguayo [Argentine-Uruguayan Catholic Congress] held in Montevideo, Uruguay, where Catholic women received invitations to speak for the first time. Among the participants, Celia Lapalma de Emery, a prominent supporter of Catholic women's philanthropic activities, offered her views of Catholic-linked philanthropy. Her speech, another type of performance, focused on how the personal tenderness that she and other Christian mothers felt toward their own children potentially inhibited them from participating in public activities exposing them to immorality and confusing ideas. She believed that loving one's own children differed profoundly from loving an abandoned child.

Lapalma de Emery identified contemporary social problems as a combination of the plight of the working classes mixed with the influence of socialism and liberalism. To neutralize them, she proposed Catholic action in which all Catholic mothers needed to participate. Within the parameters of existing Catholic child welfare activities, she mentioned the Society of Beneficence as well as the Patronato de la Infancia and specific Catholic organizations. But their combined presence only represented a tiny proportion of all Catholics in Argentina. More women needed to be recruited. Lapalma de Emery believed that Catholics should also focus on aiding the working woman. She defined 1906 as the moment of confrontation between religious and secular authorities, one that *cristianos sin miedo* [Christians without fear] needed to form an army to fight and that mothers needed to join. For Lapalma de Emery, helping street children formed a critical part of a modern religious crusade.[7] She directly linked mothers and children to the glory of the Argentine state; these crusades of love inextricably allied them to the Catholic Church. Performing charity as a crusade became "the exercise of a duty imposed by God." In her description of such Christian charity, she mentioned names from among the most elite women in the country, many of whom belonged to more than one charitable organization.[8]

Like the damas of the Society of Beneficence, Lapalma de Emery quickly criticized insufficient state funding for poor children, and her own biography demonstrated how she performed charity. In 1908 she replaced the noted feminist socialist Gabriela Laperrière de Coni, wife of Emilio Coni, as honorary (i.e., unpaid) inspector of factories. Both women deplored the situation of women and children in the factories of Buenos Aires. Lapalma de Emery also particularly chided officials for not giving defenders of minors sufficient funding to prevent the incarceration of homeless street children. The pitiful sight of "this sad portion of our future citizens . . . without homes and without affection, without help and without education, is so sad that one cannot look at them without choking one's voice."[9] She clearly saw state aid to street children as essential. In the meantime, private charity could deal with poor mothers and their families.

At the Primer Congreso Nacional de Asistencia Social [First National Conference of Social Assistance], sponsored by the Argentine Ministry of Foreign Relations and Religion in 1933, Cármen P. de Nelson and Angela S. de Cremata further elucidated the theories of Lapalma de Emery. They identified themselves as "those called upon by public opinion to fulfill the functions of mothers for those who have none. We propose, therefore, the formation of an organization with the sweet name of Social Maternity already given by the erudite Prof. Mrs. Celia L. Lapalma de Emery." With this announcement they suggested sponsoring a girls' home where minors could be rehabilitated. They noted that it should not be too expensive because a place too comfortable "runs the risk of making them too used to a situation that life will not offer them." Above all, they wanted a modest place where there were only a few wards.[10] Once again, Catholic women activists tried to enlist the aid of other Catholic women in the service of childhood and motherhood. This campaign foreshadowed Eva Perón's efforts to enlist women in the performance of politics in the name of her husband Juan.

The more traditional attitudes of the damas of the Society of Beneficence toward their charges rarely appeared publicly. The damas ran institutions rather than campaigns, and they often expressed their attitudes in private or through their attorneys. However, they implicitly recognized the impossibility of providing the love and nurturing necessary for the well-being of their charges. For one thing, their institutions housed too many children. Furthermore, foundlings who survived infancy went into foster homes where their status could range from that of servant to beloved adoptee. The Society's concern for the fate of children entering private homes reflected the way that they collected statistics on foster care. Perhaps in an effort to protect themselves against accusations that most girls in care ended up serving as maids, the damas consistently claimed that foster parents treated the great majority of their wards as family members. Until 1912, they simply listed the numbers of children sent into care.[11] Thereafter, the damas devised a new classification scheme to reflect how many children had been taken in as sons or daughters [hijos] as opposed to servants. According to their revised accounts, out of 703 children sent out into foster care, 613 received care as hijos, 60 became companions, and only 4 ended up as servants.[12] In fact, the damas could not guarantee that the children would be treated as promised and they did not have enough social workers to keep track of all the children under their control.

In 1933, the Primera Conferencia Nacional sobre Infancia Abandonada y Delincuente [First National Conference on Abandoned and Delinquent Children] invited specialists who proposed unifying legislation dealing with child welfare along with professionals who aimed to create the basis for new educational establishments. Sra. Rosa del Campo de Botet, secretary of the Society of Beneficence, spoke to the former issue. She began by describing her affection for the Society, her devotion to its traditional activities, and the fervor with which she helped the downtrodden. She found it a great comfort "to do good deeds within the ideals of Christian faith, love for one's neighbor, and devotion to the nation."[13] She then went on to describe her activities within the Society, ones that filled legal requisites as well as providing succor. She criticized the civil code's silence regarding adoption by arguing that it had limited possibilities for many of the orphans who might have been taken in by married women and, further, that it caused emotional pain for children taken into care. She told the story of a young girl who discovered her parents not to be her biological kin and thus felt shame that no one would want to marry her under such circumstances. Campo de Botet argued fervently that foster parents needed access to the same legal rights as biological ones. She concluded by linking the Society directly to political groups that favored adoption as a legal process.[14] In this way she demonstrated that the damas could perform their politics in the legislature as well as in the vernacular of Christian charity.

According to the Society's logic, and in contrast to some women who argued that more orphanages and homes solved the problem, true caring could only occur in a family where children had legal connections to their guardians. They believed love needed to be privatized and protected by the law. For those reasons, the damas urged the state to legalize adoption so that all parents could protect their offspring against the social prejudices associated with a lack of family and status. While the Society of Beneficence advocated adoption legislation, the damas still insisted on their right to operate their establishments. They truly believed that they offered the best care possible for their wards given the political climate that opposed adoption. Furthermore, they, like many but not all philanthropic groups, constructed huge, impersonal institutions that reaffirmed their own power.

Not all Catholic women believed in the value of the Society of Beneficence and its strategies for the poor. Several examples demonstrate this
diversity. The Sociedad Damas de Caridad de San Vicente de Paul opened
day schools for children with working parents. Between the three schools
already operating in the 1880s, they provided day care for thirteen hundred
children, thus reducing the need to abandon children.[15] Similarly, not all
Catholic women performed charity in the name of religion. The Casa del
Niño, founded in 1910 by Julia S. de Curto, operated specifically to house
street children of both sexes. Allied neither with the Society nor with feminists or the church, Julia and her sister, both prominent women from a
family of educators, worked diligently to rehabilitate children who got into
trouble. Remitted to them by the police and defenders of minors, by parents who could not handle their children, and by people who found children living on the streets, minors inhabited a building that, unlike the
orphanages, allowed them to go in and out at will. The children attended
public schools and did not have to wear uniforms. Furthermore, the number of children living at the Casa del Niño, which eventually opened other
facilities, was relatively small. The idea of offering conditions similar to
those found in family environments where relatively few children resided
was revolutionary for the times, and it clearly reflected more middle-class
values than did the grand orphanages. And, by the 1930s, the smaller home
became the new model for institutional care as large orphanages became
less needed and more criticized.[16]

In the 1930s new groups of Catholic women associated with Acción
Católica began to provide nuance in ways that distanced themselves from
the Catholic damas who ran orphanages. Rather than focus on orphaned
children, these women discussed the ideals of Catholic motherhood and the
need to supervise children's activities, particularly adolescent girls. The
membership of these groups included women from all walks of life committed to ideals of social amelioration guided by the Catholic Church. In
1937 they changed their official name from the Liga de Damas Católicas
[League of Catholic Ladies] to the Asociación de Mujeres de Acción Católica
[Association of Catholic Action Women]. Thus by the 1930s two distinct
groups of Catholic women engaged in child issues: the elite damas who ran
charities and the more diverse middle-class group of *mujeres* [women] who
wanted to nurture the traditional Catholic family in Argentina.[17] These
women advocated distinct strategies: while one group (the damas) contested men and operated orphanages, the mujeres staunchly remained sub-
ordinate to the men in their organization and did not engage directly in

child welfare work. Together they formed a powerful Catholic discourse on children, with each performing charity in a distinct way.

Feminists and Child Welfare

Although more traditional upper-class women stood by and watched over poor children, middle- and upper-class feminists opposed all orphanages. Their disapproval meant that they had almost no contact with orphans and street children and their daily lives. The contrast between the female philanthropists and the Argentine middle-class feminists was striking because these coteries performed their child welfare policies with very different styles. Although such groups as the Society of Beneficence aided orphans and poor women, Argentine feminists, in line with other Latin American feminists, devoted an extensive amount of energy to improving the legal and social conditions of all mothers and to providing education for all children so that biological mothers could help their own children and thereby avoid the need to abandon them or place them in institutional settings. In their own way, and neither supporting adoption nor acknowledging the Society's support for it, feminists advocated the privatization of child welfare under the supervision of caring mothers.

Feminists also advanced notions of scientific modern motherhood that placed high value on social motherhood that led to wise mothers and healthy adults and often bolstered the Latin American eugenics movement that favored policies such as prenuptial wedding examinations.[18] Many of the first Argentine feminists trained as public health physicians as well as educators, and they served as role models as both educated professionals and teachers to other women. Lowering infant mortality rates, from the feminist perspective, supported the birth of future citizens and gave women more control over their children. At the same time feminists supported legislation to give women equal pay and equal access to education. Their political campaigns included child welfare as a component of mothering and made no distinctions between political and social feminism.[19]

Feminists' views did not fit into traditional upper-class notions of charity. Instead, they reached out to women of all classes to help them solve personal and family problems as modern individuals. Rather than dealing with the women as individual cases, the first generation of feminists, those who began to profess feminism before 1920, preferred that the state perform this task by offering more equal rights for married women. They performed child welfare indirectly as proponents of new socially encom-

how "radical" are feminist flus?

passing laws empowering mothers. Feminists would divide on this issue in the 1940s, however, as the second generation of feminists used notions of social work and case studies to help children, with or without parents.

For the first generation of feminists, children became future citizens at the same time that their existence helped women fulfill their social, civic, and reproductive destinies. Children provided legitimation for feminist entry into public life. As Asunción Lavrin put it, "Public health and child care constituted a unique arena where feminists could make a case for women's special role in any scheme of social change. . . . Children's health was one of the most important issues raised by physicians and by feminists, who found in the care of children a key source of legitimation for women's emergence in the public arena."[20] Feminists believed that mothers were better suited to help children than were orphanages, and medical science and feminist principles provided the educational and legal strategies to achieve that goal.

One of the first female physicians, Elvira Rawson de Dellepiane, believed that medically defined hygiene offered the ideal method to advance the biological and social missions central to modern motherhood. Her doctoral thesis, published in 1892, began by contrasting women's reproductive role with their absence of civil rights: "Women are destined to fulfill the most important role in the reproduction of the species. [Nevertheless] they have a delicate constitution and have been reduced by their delicate mission and by customs to carry out a secondary public role. They are deprived of the freedoms enjoyed by the other sex, forced to suffocate their passions, provided a constantly insufficient education . . . [They] are deprived of exercise and confronted by dangers that compromise their life and destiny. In hygiene they find the saving guide to emerge unscathed from the various stages of their evolution while maintaining the functional integrity of their organs generally and particularly those that dominate their existence, i.e. their reproductive organs."[21] When Rawson de Dellepiane discussed marriage, she perceived it as another state of evolution, one that transformed women's emotional lives. "With this act [of marriage] not only does one fulfill the sacred mandate to be fruitful and multiply, a woman develops new sentiments such as caring for her husband and motherly love, ones that purify all sentiments [and] moralize customs."[22] If poor women did not love their husbands and abandoned their children, then poverty, not the women, was the cause. Only a noble society could resolve the problem.[23]

The biblical reference in the section on marriage offered Rawson de Dellepiane the opportunity to both acknowledge and contest Catholic views of abstinence and celibacy as women's mostly spiritual condition. In a latter part of the chapter she argued that single, celibate, unmarried women died earlier than married mothers and that poor unmarried women faced a life of libertinage and decadence. To prove her point, she examined mortality statistics for 1892 by sex and marital status and found that despite the rigors of childbirth, only 319 married women died during the year in comparison to 377 single women.[24]

Rawson de Dellepiane's long career as a feminist and freethinker enabled her to challenge the moral high ground of Catholicism through a strong feminist belief in woman's multiple missions as productive, educational, and reproductive. Trained as a physician, she also advocated educational reforms and championed political projects to promote female equality. Rawson de Dellepiane also played a pivotal role in the formulation of modern motherhood through scientific understandings of childbirth and mothering. In 1910 at the Primer Congreso Femenino Internacional de la República Argentina [First International Feminist Congress of Argentina] in Buenos Aires, she proposed the construction of residences for needy women who were pregnant or who had recently given birth. Rawson de Dellepiane obtained a declaration published by the conference that criticized foundling homes and argued that mothers, single or married, qualified for social assistance. She also proposed that new laws permit investigations of paternity and give all women the right to be guardians.[25]

Rawson de Dellepiane's philosophy conformed to the Argentine feminist beliefs that needy women and their children needed to be defended and these principles authorized feminists to empower women. In 1914 Raquel Camaña, a well-known educator and feminist, published an article entitled "Femeninidad." In it, she directly linked motherhood to democracy as well as to the need for mothers to care for their own children: "When a woman realizes she is about to become a mother, she will understand that it is her duty to nourish this future child not only with pure air, proper foods, and appropriate exercise, but also that she must mold this little soul with spiritual tranquility, good character, wholesome happiness, and with never ending optimism; that she should avoid the consequences of downtrodden spirits, anger, and nervous crisis. And under the influence of the laws of love, she will improve herself as well as her child. This is the solution of the human condition, one that will create a vibrant democracy more important than political or industrial democracy."[26] Argentine feminists were so supportive of scientific motherhood and its promise to reduce infant mortality that they banded together in 1911 to found the Liga de los Derechos de la

Mujer y el Niño [League for Women's and Children's Rights], and the following year organized the first Congreso Nacional del Niño [National Child Congress].

The principal newspapers of Buenos Aires covered the speeches and official vists of the delegates, and on November 16, 1912, pictures of the organizers appeared in *Caras y Caretas*, perhaps the most widely read middle-class magazine of the time. At the 1912 congress Rawson de Dellepiane openly opposed the efforts of male public health physicians to set up homes attached to hospitals for recent mothers. Instead she argued that mothers needed to return to their own homes and recuperate there. Of course, this argument presumed that they had an appropriate home to live in and thus medical aid should be provided on an outpatient basis. She and other feminists had more confidence in women's innate mothering abilities than in the ability of male doctors or orphanages.[27]

The comments of the educator Dr. Ernestina López de Nelson in an article entitled "Nuevos ideales filantrópicos," published in 1914, clearly spelled out the early feminist position on orphanages. She argued that street children became a public concern because abandonment led to infant mortality, degeneracy, pauperism, and delinquency, "the four great phantasms of modern societies." However, she believed in a new kind of philanthropy, one that did not come from elites but rather from "collective and democratic endeavors."[28] This proper education of parents freed from class prejudices would ensure the well-being of their children and necessitate rights for all married women.

By the time the first Congreso Americano del Niño [Pan American Child Congress] took place in Buenos Aires in 1916, the battle lines over mothers and children had been drawn by female and male philanthropists, by feminists, and by male doctors and lawyers. Presided over by the feminist Dr. Julieta Lantieri, the congress cordially (although with intrinsic distrust) invited distinguished Argentine male lawyers and physicians to head the sections on law, hygiene, infant psychology, and assistance and protection for mothers.[29] All of those present at the congress agreed that legal reforms needed to tackle problems of street children and juvenile delinquency, and further, that better hygiene and greater understanding of child development would lower infant mortality rates and promote better-adjusted children. The category of assistance and protection for mothers was the area of greatest conflict because it revealed strong gender disagreements as well as tensions between secular and religious institutions (schools, orphanages, and hospitals). These sections, nevertheless, defined the basic interests that both women and men shared in the child rights movements at that time, and the feminists sought to reveal the inappropriate views of their opponents.

Groups labeled Social Assistance and Sociology examined the mother-child link. The former addressed how to protect maternity and childhood through protective labor laws, the reduction of infant mortality, efforts to help abandoned children, the elimination of child labor, and the formation of clubs for both mothers and children. The latter examined the social factors that affected these issues, including the role of orphanages, poverty, state protection of mothers and children, the sociology of public education, eugenics, and the value of temperance societies.[30] Official findings offered recommendations to establish special schools for physically weak children, provide sex education for adults as well as children, create breast milk dispensaries, and promote laws to reduce alcohol, ether, cocaine, and morphine consumption. Asunción Lavrin described the 1916 meeting as "a departure point for considering the state as responsible for the protection of women and children. It reflected the concerns of social reformers in several walks of life and their convictions about the vulnerability of the 'weaker' members of the social body."[31]

This meeting also received extensive newspaper coverage. Some controversial speeches, however, were not covered by the newspapers. Among them was the Uruguayan physician Paulina Luisi's exhortation to advocate sterilization for genetically and mentally unfit individuals as well as her promotion of abortion on demand for married women forced to submit to the sexual demands of their husbands. Luisi supported her views by arguing that children born to defective parents, as well as those conceived in violence, would never be strong enough to survive the Darwinian struggle for survival. Although she believed that the best way to deal with these issues linked personal responsibility to reproduction, her talk probably shocked both feminists and anti-feminists for its specific mention of women's right to decide whether or not to carry a fetus to term. Her strategy ultimately advocated women's need to control their reproductive activities at the cost of advocating state-sponsored eugenics laws.[32]

After the child congress, Elvira Rawson de Dellepiane shifted her desire from providing homes for parturient women to participating in the kindergarten movement. She ran a preschool in the working-class neighborhood of La Boca. In this way she performed child welfare through education. She made all kinds of suggestions to the Consejo Nacional de Educación [National Board of Education] because it funded the kindergarten. She wanted baths installed with hot and cold water so that neighborhood mothers could bathe their children at the school, but funding was not approved. Other goals she identified included Spanish for nonnative speakers, hygiene classes, the need to instill concepts of nation and fraternity, and better manners. In effect she wanted to teach in school what should have been taught at home. Her plans went unheeded.[33]

Sara Justo, another feminist interested in children's issues, was associated with *Unión y Labor*, which appeared from 1909–1913. This journal supported the educational strategies expounded by the world-renowned educator María Montessori. In line with this educational philosophy, Justo and others established their own Casa del Niño in the Barracas district of Buenos Aires, which lasted until the journal closed. There working-class children learned the Montessori method, which emphasized child creativity and independence.[34]

The differences between the feminists and the Catholic damas proved to be irreconcilable. The Catholic damas wanted to keep their institutions and support private adoption, and the Catholic mujeres wanted all women to be good Catholic mothers. In contrast, the feminists wanted all women to have their social rights as mothers guaranteed by the state, not the Catholic Church. Perhaps because of their distinctive approaches to child welfare and religion, women remained at the forefront of all types of campaigns to promote state help for poor children. Interestingly, charity groups and the municipality of Buenos Aires eventually constructed the shelters for parturient women and mothers with infants, as did the Patronato de la Infancia. The city also developed institutes of puericulture to teach scientific child rearing. And, in 1927, the Society of Beneficence with great fanfare opened the Maternity Institute within the Hospital Rivadavia. The first of several such institutions, it included a residential refuge for single and poor mothers as well as the Asilo de Lactantes [Nursing Mothers' Ward], a ward where mothers could live while nursing or, if unable to nurse, have access to wet nurses, usually other female residents. The Institute also had a legal office, principally for encouraging marriage.[35] National government subsidies paid for most of the building's costs.

The fact that it was the Society of Beneficence damas rather than the feminists who opened the institute testified to the ability of elite women to obtain governmental funding. It also testified to the fact that by the 1920s the feminists directed more of their energies either to reforms of the civil code or to female suffrage. Furthermore it indicated that women who did not have professions found it easier to organize and manage large institutional endeavors compared to the feminists who often had jobs as well as their own political agendas. Indeed, one consequence of the rise of professional women was the loss of female control of child welfare organizations subsequently organized by the state.

Damas of the Collectivities

At this point it is relevant to add to the comparison of feminists and female philanthropists those women who engaged in child welfare due to their interest and links to an immigrant or religious *colectividad*. Many such groups existed, and it would be difficult to define a "typical" experience for these women. Nevertheless, their presence in Argentina had tremendous implications for child welfare projects.

Such was certainly the case of the Patronato Español [Spanish Assistance Society], which arose from the efforts of female members of the Sociedad Español de la Virgen del Pilar [Spanish Society of the Virgin of Pilar]. In September 1912 these women formed the Comisión de Damas Españolas [Commission of Spanish Ladies] consisting of many of the most well-known, upper-class women of Spanish origin. Members of this group immediately changed their name to the Comisión de Damas Protectoras de Inmigrantes Españolas [Commission of Ladies to Protect Immigrant Spanish Women] and they identified their task as helping young Spanish women in need who were far from their paternal home. Led by Sra. Isabela B. de Sáenz, and later by Sra. Pilar López de Ayala de Durán, Sra. Luisa Canale de Cibrián, Sra. Presentación Ortiz de Bayona, and María Caparrós de Llorente, they met once a week for several years under the supervision of a priest, Father Masferrer, who rarely intervened.[36]

During the early years members of the Patronato Español constantly kept in touch with contacts in Spain to obtain support and to link the children with their heritage. In this way the women maintained a national-ethnic identity and guarded their cultural heritage by performing child welfare. The Spanish damas often repatriated orphans to their kin in Spain. And at Christmas Spanish families in Buenos Aires donated large quantities of basic foods such as sugar, rice, and other items through contributions from Spanish-identified businesses as well as from individuals. Spanish physicians gave their services without charge.[37]

From the very beginning and for many years thereafter, Sra. Isabela Briones de Sáenz led the Patronato Español. There seemed to be no objections from the community that this woman be the visible leader of the organization. In 1930, the king of Spain granted her the Gran Cruz de Beneficencia [Great Cross of Beneficence] to reward her selfless activities. Although she stepped down from her position in 1938 to enable Doña Presentación Ortiz de Bayona to take over, Sra. Briones de Sáenz was well remembered in her community until her death in 1960.[38]

By 1918 so many girls lived in the Patronato Español's shelter that the Spanish damas decided to admit only complete orphans and reject the admission of the rest. Finally, in 1919 the Spanish damas judged their old building on Córdoba Avenue to be too small and in poor condition, and in June they purchased a religious institution in the Federico Lacroze neighborhood, thanks to the financial help of the men in the society.[39] Eventually additional purchases enabled the Patronato Español to construct a building that spanned an entire city block and stood as testimony to the power of the women of the Spanish immigrant community. It also reaffirmed that no matter how independently they performed child welfare, as women they remained submissive to the demands of the collectivity and the generosity of the men.

The Jewish female philanthropy group known as the Sociedad de Damas de Beneficencia Israelitas, or the Jewish damas also proved quite successful in their endeavors, which was no small feat in a predominantly Catholic society. Eventually they decided to open a girls' orphanage, and they were aided in their search for a suitable property by four distinguished male members of the Congregación Israelita [Israelite Congregation], the principal synagogue of Buenos Aires, specifically Hermann Goldenberg, president of Congregación Israelita, Gustavo Weil, Max Glücksmann, and S. Krämer. In 1919 Goldenberg purchased the building at auction for the women, and Gustavo Weil contributed 1,000 pesos in his wife's name. Thereafter the women always acknowledged these men and others as key benefactors at critical moments in the history of the orphanage.[40] After World War I, the expected influx of impoverished Jewish immigrants to Argentina meant that the number of children abandoned or orphaned kept increasing. By 1923 male leaders at the Congregación Israelita once again offered to help by lending 21,973 pesos without interest to construct a new building in a fashionable neighborhood.[41]

The Jewish damas raised money for the orphanage by organizing raffles, sponsoring dances and kermesses [fairs where money was raised through raffles, races, etc.], asking for donations from the Jewish communities of the interior, and collecting special donations from the wealthier members of the congregation. A frequent contributor in the early years was Max

Glücksmann, who also often held special benefit performances for the Sociedad in his movie theater. His wife Rebecca became fourth president of the Sociedad in 1914, replacing Sra. Francisca R. de Krämer whose husband helped select the site for the first orphanage.

In her role as president of the Jewish damas, Rebecca R. de Glücksmann provided unwavering assistance to the home until 1954.[42] Her lengthy administration, however, led to criticisms within the Jewish community that a select group of rich members controlled the orphanage for the satisfaction of their own status. This meant that collections and donations in Buenos Aires beyond the circle of founders and those who attended the parties at the fancy hotels rarely met either needs or expectations, and the Jewish damas had to hire a male representative to travel to the interior to collect money from the Jewish communities scattered throughout Argentina.[43] However, well into the 1950s no one stepped up to oppose Sra. de Glücksmann, and she continued to run the organization with the unpaid help of hundreds of women and men. The case of the Jewish community demonstrates that the status affirmation obtained by Sra. de Glücksmann was recognized, and some resented the fact that others could not achieve it as well.

Despite the elitist accusations lodged by the Jewish community against the board of the orphanage, the women's group contributed to the welfare of the Jewish community through many venues and helped define it in a public way. As their motto, and repeated in each report, they adopted the following words: "We engage in welfare work not for charity, but for human solidarity. Poor people who are helped by us in their moment of need tomorrow will be able to give aid to others. And, as a consequence of these principles, no one should ask for help they don't need so that they end up making charity a vice." The Jewish damas followed this principle when they shared the expenses of sewing machines and small business loans to women with the philanthropic Ezrah Society. Besides sewing layette clothing for poor pregnant women, the Jewish damas also attended to Jewish immigrants of both sexes who arrived from Europe during and after the war. Among these immigrants, thirty female Ukrainian orphans had arrived by boat from Europe. Their presence at the orphanage in the 1920s led the women to request double the annual contribution of each patron as well as to plan the construction of a new wing on the property.[44]

Led by prominent women, the Jewish community joined other Argentine groups in the battle against infant mortality and child abandonment. The Jewish women did so by imitating the Society of Beneficence. They also

argued that the Jewish community needed to support the orphanage; otherwise the girls would be baptized as Christian if sent to the Society of Beneficence. In 1926 the plight of Jewish children in Catholic orphanages still
preoccupied the Jewish community. Members of the board of the boys'
orphanage met with Rabbi men on July 18 to discuss the situation. They
estimated that approximately three hundred Jewish children lived in Catholic orphanages, but it would be very difficult both politically and financially to retrieve them. To rescue the children, Jewish orphanages had to
pay for each child's room and board at fifteen to twenty pesos per month for
their entire stay in other institutions. The Jewish orphanages could barely
pay for children in their care, let alone rescue others.[45] Thus for the Jewish
damas as well as their male counterparts, their efforts to keep Jewish children in Jewish orphanages helped keep the colectividad intact.

For Jewish elite women, charity work offered several attractions. First,
their good deeds acknowledged and reaffirmed their conception of Jewish
solidarity in Buenos Aires and provided the women with social status un-
achievable in other ways. Second, they often organized programs along
with their husbands, and their presence as married couples further reinforced their status within the community. Finally, they created a social
space within the Jewish community that paralleled that of the Catholic-
focused Society of Beneficence. Jewish women who copied these groups
legitimated their presence and performed charity in some of the most elite
social spaces in Buenos Aires, particularly the Plaza Hotel and the Alvear
Palace Hotel. The fact that these Jewish women had no problems sponsoring activities at elegant hotels indicated that high society in Buenos Aires
accepted this Jewish women's group at a time when anti-Semitism was
becoming increasingly visible.[46]

Like the Society of Beneficence, other Jewish female philanthropists
extended their activities during the 1930s. Their expansion, however, resulted from different reasons. In the midst of the world depression, Jewish
immigrant women banded together to found a home called the Hogar Infantil Israelita [Jewish Infants' Home] to provide day care for children of
poor mothers. On the surface the infants' home appeared to be a competi-
tor to the Jewish girls' orphanage, but in fact it evolved into a multipurpose
organization that operated a day-care center and kindergarten for poor
Jewish children that lasted until the 1980s. The Hogar, designed as a temporary place to house or school young children with ill or working parents,
enabled Jewish children to stay off the streets and avoid the scrutiny of
police or other public officials.

The founders, Rosa G. Gierson (who within several years became president and, like Rebeca de Glücksmann served for many years), Ana S. de Gaversky, Tany B. de Svartz, Esther de Fischer, Sofía de Milleritsky, Paulina Goldfard, and Eva Priluk, planned to admit the children individually, and Esther de Fischer served as the first president. The kindergarten received children between the ages of four and six, and a school bus picked them up each day. Within one year, the home provided day-care facilities for seventy children under the age of six, mostly during the day, at their establishment in the Flores neighborhood of Buenos Aires. To help poor families, the home advertised in Yiddish pamphlets. The women accepted Jewish children from the interior provinces to justify the donations solicited there; they even gave monthly contributions to the local police home for children.[47]

Since the children had legitimate parents most stayed at the institution only while parents were hospitalized, or they attended the day-care facilities as needed. When individuals approached the group seeking a child to adopt, these women quickly noted that they did not deal with such issues. Indeed, no Jewish institution caring for female children sent them into foster care or adoption, although the Jewish boys' orphanage occasionally sent boys into apprenticeship situations.

Like the Jewish damas, the Idischer Frauenhilfsverein [Yiddish Women's Group] raised money through dances at fancy hotels, but more often events were held on the grounds of the Hogar, a tactic that saved them from much of the criticism of upper-class behavior leveled at the Jewish damas.[48] In fact, there never seemed to be any accusations of elitism lodged against these women.

In 1933 members of the Hogar acknowledged the need for an infant dormitory [sala cuna], and even before they added one to the property they began to hire wet nurses to help working mothers "whose husbands have taken up drinking and cannot support the family."[49] Unlike the Jewish girls' orphanage, these children did not remain at the home until they reached the age of majority. Instead they returned to family members as soon as the problems had been solved.

Three years later Ana de Gavensky became president of the Hogar. By then the institution cared for 100 to 130 children daily, and two buses transported the children to and from their homes to the center. At that point the Hogar owned no buildings and relied on rentals, thus women's performance of charity rested solely on the provision of services. Yet in the midst of economic uncertainty, the Hogar began a building campaign that continued into the 1940s. Eventually they purchased a building at Monte 2150.

By 1938 the missions of the women who operated the Hogar Infantil Israelita seemed to be very similar to those who ran the girls' orphanages. When Jewish damas approached the Hogar ladies regarding possible unification, the women's group rejected this path. Instead, in 1940 they formalized their ideas and proposed statutes for the Hogar that defined itself as an organization of Israelite women that operated a children's home designed to help indigent parents of preschool children. They envisioned the establishment of similar institutions throughout the capital city. In addition, they operated a ward for children under the age of two.[50] By that time the Hogar had moved to a new, larger location at José Bonifacio 2016, and it defined its function as a kindergarten with more than ninety children, mostly offspring of working parents. They opened their doors to Sephardic children, although the majority of the children were Askenazic.[51]

While the Jewish damas patterned their name and social activities on the Catholic model, their attitude toward their charges, as well as their willingness to acknowledge their husbands' roles in their activities, set them apart. Historically the damas of the Society of Beneficence only warily shared power and/or authority with anyone. In the late nineteenth and early twentieth centuries they vigorously opposed efforts to remove female education and the medical care of poor women from their responsibility. Their disputes with male public health physicians became notorious, and in the 1930s and 1940s they struggled with national officials who wanted to incorporate the Society's institutions into the nascent national welfare system. They rarely acknowledged any role played by their husbands, and only when necessary did they rely on the recommendations of male legal counsel and of powerful politicians. If friends or relatives left property or money to the Society, the donations were never discussed in terms of family.

The principal reason why the Catholic damas had no need to rely upon their husbands for help in their activities was that their *apellidos* [surnames], so well known, meant that any Argentine would recognize the woman as a member of the elite establishment. In many ways they implicitly carried their husbands' approval and support through the use of their names. Curiously, many of the feminists also had famous husbands, such as the founder of the Socialist Party (Alicia Moreau de Justo and Juan B. Justo), a prominent specialist in juvenile delinquency and education (Elvira López de Nelson and Ernesto Nelson), and a prominent public health physician (Gabriela Laperrière de Coni and Emilio R. Coni). This situation did not apply to the Jewish damas, whose husbands had apellidos unfamiliar to people outside the collectivity.

Equally important, the damas of the Society of Beneficence and those in the Patronato de la Infancia never felt a close personal bond with their charges. In contrast, the Jewish damas often celebrated the religious holidays at the orphanages with their family and charges. They organized parties attended by some of the most respected members of the Jewish community and their families. The Jewish damas encouraged members of the community to celebrate events such as a bar mitzvah by offering hot chocolate to the orphans and by participating in the act with their family and friends.[52] They also refused to send any child out to foster care. Their performance style clearly marked both themselves and their wards as part of a distinct community. This meant that all children who entered as foundlings or orphans stayed until the age of majority (twenty-two) or until they were married. In 1927 the first female orphan, Dora Verona, got married. In celebration the temple waived all fees, and the chief rabbi, Samuel Halphon, wed the couple in a ceremony attended by many people from the Jewish community. After the wedding, the community hosted a luncheon and reception, and the bride received a complete trousseau and a gift from each woman on the commission of the damas. In addition, Gustavo Glaser gave furniture as a gift, and donations for the couple arrived from all over Argentina. As the Jewish community put it, "In a word, the Israelite collectivity married off an orphan in the same way they would have done for a daughter."[53]

Sometimes the girls stayed on long after they reached the age of majority because there simply was no other place for them. In the case of the Ukrainian orphans, some had reached the age of twenty-five and still lived in the orphanage. In the midst of the world depression neither work nor lodging was available for these women, yet *Mundo Israelita*, one of the local Jewish newspapers, urged the damas to have the twenty women leave the asylum and not live together outside the institution. That way, the girls would learn the meaning of independence. The fates of these women were not addressed in annual reports, but it is probable that, as often was the case, they stayed on as employees.

The distinctive treatment of female Jewish orphans did not mean, however, that the girls were raised with middle-class identities. Instead they learned manual labor, just like the girls in the charge of the Society of Beneficence. All of the girls had to work, both to help pay for their lodging and to receive small salaries that were deposited in a bank account. Later, the older girls received secretarial and nursing education. By 1943 the asylum offered classes to girls from kindergarten to sixth grade, and girls were sent out to learn nursing, decorative arts, and secretarial and book-keeping skills.[54]

As with the Catholic damas, it is very difficult to find explicit statements about how the Jewish damas felt about their charges. However, they stated their mission linking child welfare to the colectividad. For example, in a 1930 advertisement in *Mundo Israelita* seeking new members, the Jewish damas argued that "all Israelites should always have present in their spirit and their heart the supplicating image of our orphan girls." This statement appeared in boldface and capital letters. After making the reader aware of the daily arrival of orphans to their asylum, the women commented, also in boldface but not in capital letters, "Each of you reading this, who is a good Israelite and an excellent patriarch, sensitive to suffering, should not forget that your happiness is dependent upon the happiness of an orphan." Thus they reached out to the male community, in a way that the other damas and feminists never did, to contribute to the asylum. They also mentioned in this large advertisement that the damas worked to protect "widows, par-turient women, and ill women." Their final statement, in large letters, read "Keep Safe, Immaculate, and Well the Great Name of the Jews." Such rheto-ric clearly placed their child welfare performances in the framework of collective benevolence.[55]

Eva Perón, the Dama de la Esperanza:
Performing Emotive Philanthropy

In all the activities of the various damas and feminists, notions of perform-ing public demonstrations of love never appeared as part of praxis or rheto-ric. Duty, benevolence, charity, equality—all of these words resonated in one way or another, but love remained outside the quotidian vocabulary of elite and feminist reformers. Love became identified with biological chil-dren, not with others. So where and when did love enter the political dis-courses of child welfare? Most Argentines, whether supporters or detrac-tors of Peronism, would identify that realm of emotive philanthropy with Eva Perón, who was often called the Dama de la Esperanza [Lady of Hope]. The true history of performing love as part of philanthropy, however, be-gins a bit earlier.

To answer the difficult question of origins, written documents provide no evidence. Photography offers yet another way to document caring public attitudes toward street children. Which Argentine public official first had a magazine cover depicting himself or herself with a child that was not biological kin? The somewhat provocative answer to this question is President Agustín P. Justo, the leader of the Concordancia military-political alliance of the 1930s. The picture appeared in a 1937 issue of *Infancia y Juventud* published by the Patronato Nacional de Menores. In the photo, the president receives a bouquet of flowers from a young female child. Underneath the picture, he personally wrote "For the magazine 'Infancia y Juventud' with my warmest wishes for the children of the Patronato."[56]

Although kissing babies and chatting with youngsters have long been characteristic of U.S. ward politics, Argentine political campaigns had traditionally been matters for men, and kissing babies did not form part of the public vision. Furthermore, until Eva Perón no president's wife had developed a public persona. Argentine presidents had a record of attending openings and special events of key orphanages in Buenos Aires, but no recorded personal encounters with the children are evident. Added to the mystery are historical rumors that, before Eva Perón, wives of Argentine presidents served as automatic presidents of the Society of Beneficence.

Most of the early photos of Eva Perón consist of family pictures or of publicity pictures taken of her as part of her early radio and modeling careers. The first official public photo of Eva Perón found to date was taken in December 1946 as part of the Christmas festivities she participated in as First Lady. This does not mean that no earlier photos exist, as photos from her modeling and cinematic career exist, but early photos of Eva, especially with poor children, do not form a part of her photographic rhetoric.

As an illegitimate child scorned by her father's official family, many stories linked Eva's private life to her public career. Since the military destroyed so much of her private correspondence, the significance of personal motives in her public activities forms part of her legend rather than reality. Most likely the decisive public event that led Eva Perón to symbolically adopt children as a keystone of her public personality proved to be the devastating earthquake in 1944 that practically destroyed the capital of the province of San Juan. Horrific pictures taken after the earthquake showed thousands of children orphaned as a result of the collapse of buildings that killed their parents. The photos prompted prominent figures from all over the country to help raise money for the victims. Indeed, Eva Perón met her future husband Juan at a benefit held in Buenos Aires shortly after the earthquake. Furthermore, according to Juan Perón's oral testimony, Eva paid her own way on one of the medical planes that set out to San Juan, "and in this way [she] brought back an impression of what was happening and how one could make improvements."[57] Juan wrote of how much Eva's commitment to helping the orphans impressed him. Eva spent the rest of her short life performing welfare and consolidating power.

Juan Perón also became interested in the plight of these children, and he went to San Juan in 1944 as part of an investigative team. There he supposedly viewed the earthquake's devastation, and after he returned he met a train carrying many of the orphaned children.[58] Subsequently, most of the public pictures before 1947 involving children have Juan in the photo, not Eva. Yet Eva became legendary for the construction of a children's village designed to teach youngsters how Argentine society and politics functioned through their exploration of miniature versions of Congress, the presidential palace, the main post office, and other governmental facilities.

In 1947 Eva obtained an office in the Secretariat of Labor and Welfare. From that venue, she claimed that of all the social injustices that caused her pain, "the problems of children are, by far, the ones I will pay the most attention to, and [offer] the most caring." She attributed children's problems to the economic situation, mothers working outside the home, poor-quality food and housing, and the dehumanization of the individual.[59] In contrast to the public formality of Argentine officeholders, the use of caring language and a desire to share the pain experienced by poor children must have resonated among Argentines as revolutionary statements, something Eva intended. She also identified herself as the "spiritual mother of all children" and as a woman who worked faithfully with her husband "our great President Perón" to solve these difficult problems.[60]

Although Eva eventually had an impressive building in downtown Buenos Aires to house her foundation, and her foundation constructed equally luxurious transit homes to house migrant women who arrived with their children but without resources, most recollections of Eva Perón by her supporters (as opposed to her detractors) talked about her accessibility, the ability of the public to set up appointments to see her, and the fact that she publicly demonstrated concern for the people who pleaded for favors. Videotaped interviews of famous and not-so-famous people, made available to the public during the homage to Eva that took place in Buenos Aires at the Palais de Glace exposition hall in 1996, spoke of her caring nature.[61]

Correspondence (ironically found in the Society of Beneficence archive in the Argentine National Archives) indicates that poor relatives of the famous, as well as the simply poor, wrote to Eva. In 1950 Sara Rebollo wrote to Eva asking for help. She had no money of her own, and she lived with a cousin in the city of La Plata. Since 1950 marked the official year of the independence leader José de San Martín, Sara noted that she was a descendant of both José María Paz and Doña Rufina Orma de Rebello, one of the many upper-class women who donated their jewels to the independence effort. Evidently she had donated too many jewels and left her descendants in poverty.[62]

A more typical letter, dated July 20, 1951, invoked Eva's role as the defender of the humble poor: "The Lady of Hope named by the humble, the ones whom we call the needy, we turn to you because we know that you are great and have a heart full of tenderness and nobility. For this reason Señora, my poverty forces me to rely on your benevolence. I am a single woman, 52 years of age and sick from heart disease, and I ask you to give me something that is within your reach so that I can live my last years (A pension)."[63]

The poor with the most luck were those who met Eva in person at her public sessions at her foundation, or in one of the transit homes she helped establish. In these cases, rather than wait for the bureaucracy behind the foundation and the welfare state to verify the poverty and need of each supplicant, Eva often handed out cash, authorized the distribution of furniture, and made other wishes come true. It was the stories of these individuals that formed the basis of Eva's reputation for performing charity.

It is hard to imagine Eva Perón having much in common with the elite women whose efforts led to the construction of impressive orphanages to care for poor children. After all, Eva Perón constructed monuments to her own activity and to her dedication to children and the poor, but utilized a public performance style of caring to make her actions look different. And, for this reason, stories abounded regarding the snobbish response of elite women philanthropists to the young First Lady. Nevertheless, photos taken of Eva's institutions reveal that children dressed with the same white smocks found in all orphanages and public schools, and children who participated in Eva's athletic competitions all wore uniforms donated by her. It was the element of public love, rather than distinct notions of charity, that distinguished her approach from others.

Eva's performance of child welfare thus set her in the same mold as that of the upper- and middle-class damas of the collectivities and of the Society of Beneficence. Eva solved problems individually and used committees of unpaid volunteer friends to sort through the many requests she received. Just like the damas of the collectivities, throughout her life Eva remained the head of her own institution, thereby refusing to share the social status she accrued from performing welfare. At the same time her husband, unlike the husbands of the damas of the collectivities, devised his own efforts to consolidate the impersonal, bureaucratic, rights-based welfare state that had begun in a more preliminary way by his predecessors. Ultimately the performance of welfare by women and the creation of the welfare state designed by men came into conflict.

By the time Eva began to perform what she preferred to call social justice rather than charity, the modern Argentine nation found itself in a difficult dilemma. The nature of its society and inhabitants had changed since the early twentieth century, yet the distribution of child welfare, as well as other welfare projects, continued to remain in the hands of philanthropic women, both religious and secular. The immigrant community, another important component of philanthropy, had matured. By the election of Hipólito Yrigoyen in 1916, second-generation immigrants identified themselves more by their patriotism and connection to Argentina than had their parents. These children of immigrants now voted, had access to government jobs that demanded political loyalty, and joined labor unions that had their own political and social demands.

Among the women of the second generation of immigrants, the accessibility of public education meant that many had been able to prepare themselves for professional jobs as educators, social workers, and physicians, and they now expected to receive a salary, just as the feminists had predicted. Women of the working class had the opportunity to study at socialist universities, and many wanted to work in the ever-changing industrial and commercial worlds available in the capital city. With these realities, their connections to volunteerism, whether religious or community based, began to fade. Eva Perón attempted to co-opt this group by looking for supporters for her Women's Peronist Party, but feminist opponents would not join such a group. In other words, the rise of Peronism coincided with women's new attitudes toward volunteerism at the very same time that the collectivity damas tried to once again expand their facilities to meet what they presumed would be postwar needs.

Similarly, political groups in the 1930s and 1940s tried to anticipate the demand for welfare that became even more obvious after the worldwide depression began to affect Argentine industry and exports. Some envisioned a real welfare state controlled by the government, while others still believed that subsidized public philanthropy operated by women offered the best solution. No matter who won the political battles, the future of female-focused child welfare would inevitably change.

CHAPTER 4

Juvenile Delinquency, Patriarchy, and Female Philanthropy

Which children . . . are most likely to be given [state aid]? Undoubtedly they are the ones whom cruel destiny has left orphans or whose fathers, forgetting their responsibilities or sunken into vice, leave the children to their own devices. These children form a great legion in our society, and we must monitor those who give them the aid they don't receive from their parents. The good children will be helped to realize their own best inclinations, and those who have lived among the bad environment of an anarchistic and immoral home will be inculcated with habits of work and morality, the only means of regeneration.

—*Dr. Agustín Cabal, Buenos Aires defender of minors, 1910*

Although female philanthropists and feminists in Argentina created orphanages and proposed laws to benefit mothers with infants or women who wanted to adopt young children, they initially found it difficult to help older children on the streets. This chapter examines how juvenile delinquency necessitated new social policies and how women's groups expanded into juvenile reform schools precisely at the time when the state contemplated finally implementing a rationalized welfare state. Both the women's groups and the state accomplished this expansion by supporting commonly held views that patriarchy could be replaced by work or by patriotism. What divided the state and women's groups was the question of who should set policies to rehabilitate the youngsters in jail or in glorified workhouses.

The effort to persuade public authorities that female philanthropists could do a better job with minors, particularly girls, conflicted with legal practices but not with social traditions. Children over the age of five usually came under the control of their fathers, not their mothers, and male defenders of minors along with the police periodically gathered up street children, not philanthropic women. Since 1823 groups of women had sought to interrupt this reallocation of children by placing themselves in positions of authority, establishing their own workhouses or day-care centers, and offering their services to the police and other juvenile authorities.

The situation with older children at risk and on the streets, however, was very different from that of babies. The gendered identities of the children associated them with criminality and deviant sexuality, where boys were more dangerous than girls. Treatment, accordingly, had different solutions. For boys, rehabilitation resided in the world of work. For girls, marriage or domestic service became the panacea. Thus although the sight of abandoned infants elicited sentiments of charity and benevolence regardless of gender, urban dwellers reacted to older street children with fear and a firm belief that immoral parents or deviant sexuality had turned them into delinquents. Normal children would neither be rebellious nor live unsupervised. Those who diverged from this behavior needed to be incorporated into the diverse social policies that preceded the Peronist welfare state.

Patriarchy and battles among defenders of minors, the police, and women's institutions retarded the growth of state reformatories. Civil codes that gave male heads of household custody rights stymied state solutions for wayward or poor children prior to 1919. Single mothers obtained greater legal control over their children after 1926, but this right could easily disappear. Yet institutions operated by women traditionally had provided housing for orphaned abandoned children, including older ones. From the 1890s until the rise of Peronism a series of municipal and national child welfare organizations struggled to reform children by sending boys to reformatories and girls either to jail or to Catholic organizations—as often at the behest of parents as that of the police or judges. By 1930 it became clear that governmental efforts paralleled and subsidized many communal organizations that founded schools, orphanages, or reformatories to house the waifs identified as part of their community, and Catholic-based charities continued to set up other institutions. Girls remained a low priority for state and municipal governments, but they formed a strong target for philanthropists until a presidential decree banned female minors from the Casa Correccional de Mujeres [Women's Jail] after 1932. This reality drew Catholic philanthropic women further into the evolving child welfare regime, while women from other religious groups refrained from this activity.

Throughout this time, male experts debated the nature of delinquent children from the perspective of biological rather than psychological

El día de los niños pobres

La señora Teodelina Alvear de Lezica, presidenta de la comisión de damas del Patronato de la Infancia, presenciando el desfile de los niños asilados por la institución

Grupo de niños y niñas entregando sus alcancías en teatro Colón

En el foyer del mismo teatro, después del reparto de juguetes

Rendición de cuentas

Las colectas del 2 de octubre para los niños pobres no se han detenido este año en la progresión creciente marcada por los anteriores, y han subido aproximadamente hasta 150.000 pesos. Las alcancías intervienen mucho en tan notable resultado, según lo dicen las cifras con brillante elocuencia. En 1903 sin alcancías, la colecta ascendió sólo á 46.000 pesos, y saltó con ellas á 132.000 el año siguiente. Añádase á esto que algunas alcancías lograron reunir una suma mayor que ciertas comisiones, y habrá completado su justo elogio. La alcancía más afortunada fué la de la niña Mar...

1. Teodelina Alvear de Lezica, president of the Women's Commission of the Patronato de la Infancia, leading a parade of poor children for the "Day of the Poor Children." (*Caras y Caretas* 11.523, October 10, 1908)

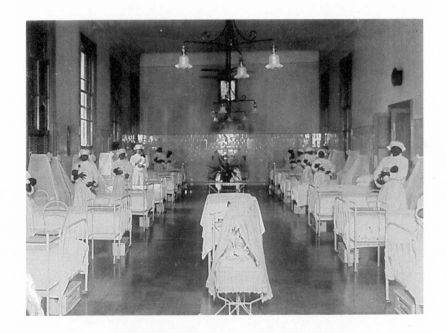

2. The foundling home run by the Society of Beneficence, Montes de Oca
Street. (Archivo General de la Nación, Argentina; photo by G. Hearn.
Casa de Expósitos, Montes de Oca)

3. The French orphanage. (Archivo General de la Nación, Argentina)

4. The Irish girls' orphanage. (Archivo General de la Nación, Argentina)

5. Kindergarten run by the Patronato de la Infancia. (Archivo General de la Nación, Argentina; photo by G. Hearn)

6. The Catholic activist
Cecilia La Palma de Emery.
(Frontispiece from *Acción
Pública y Privada en Favor de la
Mujer y del Niño en la República
Argentina* [Buenos Aires: Alfa
y Omega, 1910])

7. Cantina maternal, Buenos Aires. (Archivo General de la
Nación, Argentina; photo by G. Hearn)

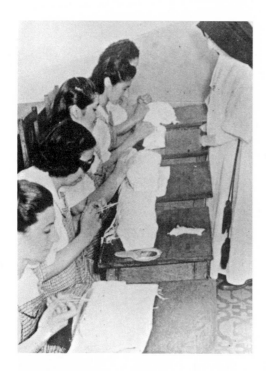

8. The Saint Felicitas
workshop in the 1920s.
(Archivo General de
la Nación, Argentina;
photo by G. Hearn)

9. Elvira Rawson de Dellepiane performing motherhood.
(Reproduced with permission from the Asunción Lavrin
collection)

10. The feminist Alicia Moreau de Justo (third from right).
(Archivo General de la Nación, Argentina; photo by Juan Barreneche)

(left) 11. The Peronist feminist Lucila Gregorio de Lavie.
(Archivo General de la Nación, Argentina; photo by Juan Barreneche)

(right) 12. The Peronist feminist Blanca Azucena Cassagne Serres.
(Archivo General de la Nación, Argentina; photo by Juan Barreneche)

13. The Asilo Argentino de Huérfanas Israelitas in 1927.
(Photo by author at Templo Libertad Archives)

14. Girls admitted to the Jewish girls' orphanage (Archivo
General de la Nación, Argentina; photo by G. Hearn)

15. Eva performing charity. (Archivo General de la Nación, Argentina; photo by G. Hearn)

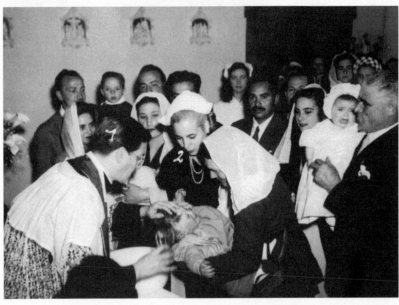

16. Eva as godmother. (Archivo General de la Nación, Argentina; photo by G. Hearn)

17. Tribute to Eva by the Confederation of Labor:
"I will return and be millions." (Photo by the author)

development; adolescence did not appear as a general fixed category in the minds of specialists or the public. For example, as late as the 1930s, the child specialist Aníbal Ponce defined *infancia* as "the period from birth to the age of seven," and in 1952 another specialist, Ismael Dulce, also defined the term in a general way as "the time that passes between birth and puberty." Ponce divided this period into segments: *lactante* [unweaned; birth until six to eight months of age]; *primera infancia* [eight months until seven or eight years, or the loss of the first teeth]; and *segunda infancia* [the arrival of permanent teeth until puberty]."[1] At the same time he used the word "adolescent" in the title of his book. Without a popularly accepted term for adolescence, it became difficult to separate children into different age groups, which in turn gave female reformers the opportunity to expand their activities.

This chapter focuses on the care of children for whom most child welfare legislation and institutional structures failed, as well as on the women who sought to rehabilitate them. Children became clients of state-subsidized religious and secular caretakers who above all valued submissiveness and dedication to work. It is here that romantic feminist and female philanthropic goals both failed because they could not bring themselves to attribute positive characteristics to wayward children, support Freud's theories of infant sexuality as the norm, or accept Piaget's theories of incremental child development. The system that emerged with women's help could neither rehabilitate the child nor replace the family. Although reformatories effectively removed child labor from the public view as well as the factory, they did not promote the psychological development often found in children of all classes, and the education provided to them geared them toward lower-class employment, service in the military, or, in the case of female minors, marriage. Different types of reformatories and workshops opened, but they all provided similar treatment.

Early Bureaucratic Efforts

Since child specialists categorically defined older children on the streets as male, the first national project to deal with juvenile delinquency consisted of a plan to construct a boys' reformatory. Proposed by President Carlos Pellegrini in 1892 and opened in 1899, the plan identified street urchins, particularly young males, as potential criminals, and suggested that a jail be constructed and dedicated solely to young male offenders. The president noted that the overcrowded existing facility held adults and children, and that "the growing number of corrupted children sent there daily by defenders and judges" could never be contained.[2]

Originally called the Casa de Corrección de Menores Varones de la Capital [Correctional Home for Minor Boys of the National Capital] when it opened in 1899, it soon became known as the Asilo de Varones Menores de la Capital [Reform Asylum for Minor Boys in the Capital]. Its purpose was to house boys indicted and sentenced, those sent by defenders of minors, and those sent directly by the police—all of whom were supposed to be between the ages of eight and eighteen. The task of the asylum was to shape the boys into "virtuous men and good citizens."[3] In 1902 over one thousand youngsters lived in cramped quarters, with some housed in corridors. At the time, it was believed that the number could increase precipitously if all street children landed there. In the institution the children labored in workshops, with the proceeds of their labors helping finance the institution. In addition, upon their release they received a token payment in lieu of wages.[4]

Particularly dangerous or recalcitrant boys continued to be sent to the penitentiary. In 1903, fifteen-year-old José Almada was transferred from the Casa Correcional de Niños Varones [Reform Asylum] to serve out his sentence of seven and a half years for attempted homicide. Prison authorities said that they had no special facilities for minors. The Casa Correcional de Niños Varones accepted the child and claimed that he had been sent to the penitentiary under a judicial order that they had opposed. José returned to the asylum where he stayed until he celebrated his eighteenth birthday. The institution underwent various transformations and gradually disappeared as a jail for delinquent boys, particularly after the 1905 creation of the Colonia de Menores Varones de Marcos Paz [National Boys' Reformatory in Marcos Paz].[5]

In Buenos Aires boys found on the streets usually ended up in jail because neither family nor kin kept children responsibly out of public spaces. Adrift in the streets of the rapidly growing capital city they became targets of the police and reformers, but neither could resolve the economic and social problems that plagued the youngsters and their families. Public authorities wanted them returned to their homes and fathers, but many either preferred to live on their own or had no homes to which they could return.

By 1906 observers in Buenos Aires commented on the presence of gangs of male street children, believing that their visibility offered an inappropriate first impression for visitors. According to the description offered by Gabriel Carrasco in 1906, children hawked all kinds of products and they seemed to have a ubiquitous presence in the city, including on the streetcars and hanging around doorways—just about everywhere except in school.[6] Three years later, Roberto Levillier urged readers of the 1909 Buenos Aires census to be concerned about delinquent minors, the "most important element in the present and in the future," because in the future they would become adult criminals. He defined these youths as exclusively male, and those who had committed more than one crime particularly concerned him.[7]

Defenders temporarily shipped out juvenile boys to the southern territories to work on sheep and cattle ranches in the belief that urban areas offered greater potential to corrupt young boys than did jobs in rural areas. Some boys left without their parents' permission. The Buenos Aires defender of minors charged with the lower-class southern side of Buenos Aires announced in 1907 that during the previous year he had petitioned courts to remove the patria potestad of parents "unable, inappropriate, or who had abandoned" their sons. During the next few years an intensive campaign attempted to rid the city of these boys by sending them, under court order, to work on ranches or agro industries in the national territories. A report in 1933 noted that the boys stayed on the ranches in only two or three cases, while the rest ran away from the caretakers who used them as cheap labor.[8]

In the world of adolescent street children, the zeal for child welfare seemed more muted than the concerns for abandoned babies, partly because Argentine reformers and professions rarely differentiated the needs of children between the ages of five and twenty-one. Public officials and specialists alike frowned upon rebellious youths and treated them with harshness. The sociologist Roberto Gache was one of three specialists who distinguished youth offenders from juvenile delinquents. In his prize-winning study from 1916, *Precocious Delinquency (Children and Adolescence)*, he noted that adolescent crime in Buenos Aires had increased during the period from 1900 to 1913.[9] In arguing that "true criminal inclinations only revealed themselves after age 15," a time during which young people developed a sense of personal identity, Gache clearly recognized the concept of adolescence as a process. The public, however, ignored this idea.

Nevertheless, Gache cited family influences as the most important factor in child development, particularly if the child in question had many siblings. To prove his assertion, he recounted the story of an elderly woman with ten children who bitterly complained to the police that one son had been unjustly imprisoned. Why imprison an innocent child? Gache pointed out how the boy, in a state of complete abandonment, had been arrested for vagrancy. He used the case as a justification for removing patria potestad from mothers and fathers who could not care for their children. Gache preferred to incarcerate a child in a reformatory rather than have him live in an unacceptable home, and discipline served as the only solution for adolescent troublemakers.[10]

In the meantime, children who did not obey their parents landed in the care of defenders of minors. Many parents willingly gave up child custody because they believed their boys to be "incorrigible." In jail, the boys accused of no crimes lived alongside delinquents, "contrary to the morality that is so necessary to inculcate in these minors."[11] Nevertheless, the universal focus on family reform perpetuated the mixing of various groups of juveniles whether they had committed an offense or not.

The belief that home created the best environment for children, according to Gache and others, guaranteed neither child safety nor good behavior. If the children had homes then there might be abuse, irresponsibility, poverty, and the consequences of alcoholism or abandonment of one parent, usually the father. If mothers could not make up for the poor performance of the fathers, or if they too were labeled irresponsible or immoral, the children ended up as criminals.

Argentine public officials continued to maintain that dysfunctional families produced youths who committed crimes. Several examples exist in the records. Poor "Horacio" D., for example, suffered from many of the issues cited by Gache. Arrested for theft in 1904, he spent five months in jail. His father, an alcoholic, had died—leaving Horacio's mother with fifteen chil-

dren.[12] An article on male juvenile delinquents that appeared in 1908 in
Caras y Caretas described a family in which the father and his sons all ended
up in jail accused of criminal behavior. The editors published photographs
of the recidivist children along with their names and family histories as
classic stories of inherited degeneration. The magazine offered neither pri-
vacy nor succor.[13] A case sent to the Society of Beneficence also reaffirmed
these dysfunctional family patterns. "Arturo" R., an eleven-year-old boy,
found himself arrested in 1935 and sent to the boys' jail for "wandering on
the streets all day . . . vulnerable to bad habits." The judge then sent him
to the boys' orphanage along with his brother. No one seemed to know
the whereabouts of the boys' parents, and the boys ended up in jail again
after the Society of Beneficence rejected them because of their rebellious
behavior.[14]

When the children became targets of government campaigns to "rid"
the streets of children, police accused their parents, if they had any, as having abandoned them morally and materially. The Argentine courts based
the concept of moral abandonment on poverty in order to remove the
parental custody of children. This reality "explained" Horacio's desire
to steal, as opposed to the view of the dire French definition enacted in 1889
for the express purpose of removing patriarchal custody from fathers.
There the law required that "parents convicted of certain serious crimes, be
stripped automatically of their right—especially when convicted for the
sexual or economic exploitation of their own children . . . [The law] also
allowed the court to act where there had been no criminal conviction' . . .
but where behavior might 'compromise the health, safety or morality of
their children.' "[15] The Buenos Aires police chief clearly expressed similar
views in his annual report for 1913–1914: "Vagrancy, begging, and abandoned children are social plagues that my predecessors have reported on
many occasions . . . and yet we still need to work on these issues so that this
capital can be socially cleansed . . . The legislation regarding guardianship
of these children has already been initiated and along with the measures
adopted by the national government regarding the habilitation and expansion of buildings needed to house them, allow us to hope that this problem
of minor children . . . will soon be solved."[16] According to this logic, children found on the streets might be separated from parents if the state could
provide a good argument to remove patria potestad.

The police of Buenos Aires and other cities initially did not relish the idea
of having boys wandering about on the streets. Nor did they want to interfere with private family matters. They only investigated the circumstances

surrounding the presence of these children in public places and, if the children had parents, verify whether the youths had been forced out of their homes. Even if children were labeled incorrigible they should remain at home, and the Buenos Aires police in the 1880s were instructed to tell parents that public jails and institutions were not *lugares de corrección* [correctional institutions].[17] Soon jails become just that—correctional institutions —as juvenile delinquency experts identified the family and heredity as the source of the problem. And urban police began advocating anti-vagrancy laws for children.[18] Child incarceration became the initial response of public officials after 1900. And although police did not consider all vagrant children to be delinquents, they participated in a system that incarcerated youngsters.

The Colonia de Menores Varones Marcos Paz, which eventually was renamed after its physician Ricardo Gutiérrez, educated as well as rehabilitated young boys. Seen as the wave of the future, the organization linked agricultural education with regular schooling. Rather than being placed together in large units, the boys were separated into groups of fifty individuals, each with a family to guide them.[19] By 1913, there were 250 boys lodged in different wings, and only 50 boys in the wing for convicted boys. By 1919 the Marcos Paz institution housed 454 boys. Of the children who left, 172 had run away, compared with 191 placed by defenders. By then defenders had set up a plan to contract the children's labor to rural endeavors that included ranching, commerce, and domestic service. Out of the total number of youngsters placed by the defenders, 162 out of 191 were placed in rural tasks out of the belief that a healthier environment "morally disinfected" them from their earlier learning experiences.[20] Furthermore, all entering boys would be studied from the perspective of individual and family characteristics.[21]

The national Departamento de Menores Abandonados y Encausados [Department of Abandoned and Indicted Minors], an early bureaucratic effort from 1913, tried to place both accused and nonaccused jailed minors in reformatories or school environments, but once again only boys benefited from these efforts. The Departmento de Menores Abandonados y Encausados's successor, the Instituto Tutelar de Menores, continued this laudable but gendered effort and focused mostly on boys convicted of crimes. The following year, 311 boys between the ages of six and fourteen had been turned over to the Instituto. Many went to foster families to work as house servants, and the rest, approximately 191 in December 1919, lived at Marcos Paz.[22] By 1922, a total of 251 boys under the jurisdiction of the

Instituto lived in reformatories. They ranged in age from seven to sixteen, and most were under thirteen. Among them, the majority lived with their single mothers or were orphans.[23]

In 1922 the Argentine government opened the Colonia Para Niños Abandonados y Delincuentes [Boys' Reformatory for Abandoned and Delinquent Children] in Oliveros in the province of Buenos Aires. That year 496 boys ended up there, almost half from defenders of minors and only 126 from judges. Seventy-five families turned their youngsters over to the institution. Almost half of the children could not read, but within a year only twenty illiterate boys remained. During this time, most of the boys ran away from the institution, which operated more as a workhouse and farm prison than a school. Nevertheless, the boys who remained learned how to read.[24] In contrast, no public institutions beyond the women's jail provided for wayward and homeless older girls.

Workshops and Correctional Facilities Operated by Women

The absence of secular public facilities opened the way for women to become involved in female juvenile reform. There are four reasons behind this fact. First, from the outset the nineteenth-century Argentine state contracted female members of religious organizations to supervise the moral reform of female women and minor offenders, which offered secular Catholic women an important precedent. Second, the Society of Beneficence and other groups of female philanthropists devised their own system of workshops to monitor the behavior of male and female children in their care, and the absence of a strong public mandate to open state-operated facilities beyond the prison system meant that women could expand their activities. Third, a new group of professional women trained in the 1920s and 1930s joined the ranks of feminists and began to interject their views of juveniles from their vantage point as professional social workers and educators. These professionals often criticized the state and religious systems that provided no possibility that poor children could work in public places, but their analyses failed to change the environment for delinquent or wayward children. And fourth, mothers with children considered incorrigible played their own part throughout the first half of the twentieth century by demanding more public reform institutions to turn their errant children into appropriate citizens.

Female philanthropists often found themselves increasingly concerned with the rehabilitation of older minors. They joined organizations to assist children released on parole, and they became directly involved with the operations of more reform schools. Their increased petitions for government subsidies for these expanded activities made philanthropic women particularly susceptible to calls for nationalizing child welfare. Others, horrified by the conditions of boys' prisons, believed that judges could not rehabilitate youngsters. During the Yrigoyen administration (1916–1922), the damas of the Conferencias de San Vicente de Paul offered their services to the country by suggesting that they operate the Marcos Paz facility rather than the recently created Instituto Tutelar de Menores. Although President Yrigoyen believed that the facility did more than provide charity because it helped promote public stability, he also believed that the women could help the waifs once they left the facility. Therefore he decreed on October 14, 1918, that the Consejo General [General Council] of the Conferencias could help with the entry and release of boys, as well as stimulate their good conduct.[25] But the women had the best luck operating institutions for girls.

The Women's Jail

Until the 1930s, the only public institutions for girls consisted of women's prisons and Catholic houses of correction. Here women played key roles and interacted with public officials involved with vagrant and delinquent children. For these reasons, before the turn of the twentieth century, religious institutions and the Society of Beneficence bore the primary responsibility of reforming female minors. The case of the women's jail in Buenos Aires serves as a model for the history of the treatment of wayward girls by female religious groups. From 1873 until 1888 nuns had operated the Asilo del Buen Pastor [Good Shepherd Asylum], a jail originally under the control of the Society of Beneficence. The Casa de Ejercicios [House of Spiritual Exercises], a convent dedicated to rehabilitating delinquent females, provided reeducation for girls deemed immoral, while those considered "incorrigible" went to the women's jail.[26] Outside Buenos Aires, police and judicial authorities had similar arrangements. For a short time, between 1873 and 1887, the Society also operated the Asilo de Pobres [Work House for the Poor], a place for young girls and women.[27]

The secular Casa Correccional de Mujeres operated by the nuns of the Good Shepard officially opened in 1892. During the early years, basic repairs, painting, and remodeling made the building habitable. Later, the addition of wings provided more space for inmates. By the time of the first national prison census in 1906, the jail had the capacity to hold 100 adults and 150 minors at one time. First and second grade primary school classes were offered for illiterate women and children, and training was provided in laundry and sewing workshops.[28] Eventually the prison offered both women and female minors classes through the fourth grade.

The number of girls who passed through the jail varied tremendously from year to year, but it always exceeded the number of adult inmates. In 1889, for example, several years before its official opening, 466 entered the jail, and most of them left during the same year. In 1892, a total of 694 girls spent time in the jail, compared with 317 in 1893. In these years the great majority arrived under judicial orders from one of three defenders of minors, a phenomenon invisible to the public. This trend continued as the numbers of minors soared to over 1,138 in 1911 and peaked in 1917 with 1,874 admissions. Until the mid-1920s fewer girls arrived, although in only one year, 1922, did the number of inmates drop below 1,400. In contrast, until the 1930s the annual number of adult prisoners rarely exceeded 400 and tended to range between 200 and 300.[29]

The defenders, like the police, reluctantly placed young girls in the women's jail. On May 7, 1901, the defender José M. Terrero unsuccessfully asked the minister of justice to plead with the minister of foreign relations to force the Society of Beneficence to accept abandoned children between the ages of six and eight. The Patronato de la Infancia could not help the defenders, as initially it only offered day-care facilities. Thus defenders had few alternatives, and female religious workers dedicated to reforming women became the principal wardens of young girls.[30]

In order to deal with this problem, the mother superior of the Casa Correccional de Mujeres wrote to Argentine President José E. Uriburu in 1895 offering to take in more street children. Claiming that many more poor girls needed to avail themselves of such shelter, she asked for permission to admit them merely because of poverty in order to provide them with an education.[31] When informed of this request, the three defenders of minors quickly stepped in to complain that such a plan would infringe on parental custody rights associated with patria potestad, as well as with the powers invested in themselves.[32]

Even though the defenders often avoided sending girls to the prison, those incarcerated found overcrowded conditions. In June 1900 the mother superior again suggested that the nuns could provide a more extensive service for vagrant girls and thereby expand their political power over the defenders. She urged the national government to authorize the construction of a completely separate juvenile facility where the children could stay "at least three or four years so they could receive a moderate education and thereby be useful to families by offering services appropriate to their condition, i.e. cooks, maids, and laundresses."[33] Her request acknowledged the limited usefulness of existing facilities.

Occasionally some defenders supported the mother superior's views. In 1903 a new defender, B. Lainez, suggested a series of reforms, including the transformation of the Casa Correccional de Mujeres into a trade school for the adult women, with sections that would separate delinquent minors from those merely being warehoused. Lainez also argued that a school for juvenile mothers could become part of the trade school. His suggestions fell on deaf ears, however, and he did not remain long in his post, perhaps because he backed the nuns' plans.[34]

The breakdown of girls incarcerated by age makes it clear that very young girls as well as adolescents landed in jail due to judicial orders. In 1907, for example, 42 youngsters under the age of ten lived in the jail, while 320 girls between the ages of ten and fifteen also found themselves behind bars. In total, the number of girls between the ages of six and fifteen equaled more than 38 percent of incarcerated juveniles. By 1912, this proportion had decreased to only 33 percent.[35]

The defenders, highly displeased by the number of female minors languishing in jail, believed that no other alternatives existed. One defender suggested a new policy to keep girls from ending up on the streets because they abandoned their homes or places of employment. In 1910 Dr. Agustín Cabal, frustrated by the number of girls who refused to remain in the home of their employers, began to insist that all girls under his care be fingerprinted by the police. This not only made it easier to capture them, he reasoned, but it also offered an incentive to these waifs. According to him, if by the time the girl reached legal adulthood she had no files with the police other than her fingerprints then she could use that fact to demonstrate "proof of her honesty."[36] Those who could not do so ended up in jail and subsequently reentered society with a new, questionable identity.

Increased numbers of inmates and insufficient funding resulted in deplorable jail conditions. According to a report of the mother superior on April 12, 1910, there was a shortage of warm clothing, bedding, and underwear for both adult and child inmates, and all of the inmates needed new shoes. The section for girls from fifteen to twenty years of age housed 140 inmates but had only 118 beds—those who did not have a bed slept on the floor. On cold nights, each girl had only one blanket. The nuns solicited over four thousand pesos to provide basic elements for the children. Although they received the funds requested, the reports indicate that additional government funding came only on an ad hoc basis.[37]

Although legislators at the turn of the century quickly authorized funding for a special facility for delinquent boys, they hesitated to provide similar facilities for either homeless or delinquent girls. Likewise, they failed to challenge the authority of female religious orders in charge of women's jails, although they resisted the efforts of the nuns to establish where wayward girls could be educated. Unable to achieve long-term educational facilities, the nuns settled for providing some elementary education and workshops. The short stays of both the girls and the adult prisoners meant that all hopes of rehabilitating them were illusory, and the annual reports of the nuns indicated this as a justification for transforming the jail into another type of institution that offered separate long-term facilities for girls and women.

In these prisons, street children, like orphans, found work to be a replacement for family. During the short stay in the women's jail, girls labored in shops set up for sewing and laundry work. They received meager pay, partly because most did not stay long but also because they had to purchase all of the materials they used. An example of the labor issue comes from the 1913 annual report of earnings by minors at the Casa Correccional de Mujeres. The many girls who passed through the doors of that institution together earned less than 2,500 pesos. Those who left that year received only 417.48 pesos. Girls spent 279.77 pesos, mostly on clothing and shoes. Their expenses far exceeded what they actually received. The costs of thread, fabric, and other articles of production equaled 612.72 pesos, and they also had to pay almost the same amount for the use and maintenance of facilities. In other years reports of child income were quite similar.[38]

The nuns continued to believe that they could rehabilitate even the most difficult girls through education and work. In an extract of the 1919 annual report for the women's jail, the mother superior noted that the minors in her care were worthy of compassion "because the majority of them cannot aspire to the well being that comes from knowledge of the arts and sciences for the simple reason that they lack the means to obtain them [i.e., family and status]. They inevitably will have to fend for themselves and thus will have to learn to labor as working-class women and servants." For this reason the nuns wanted to educate the girls to live "honest lives and to practice their duties as Christians."[39] The language of the mother superior acknowledged that girls who entered the jail had insufficient social connections to offer them anything other than work for the uneducated and unprotected. Her words went unheeded.

The Buenos Aires women's jail continued to serve as an auxiliary to the defenders of minors. In 1914 the nuns finally segregated in a separate wing the girls sent to them by the defenders. Segregation partially alleviated the anxiety of the defenders who were loath to mix the prison populations.[40] By 1921 the nuns felt that everything operated well at the jail, and that their constant preoccupation involved training both girls and women in basic domestic skills. As they put it, "Experience has shown that indolence and luxury are the principal causes of delinquency among women, as in minor girls . . . and it is necessary to make them love their work: the majority of them depend solely on manual labor to reward them with a decorous life."[41] None were encouraged to transcend the class and gendered nature of their existence.

During this time, young girls incarcerated in the women's jail, whether street children or youthful delinquents, remained beyond the reach of the early specialists in juvenile delinquency and juvenile law. Under the scrutiny of nuns, the rehabilitation of the girls consisted of work that replicated domestic labor, and children who found foster homes received further training in these skills. The notion that children needed affection and parenting did not apply to them. For these reasons their lives resembled those of orphans taken in by the many institutions of the city. Both groups suffered social discrimination and rarely were reintegrated with their biological families unless they ran away from the institutions.

Mothers, Fathers, and Their Delinquent Children

Mothers contributed to this process of social discrimination by handing over unruly girls to public authorities. In 1917 "Marta" L. L., an orphan, ran away from the home of her custodial parents whom she accused of mistreating her. She kept escaping and finally ended up arrested and placed in the women's jail.[42] In another case, Luisa Gigena de Saldaño requested in 1920 that the government discipline her daughter, Juana Isabel. Because Luisa was destitute, she could only offer the address of the defender of the poor as her legal residence. She claimed that Juana's father had traveled to Tucumán, and that Juana took advantage of this fact by abandoning her family to engage in prostitution. Enraged, Luisa had the police apprehend her daughter and, lacking other resources, she petitioned the court to incarcerate her daughter for the amount of time stipulated by the law.[43]

"Adela" R. C., whose mother turned her over to the defenders of minors in December 1946, was considered by her mother to be a mischievous girl who lived on the streets. The eleven year old had been thrown out of several

Catholic schools for bad conduct. Instead of taking her in immediately, the defenders of minors decided to observe her for several months to see if she would not improve her behavior. According to her mother, Adela was "fond of the street, playing games with boys, [and being] contentious, rebellious, willful, and extremely restless." The following year she entered the Hogar Santa Rosa [Santa Rosa Reformatory], which opened in 1938. The nuns there judged her to be highly undisciplined, and Adela remained there until September 1949, when her mother took her back.[44]

"Mona" G. entered the Casa Correccional de Mujeres in 1947 at the age of fourteen. Her father had abandoned the family and taken the three oldest boys, leaving her mother with the responsibility of supporting the young girl. Mona ran way from her mother and stepfather and was arrested. According to the welfare report on the family, the mother lived "miserably in the most horrifying poverty with a total lack of hygiene," and the child was barefoot and suffering from impetigo. Child rescue for Mona meant living in the Santa Rosa reformatory.[45]

In February 1947 "Iselda" M. I., a sixteen year old who was unwanted by her stepmother, ended up in the Hogar Santa Rosa. The father and stepmother had left her behind in Buenos Aires when they went to Rosario with some of her brothers to look for work. When her poor conduct caught the attention of authorities, she was sent to the Asilo Ursula Ll. de Inchausti in December. The following year she was moved to the Hogar Santa Rosa as a result of behavioral problems. Eventually she ran away from Santa Rosa and was never found again.[46]

Mothers also handed over their boys. In 1947 "Agusto" P., the fifteen-year-old son of "Pilar" O. de P., was sent to the defenders of minors. His mother justified the action because she claimed that Agusto was an "undisciplined child, rebellious, who shows a lack of ability for every task and has committed reprehensible acts such as that which took place in the Colegio León XIII, damaging the machines used in that institution." Agusto's father had abandoned the family twelve years earlier, and the mother couldn't discipline the child who wanted to replace the father "in every way." A social worker reaffirmed this view, and she noted a messy, unkempt household in which the mother and son slept in the same bed. The boy was sent to the Colonia Hogar Ricardo Gutiérrez [Ricardo Gutiérrez Home] in Marcos Paz. He ran away from the facility several times, until his mother took him back in 1951.[47]

Fathers behaved in a similar fashion in relegating their children to the authorities. In Buenos Aires, for example, Roberto Gagnebien went to court in 1904 to seek help after his son David had run away several times, and often had been arrested. Since he could no longer prevent his child from getting into mischief, Roberto wanted the judge to place David in an institution. David entered the Marcos Paz facility. By relinquishing his rights over David, Roberto had acknowledged his limitations as a father.

In 1909 Ramón Domínguez wrote to the minister of justice complaining of the poor behavior of his seventeen-year-old son, Alberto. Domínguez placed part of the blame on his wife's more tolerant attitude, but now he felt that Alberto was a bad influence on his other children. After describing his "certainty that in such a pernicious environment my son will only become a prejudicial individual and even less useful to the Nation, to Society, and to the Home," Domínguez pleaded that Alberto be sent to the Marcos Paz facility to turn him into a "dignified citizen, honorable, laborious, and patriotic as the fervent desire of my father's heart."[48]

Felipe di Camillo, the father of many children, was burdened by poverty as a common laborer. He had become dismayed by the conduct of his fifteen-year-old son, Alfredo, who had developed idle habits. Di Camillo was fearful that Alfredo would not become a good citizen and, like Ramón Domínguez, di Camillo wanted his son sent to the Marcos Paz facility. Although di Camillo proved himself to be Alfredo's natural father, a lack of room in the reformatory led officials to deny the request.[49]

The Society of Beneficence Workshops

The Society of Beneficence, in its effort to provide a role model for children, also taught them how to work. Society workers treated vagrant children placed in their care in the same way they dealt with orphans and fulfilled the dictates of the civil code by paying them a tiny wage, and by turning their orphanages for children above the age of six into workshops. Since the Society operated both a boys' orphanage and one for girls, as well as other reformatories, the gendered nature of child manual labor was clear. In 1877 the Asilo de Huérfanas [girls' orphanage] reported that the girls living there had earned $16,745 pesos, mostly by washing curtains and making jams.[50] By the 1880s the training offered at the girls' orphanage had expanded to meet the needs of a modern city and included training courses for future telephone operators. In 1886 the Unión Telefónica [Union Telephone Company] asked for more girls from the orphanage. Nevertheless, washing and cooking remained the principal work for orphans, and gradually sewing replaced washing curtains.[51]

Education for girls focused more on vocational manual training than on basic educational skills. By 1900 orphaned girls received six years of schooling, and in each grade they learned different sewing skills. For example, fourth-grade girls learned basic embroidery and some cooking skills, while their fifth-grade counterparts learned how to embroider in white, silk, and gold threads. According to the Society's annual report, the youngest of the schoolgirls learned principles of dressmaking.[52] What began as education soon functioned as a factory routine.

In a 1910 letter from the girls' orphanage to the president of the Society of Beneficence, the work schedule precluded time for other forms of learning. By then there were five workshops: embroidery, dressmaking, laundry, the construction of underwear and clothing for the children, and the preparation of jams and pastry. Each workshop operated from 8 to 11:30 AM and from 1:30 to 4:30 PM daily, except Wednesdays when the children cleaned the facilities. Below the fifth grade, younger girls attended a "work" class [*clase de labores*] for three-hour afternoon sessions as well as evening sessions to learn how to do laundry and make clothing for other inmates.[53] Within this regime, students could select what type of work they preferred.

In addition to the general work performed in the workshops, the Society constantly sought work contracts from government or commercial entities. On a number of occasions the damas sought contracts with the military to provide employment for the girls. To make the contracts both competitive and enticing, on at least one occasion the Society tried to undercut competition from factories by offering the services of orphans at no salary. Despite the desire to obtain low bids, not even the military could accept such conditions.[54]

Boys faced very different work situations regardless of whether they lived in the Asilo de Huérfanos [boys' orphanage] or were fostered out by either the defenders of minors or the Society of Beneficence. For one thing, the damas viewed the boys as ideal recruits for military service. Lacking fathers, officials reasoned that the boys belonged to the fatherland. This policy began as early as 1874, when Sra. Jacinta Castro, an orphanage employee, created the Maipú Battalion to train the boys in military maneuvers. Taught by a man who had been dismissed for taking part in a political rebellion, the damas rehabilitated him as he taught inmates discipline and military principles. The girls sewed the boys' uniforms as well as their own, and six years later the boys received their first rifles.[55] The boys' orphanage became so committed to military education that they criticized public schools for excluding it and accused them of "feminizing" boys instead of teaching them to defend the nation. If other young men learned how to work to defend the nation then they, too, would be ideal candidates for military service.[56] This idea became popular at other boys' orphanages.

The Society may have been delighted with this form of vocational training, but receiving these boys pleased neither the army nor the navy. Although military officials occasionally contacted the orphanage for recruits for the military band, they often rejected the children because the boys could not accustom themselves to military discipline and they had learned little at the damas' institutions.[57]

Furthermore, some educators hired by the boys' orphanage believed that the military did not offer the ideal vocation for all orphans. Bernabe Perdernera wrote to the president of the Society in 1899 and stated that after fourteen years of teaching at the orphanage he had concluded that not all the boys had natural inclinations to serve in the military. He was convinced that "to select an occupation or trade is a right of humanity [that] everyone should be able to enjoy."[58] Instead of tracking students in a military curriculum, boys should be offered the possibility of both vocational and humanist education.

In contrast to the Society, defenders of minors diligently tried to place the children in foster care if no relatives would take on the burden. Once placed, little girls still ran the risk of physical and sexual exploitation. Although some families developed a warm and protective relationship with orphaned girls, as well as educated them and gave them money as dowries rather than for services rendered, most girls resented the authority of their foster families. As a result, they often ran away from their employers because they found it less risky to live on the streets than as servants. Thus children fled from poor treatment, whether in reformatories or in foster homes.

On the other hand, philanthropists expected boys to support themselves. In 1900 when the workshops received completely new machinery, the proceeds of child labor financed the purchase.[59] In its report on income produced by the boys, the Society boasted of how well the regime functioned and argued that the "education and apprenticeship" received at the boys' orphanage could be quantified and that such information augured well for the future of the orphans, since such training would serve them throughout their lives.[60] In 1922 new machinery again arrived at the workshops where up to 430 boys supplied all the shoes and baked goods for the Society's various institutions.[61]

Gradually the Society expanded workshops for children through a com-

bination of private bequests and public subsidies. For example, the damas in 1901 founded an orphanage in Mercedes, province of Buenos Aires,
which they named General Martín Rodríguez after the liberal governor of
early Buenos Aires. Originally designed to catch the overflow of the foundling home, the women soon dedicated the facilities for boys in its care. By
1942 the institution had a capacity for seven hundred boys who learned
rural tasks, carpentry, weaving, and primary education under the guidance of the nuns of the Congregación de Hermanas de Nuestra Señora del
Huerto. In 1925 the Instituto José María Pizarro y Monje opened in honor of
the bequest of Doña Cornelia Pizarro to provide industrial education for
boys and girls. There they learned domestic service and sold their textile products to hospitals and to the public. The central sewing workshop
opened on February 15, 1917, to centralize the various workshops operating
at its establishment. There women who had been inmates as children and
unable to find work could obtain jobs. By 1942, fifty such women worked to
make clothes for the minors. And in 1934, they inaugurated a workshop for
up to sixty girls aged fourteen to eighteen to learn domestic skills. These
girls were once again under the supervision of nuns, this time the Congregación de los Santos Angeles Custodios [Congregation of Holy Guardian
Angels]. These new organizations represented only a few of the twentieth-
century asylums operated by the damas for boys and girls. Each had their
own rhythm and purpose and enabled the damas to send recalcitrant boys
and girls to more disciplinary environments if necessary, thereby creating
their own disciplinary and workshop system.

By the 1930s the Society of Beneficence had a network of hospitals,
orphanages, and workshops devoted to minor children. Thus, while the
number of children living at the institutions declined, the numbers in the
care of the Society, at least during the day, increased through such organizations as the Manuel Rocca Institute that provided four hundred poor children with free day care, education, and meals at no cost. Another four
hundred boys learned agronomy, animal husbandry, and schooling through
the secondary school level in Luján, province of Buenos Aires.[62]

Other Juvenile Reformatories and Workhouses

Within Buenos Aires and in many provinces, a series of philanthropic and
religious institutions housed rebellious children whose behavior caught the
attention of public authorities. Among the citizens of Buenos Aires, the
defenders of minors dealt with most of the non-orphan children found on

the streets. Like the damas of the Society of Beneficence they believed that the military would provide the ideal home for such waifs. In 1894 the defender for the southern part of Buenos Aires complained about the experience of some thirty minors sent to several battalion units. They were supposed to be paid two pesos per month once they reached the age of fifteen. Some went as musical apprentices, because these boys could be admitted at a younger age. But the defender recommended these placements only for the most incorrigible. The vast majority became servants in private homes because businesses didn't want to take in unruly juveniles.[63] In 1911, the defender Castellanos informed his superiors that the military unit that used to admit children into its ranks, the Escuela de Grumetes [Cabin-boy's School], no longer functioned. The remaining schools might take some of the street children, but the Escuelas de Apréndices Mecánicos [Mechanics Apprenticeship School], often required skills their wards did not have, while others insisted that recruits be at least nineteen years old.[64]

In his annual report for 1910, Castellanos stated that at least 60 percent of the juvenile boys he received from the courts were between the ages of ten and sixteen and were illiterate and without a trade. He argued that they should be schooled so that not only "would the State obtain useful citizens for the nation, it would also save important sums of money spent on feeding so many vagrants and vicious boys." Castellanos defined education in terms of apprenticeships that would permit them to save some money while reducing the costs of feeding them. Unfortunately most of these boys neither worked as apprentices nor learned a trade because there was no place to train them.[65] Indeed, Argentine industry had little demand for child labor.

Since the defenders of minors operated no facilities they sent juveniles to other institutions. The Damas de Caridad de San Vicente de Paul became the first group to offer their services to the juvenile courts established under the Agote law. They received permission to accept the delinquent girls in the Hogar Carolina Estrada de Martínez, named after the ladies' president. There the girls learned domestic arts based upon the programs in a similar home in Spain.[66]

Among the most enlightened organizations, the Casas del Niño, operated on the basis of small homes where children wore no uniforms, could come and go freely, and went to public school. Limited to thirty children per home, the five homes scattered throughout the city of Buenos Aires and its suburbs carried the motto "Neither jail nor asylum" and tried to provide a homelike atmosphere under the guidance of women. Eventually the

Casas became the ideal for juvenile establishments, although it was rarely imitated.[67]

The Patronato de la Infancia of Buenos Aires, with the help of its female auxiliary group, soon started working with juvenile delinquents. In 1896 the group established the Escuela de Artes y Oficios [School of Arts and Trades] for boys abandoned morally or materially, for the offspring of abusive parents, and for children of the poor. The impetus for this school came from an 1894 newspaper article about waifs rounded up on the streets by the police simply because of poverty. The group had a long discussion about the merits of seeking subsidies from the government, and those in favor won by arguing that their "own efforts will be inferior if we continue on our own."[68] They also toyed with the idea of training boys to serve in the navy or the military. When this did not work out, in 1914 they established what they called Escuelas Patrias [Patriotic Schools] to provide wholesome education for children in unwholesome neighborhoods. Geared toward native-born children, mostly because immigrants went to Argentina as adults, the Patriotic Schools provided education and philanthropy designed to hold the family together. Eventually more than eight hundred children attended the Escuelas Patrias in the southern district of Buenos Aires. It seems that the Patronato board members constantly read articles about the condition of street children, and when a case occurred that disturbed them they offered their services to public officials. Over time, they expanded vocational training in rural schools to include farming, ranching, and textile production.[69]

The Patronato also offered to operate the Escuela Agrícola-Industrial, a juvenile reformatory for boys at Claypole in the province of Buenos Aires. With financial help from the juvenile court, Patronato officials hoped to be able to renovate the Escuela de Maestros Rurales de Claypole [School for Rural Teachers of Claypole] so that up to 150 boys could live there. They also took possession of the downtown Asilo Humberto I° [Humberto I Street Asylum], at the request of and with funding from the Devoto family. Once again, they hoped to house some 120 minors there.[70]

Expanding the prisons did little to resolve the juvenile problem. For adults, rehabilitation signified reformed work habits that would keep them from committing crimes. For minors, rehabilitation implied education for several years and staying off the streets so that they did not have to work. Prisons either had to be turned into educational institutions or the children had to be transferred to better facilities. Neither policy became popular among government officials until the 1930s. Thus traditional concepts of reform and rehabilitation made little sense for the majority of minors in the prison population, and family reform became more important than individual rehabilitation for children.

Boys in Jail and on the Streets

Street children, especially males, did not enjoy the social protection of families. Regardless of their true origins, they were presumed to be lower class and destined for the most menial occupations. When these children ended up in court or were sent by their parents to the defenders, their lack of social protection was reaffirmed by their placement in the homes of strangers, in the penitentiary or in some other reformatory, or handed over to businesses. For all parties, the act of entering a jail confirmed societal disapproval of these youngsters and their families. Similarly, the act of leaving jail involved placing the child in the home of a nonrelative, thus further marking the child as a laborer and not a protected individual. In this new home the child had no parents but rather only employers. They had no relatives, furthermore, and they received no inheritance.

The process also deprived the children of the right to develop as adolescents and find their own identities. Although child rescue projects strived to "rehabilitate," they inevitably stained the reputation of the innocent young wards under their care by associating them with the world of crime and dishonor, by taking them away from parents, and by encouraging parents to turn over custody rights to children in order to have them rehabilitated in institutions.

The experience of boys in jail preferably linked them to the world of supervised work rather than work on the streets. Indeed, making a living on the streets often led to arrest. One of the most criticized jobs for boys was that of newspaper vendor. Even though this employment was a traditional one for boys in countries like the United States, in most Latin American countries the job was seen as one step away from delinquency. In 1908 the psychologist and criminal expert José Ingenieros published his observations of newspaper boys in Buenos Aires. Conducted in 1901, his research was based on information from employment records of newspapers, from the Carcel de Encausados [Jail for Misdemeanor Crimes], from the privately sponsored shelter called the Refugio de Menores [Minors' Refuge], and from the jail that housed juveniles accused of more serious crimes, the Casa de Corrección [Boys' Jail]. Ingenieros viewed selling papers on the streets as a gateway to criminality because most families who sent their children out to work, even immigrant ones, did not need the income to survive. Instead they chose to put their sons to work because "they wanted to profit from the New World even if the price was the future of their sons." The psychologist also argued that the children were perverted because they engaged in public acts of masturbation and many of them had participated in homosexual activity.[71] It is important to note that key arguments of Ingenieros's report linked children's problems to dysfunctional families and to inappropriate parents, and linked working on the streets to inappropriate sexuality. Poor boys could work for their parents in supervised settings in industry and, ideally, out in the countryside, but not on the streets.

Within the boys' jail, overcrowded conditions and difficulties in exercising control led to severe corporal punishment. A public scandal emerged in late 1900 with the indictment of the director of the jail for his complicity in the case of a young thief beaten to death. Soon afterward, the institution reconstituted itself as the boys' reformatory. There, after 1905, youths under the age of fifteen had to be interviewed by the newly created Oficina de Estudios Médicos Legales [Office of Medico-Legal Studies]. The results of many of these interviews were published in a short-lived journal called *Revista Penitenciaria* [Penitentiary Review], which was published by the director of the reformatory.[72] The reports prompted experts to offer legal opinions as to whether the child could distinguish between right and wrong. The inability to do so constituted the only way that juveniles could receive a lesser sentence than determined by the penal code. Officials at the reformatory, however, rarely asked for such a reduction because they wanted longer to rehabilitate the child.

According to the *Revista Penitenciaria*, unacceptable sexual behavior was often the hallmark of the male street child. Not only did police accuse children of sexual crimes, particularly rape, delinquency specialists also asked about their sexual habits. "Alonso Ara" was arrested in 1905 and accused of pederasty. The fifteen-year-old sold fruit on the street at a stand with his father in the Spinetto market. The mother of eleven-year-old "Andrés Gutiérrez" claimed that Alonso raped the younger boy after he forced him into the interior of the fruit stand.[73] "Jerónimo" P., a twelve-year-old orphan, was arrested for theft, but it seems that the interviewers had more interest in his sexual life. Evidently he claimed to have had sexual relations from the age of nine; since then, he had visited bordellos and had sex with dogs and goats as well as homosexual relations. Rather than view this testimony as the excessive boasting of a child, the specialists determined that he should be considered an adult, declared degenerate and not responsible for his acts, and interned in the boys' reformatory.[74]

Within the institution, wardens constantly monitored boys for evidence of masturbation and homosexual activity. They intercepted letters of affection between boys and had them separated. They insisted that boys sleep face up with their hands outside their covers after some thirty boys were caught and forced to confess they had been masturbating. Once again, the children were stigmatized as sexual perverts.[75]

The interviewers also asked about family ties. They wanted to know how many abortions their mothers had, the drinking habits of their fathers, and whether siblings had criminal histories. "Juan" L., a shoeshine boy accused of striking someone, had been arrested at the age of nine. He was thirteen when interviewed. One of five children of illiterate immigrant parents, delinquency specialists considered him to have a good morality despite "having belonged to the guild of newspaper vendors and wandering shoeshine boys, who, given the scant monitoring of their parents are, in general, vicious, vagabonds and quarrelsome."[76] Because he had poor but honest parents, the specialists labeled Juan as too poorly educated to understand his acts. This was probably little comfort to the young boy who still had to serve his sentence.

The views of the interviewers, as well as the conditions of the children, changed little over time. In 1937 Juan Carlos Landó, a specialist in juvenile delinquency, described the classic street child as "uneducated . . . or with enormous educational backwardness, torn out of the promiscuity of the tenement house, with his sexual instincts prematurely awakened and often perverted, suffering from the consequences of alcohol, TB, or syphilis, the abandoned street child or delinquent is neither always more or less normal than his happier companions who go to school, sleep alone, have medical attention, and who are familiar with kindness and the protection of the family."[77]

For Landó, happy male street children lived in the Ricardo Gutiérrez facility in Marcos Paz—an ironic statement given the frequency with which boys escaped from this and other reformatories. Nevertheless, the unsentimental tropes about street children remained constant and linked to the absence of appropriate family members as well as of love and affection. And female reformers intended to rehabilitate boys through work and moral reform in the same way as their male counterparts.

How many boys landed in jail? Between 1898 and 1903 a total of 636 boys were imprisoned in penitentiaries, most of whom were Argentine, along with a number of Italians and Spaniards. Between 1904 and 1913 the numbers soared as 4,019 boys under the age of sixteen were imprisoned, compared with 12,015 between the ages of sixteen and twenty. Between 1919 and 1923, however, only 1,218 boys under age sixteen were imprisoned, compared with 4,302 boys between sixteen and twenty. The drop in younger boys reflected laws that mandated that younger boys be sent to reformatories.[78]

Police Campaigns to Clear the Streets

Part of the problem dealing with children on the streets of Argentine cities resulted from massive police campaigns to keep the streets free of children. The experience of Buenos Aires from 1922 to 1928 shows how police campaigns to reduce the number of street children affected the number of children incarcerated. The Buenos Aires juvenile judge César Viale, a member of the Instituto Tutelar de Menores, saw more than 2,000 children in just five years between 1923 and 1927. This number included both boys and girls, few of whom were under the care of the defenders of minors. Viale's reports indicated the growing importance of placing youths in a system of parole often monitored by philanthropic and religious women. Among the children free under parole [*libertad vigilada*], 5,903 boys and 391 girls entered the program, while 4,388 boys and 278 girls were removed from the parole list. At the same time, 3,203 boys were accused along with 736 girls. The boys went to reform schools, orphanages, a school for the retarded, and schools run by the Salesian Brothers, the Patronato de la Infancia, and the Society of Beneficence. The girls went to the Casa Correccional de Mujeres, the Asilo San Miguel (usually reserved for prostitutes), and asylums operated by the Damas Católicas [Catholic Ladies], the Damas del Taller "La Providencia" [Ladies of the La Providencia Workshop], the Society of Beneficence, and the Damas de Caridad. Once again the tight relationship between the state and Catholic charities could be seen in the distribution of children, and this made it difficult to calculate how many children lived in institutional settings simply because they were poor.[79]

Most of the boys were accused of selling newspapers without authorization (338), shining shoes without permission (250), or working on the streets without permission (21), all of which were actions that had become misdemeanor offenses. In comparison only 11 were arrested for drunkenness, and just 194 for begging, 86 for carrying arms, and 178 for disorderly conduct. The rest ended up in jail for loitering and other misdemeanors. By contrast Viale did not mention the girls' offenses.

Viale also included statistics from the 1928–1932 period. The number of children arrested decreased to 713 boys and 104 girls, while the number of children on parole expanded. This time he mentioned the crimes attributed to the girls, making it clear that the girls more likely ended up in jail as victims than as perpetrators. While police accused 12 girls of scandal (prostitution), 21 of disorderly conduct, and 24 of begging (the categories with the greatest number of accusations), 29 were victims of crimes and the rest were accused of minor misdemeanors. Although it might appear strange that female victims of crimes ended up in institutions along with girls accused of committing crimes, this occurred fairly frequently. The girls landed in asylums, and some were even sent to jail after being accused of immorality for inciting the perpetrator.

How many places were available in child reformatories? The institutional facilities for these children remained limited, which led to so many being placed on probation. A 1925 Argentine government report on juvenile delinquency noted that only 1,450 places existed within government institutions for delinquent or homeless children. The reform school in the province of Buenos Aires, the facility with the largest capacity by far (excluding the Society of Beneficence), housed 500 boys, and hoped to open a facility for 500 girls. The Instituto Tutelar de Menores housed only 350 children, while the Marcos Paz facility housed 500 more. The downtown boys' jail, the Alcaldía de Menores, had capacity for only 100 boys in two large dormitories, but it often housed more. Finally, a regional asylum for retarded children for boys and girls, not included in the 1,450 places, housed 800 adults and children. The other official institutions fell under the category of "protective" institutions, and it included all of the homes operated by the Society of Beneficence.[80]

Both private and public institutions thus rehabilitated juveniles. The city of Buenos Aires had formed yet another group, the Asociación Tutelar de Menores [Association of Guidance for Minors], which controlled the Escuela-Taller General "Benjamín Victoria" [Industrial School for Boys "Benjamín Victoria"] in the Tigre area of Buenos Aires. It had room for 150 boys, as well as two small reformatories for girls with a capacity of 90. The Casa del Niño still operated, but no statistics for its activities were offered. The Salesian Brothers ran a number of schools for boys throughout the country under the rubric of the work of Don Bosco, and the Methodists, the

Catholic damas, and a number of other organizations offered the bulk of private reformatory housing for more than 4,000 children. Gradually the province of Buenos Aires established its own reform schools.[81]

There are also some statistics for the provincial jails. In the province of Mendoza in 1926, for example, 45 children sent by defenders of minors went to the public reformatory for minors, while 200 girls went to the Asilo del Buen Pastor and 4 boys went to the army or the navy. Girls often landed in convents or labored at domestic service. In 1935 in Córdoba province, the minors' section in the jail for the indicted divided boys in age categories of ten to fourteen (30) and fifteen to twenty-five (651).

The province of Tucumán, the smallest in Argentina, also had its share of juveniles in jail. Between 1898 and 1907, only 45 boys under fifteen were jailed, but 863 between fifteen and twenty-five. In 1910 alone, 31 boys under fifteen were jailed, while in 1918, the number was 78, mostly for robbery and property crimes. Similar statistics described conditions from 1919 to 1923. Usually between 25 and 60 children were jailed, and police provided no explanation for the arrests.[82]

Imprisoned or institutionalized children did not necessarily remain under state supervision. Most of them escaped, at least for short periods of time. Take the case of "Samuel" P., a sixteen year old arrested for vagrancy in 1947 and sent to the Escuela-Taller General "Benjamín Victoria." Shortly after arriving, the young boy crossed a ditch that encircled the home and then ran to nearby hills where he hid in the weeds until he could return home. His mother refused to let him in, so he went back into the streets until a policeman caught him again. Although he was ready to leave the institution when he turned eighteen, his parents refused to allow him home (most likely due to his bad behavior). He was sent to another home where he lived until a brother promised to take care of him, and he labored as a carpenter in the workshop of the Consejo de Asistencia Social [National Board of Social Assistance].[83]

"Juan Antonio" P., an eighteen-year-old orphan who lived with an elderly work companion, arrived at the boys' reformatory after having been accused several times of vagrancy. After living at the Ricardo Gutiérrez facility he escaped in April 1950 and then remained on the streets until police recaptured him in February 1951. That November he ran away again and remained in hiding until the institution declared him officially released from the facility in 1953.[84] These stories exemplify the reality that neither parents nor institutions could deal with rebellious children whose behavior reflected developmental behavior that was not acceptable.

How to Reform the Reformatories

As early as 1920 Dr. Gregorio Bermann, a pioneer psychiatrist from the province of Córdoba, openly challenged the nation's dependence on a child welfare system that combined philanthropy and child specialists. He did not discount the concerns of the police about who broke the law, but rather he analyzed why children broke the law. For Bermann the solution to child delinquency could be found neither in incarceration nor in disinterested beneficence, but rather in the skilled analysis and investigation of specialists like himself.[85]

Bermann examined the record of the Olivera juvenile reformatory, which had been in operation since 1922 under the control of the Ministerio de Relaciones Exteriores y Culto [Ministry of Foreign Relations and Religion]. Judges, police officials, and defenders of minors sent boys there. In his opinion the reformatory was not able to achieve "the goals of educating and re-socializing boys because it is impossible to treat abandoned minors, whether due to parental disappearance or parental inability to raise the boys, in the same way and along with juvenile delinquents." He believed the same to be true of other reformatories under the Ministerio de Instrucción Pública.[86]

Bermann recommended reorganizing juvenile delinquency facilities in Argentina along with the greater use of specialists, usually males, rather than moral reformers or religious orders, both male and female. The arrival of the world depression shortly after he made his statements made that goal more important than ever before. The dilemma remained, however, as to how willing the national government would be to take primary responsibility in child reform efforts and how such reforms would be funded.

By the 1940s the treatment and housing of juvenile delinquents was in crisis. A series of national conferences were organized in order to discuss their plight, which was seen as far more urgent than that of the abandoned babies at the beginning of the century. The demography of poor children on the street had shifted. Specialists still blamed the family, but the solutions had to be different, and the Argentine state had to decide between government officials and the philanthropic private sector as the party responsible for implementing juvenile delinquency treatment. Poverty and family dislocation caused by the world depression added to the increasing migration to Buenos Aires of families as well as youngsters on their own, and this issue along with the increased visibility of street children due to police campaigns necessitated new solutions.

Adolescents on the streets in Argentina prompted philanthropic and professional specialists to study the problem of the children's presence there. Their solutions directly affected the shape of welfare regimes and served as a catalyst for the formation of the Argentine welfare state. However, the state found it financially difficult to divest itself of its reliance on volunteer and religious philanthropy, and this issue became clearer as military coups interrupted the democratic state from 1930 onward. The political groups that allied themselves with the military found it increasingly difficult to ignore the requests for subsidies, and the calls for the welfare state coincided with the expansion of government subsidies.

CHAPTER 5

The Depression and the Rise
of the Welfare State

Despite the inadequacies of the child welfare facilities in Argentina, by the beginning of the 1930s they were receiving international accolades. The Pan American Union praised the women philanthropists and their endeavors, as did other international groups that tended to focus more on services for women and infants than on state juvenile bureaucracies. When President Herbert Hoover and his wife Lou Henry Hoover visited Argentina in 1929, Mrs. Hoover visited the Society of Beneficence and lauded its recently opened Maternal Institute. Two years later the *Bulletin of the Pan American Union* published an article entitled "Child Welfare Institutions in Buenos Aires and Montevideo." The authors noted that the efforts in these regions were impressive, and they pointed out that the results "obtained are not the work of any one institution or group but rather of many institutions and groups working in complete accord and cooperation with the government of each country, [with] private initiative serving fields which public action failed to cover."[1]

Such apparent seamlessness of public and private efforts between those of municipal, private, and religious philanthropic agencies and the Society of Beneficence ignored the child welfare organizational issues that concerned the governments of the 1930s, particularly under the presidency of Agustín P. Justo (1932–1938) and his Concordancia alliance. The impact of the world depression on agriculture, combined with urban suffering and a desire to rationalize state bureaucracies, placed an enormous demand upon all branches of the Argentine government to respond. This chapter focuses on the ways that new government agencies threatened the philanthropic women's contribution to maternal assistance and juvenile reform, while it created more jobs for professional women. Ironically, at the very time that government-subsidized child welfare reached new heights, government social policies co-opted their mission and empowered professional women.

Aware of the impact of the world depression on Buenos Aires, the Concordancia government understood how it affected children and used it as a justification to change state policy toward abandoned children. On January 24, 1931, a decree finally reorganized and funded the Patronato Nacional de Menores and empowered its board to reorganize the juvenile justice system. The people named to the Patronato included prominent male specialists in child rights issues, and with President Justo's support they convened a major conference to bring together national and provincial authorities interested in reforming juvenile law.

Held in September 1933, the Primera Conferencia Nacional Sobre Infancia Abandonada y Delincuente [First National Conference on Abandoned and Delinquent Children] attracted the attention of the public at large, not only because of the topic but also the attendance of the president and his cabinet. In a speech at the event Dr. Manuel M. de Yriondo, the minister of justice and public instruction, cited the argument of the juvenile delinquency specialist Judge Carlos de Arenaza, who stated that "by protecting children, the state consolidates its own principles." Yriondo also recognized that private philanthropic groups had been in charge of child welfare since the passage of the Agote law in 1919, and the results of these efforts indicated a lack of coordination.[2]

The specialists discussed juvenile delinquency and the need for a system of supervised parole for minors, a technique until then used mostly for adult female offenders. The socialist deputy Angel Gímenez attended the sessions and lauded the proposals of specialists. On subsequent days juvenile specialists debated the merits of reform schools as compared to children left at home with biological parents, and they suggested legal adoption as an alternative to reform schools. They went out of their way to praise the Casas del Niño as a model for minors, although they did not discuss the increased costs of such a system. For these child rights advocates, the needs of children had to be met regardless of cost. Before the end of the conference, the legal specialist Jorge Coll presented his comprehensive child welfare reform proposals. The legislation covered the gamut from patria potestad reforms to complete adoption; regulations for child labor; and penal code reforms that covered child abuse. Notably, his plan did not discuss female philanthropy as an essential item. For Coll and others, the future of female philanthropy was no longer tied to social policies related to children.

Members of the Society of Beneficence and the damas of San Vicente de Paul injected their opinions at the September 28 session about the rehabilitation of girls. The perceived difference between the genders emerged when participants discussed whether vocational education should be different for boys and girls. Some argued that girls should not be given professional training but rather preparation for domestic life. No one refuted this idea because feminists did not attend the conference.[3] Furthermore, one of the damas of San Vicente de Paul reiterated the special challenge of helping girls in prison, and she offered the society's services to attend to these girls, much like the nuns of the Good Shepherd had done many years before. In noting that the damas of St. Vincent de Paul had been accepting girls recommended by the juvenile courts created in 1919, she pointed out that the few girls they could accept lived in family settings of thirty girls where they were given a basic education as well as lessons in housekeeping and child care.[4]

Even before the conference took place, public officials recognized the precarious situation of female minors. In 1932, economic conditions had made it very difficult to place the youngsters in homes as domestic servants, and a higher than usual number of homeless girls went to the women's jail. For those reasons, even before the conference President Justo in 1932 decreed that the Patronato Nacional de Menores establish an institution for the girls in the women's jail "so that they can get work in industry or commerce." To that end, the government donated a property to the Patronato Nacional.[5]

Given the number of girls still incarcerated each year at the women's jail, Buenos Aires needed more than a few model homes to deal with young girls forced onto the streets. The alliance between the Patronato Nacional de Menores and the state ultimately led to the formation of larger girls' homes under the watchful eyes of penologists and sociologists rather than the nuns of the Good Shepherd, who operated the Casa Correccional de Mujeres, and this directly challenged subsidized philanthropic efforts. By the end of Concordancia rule in 1943, the Patronato operated three homes for girls compared with six for boys.

The Hogar Santa Rita opened in 1938 under the auspices of the Patronato Nacional de Menores, headed by Susana Fernándes de la Puente. The home in downtown Buenos Aires operated under the auspices of the Patronato Nacional, and judges or defenders and specialists assessed the minors and sent them elsewhere. Shortly thereafter, the Patronato Nacional also opened the Asilo de Niñas Menores [Girls' Asylum] and the Escuela Hogar

Santa Rosa [Santa Rosa Home and School] in the province of Buenos Aires. These homes housed 390 girls, far too few to address all the delinquent girls' problems.[6]

New Mother-Child State Agencies

By 1943 the Argentine national government had also created a series of mother-focused agencies including the 1936 Dirección de Maternidad e Infancia [Mother and Infant Bureau] and the 1933 Caja de Maternidad [Mother's Pension Fund], which was established to ensure that working women could take time off to care for their newborn children. A governmental shift from principally addressing child welfare to more attention to maternal assistance and mothers' rights thus occurred at the same time that the government expanded resources for minors arrested by the police or placed under the custody of defenders.

Many state-controlled child and maternal welfare ideas obtained strong support from the Concordancia's ally, the Independent Socialists, along with its devoted enemy, the Socialist Party. Indeed, socialists under the leadership of Alfredo Palacios introduced many rights-based proposals for working mothers (which also were advocated by feminists) along with those that came from official quarters. At the same time, in response to the impact of the world depression, individual provinces supplemented municipal programs to expand existing local services, and the national government augmented these actions with extensive subsidies. By the end of the 1930s a welfare state shored up but did not replace social policies based on national government subsidies. By late 1937, however, serious questions emerged once again about the efficacy of a welfare state still reliant on subsidies to philanthropic organizations.

Although the many government agencies established during this time were poorly funded and far from effective, they provided the blueprint for the Peronist welfare state. Equally important, they showed the shared political commitment to state-directed mother and child welfare that tenuously linked sectors of conservative liberals, public health officials, philanthropic women, feminists, socialists, members of the Radical Party, and right-wing conservatives. National conferences devoted to child welfare, and the entry of new groups hoping to shape government welfare policies, facilitated public discussion of the welfare state. Conference organizers often approached child welfare from opposing ideological viewpoints but still found grounds for cooperation. Nevertheless, the consensus on child welfare did not translate into a full-blown welfare state of any kind until the accession of Juan Perón to the presidency in 1946 and his ability to direct revenues into the welfare budget. The desire and demand already existed, but scarce funding during the 1930s impeded major state investments in welfare.

Families, Minors, and the Depression

Initially, the impact of the world depression on Argentina became evident in the massive influx of migrants from the interior of the country to the city of Buenos Aires—men, women, and children seeking work. This migration to Buenos Aires occurred relatively late as families and individuals first tried their best to survive in the Argentine interior. Before 1936 the city annually welcomed 8,000 migrants each year, but between 1936 and 1943 it had to provide housing, work, and welfare for an additional 72,000 migrants, or an average of 12,000 migrants per year. Between 1929 and 1934, the average wage fell 77 percent, and wages only returned to their 1929 levels in 1939. The cost of living paralleled these changes.[7]

Tough economic conditions thus did not immediately translate into more cases of infant abandonment and increases in the number of street children. Unlike the late nineteenth century, by the 1930s many mothers had learned not to rely on infant abandonment at the state orphanages. Indeed, during that decade the number of infants abandoned at the foundling home of the Society of Beneficence declined from 1,131 in 1932 to 830 in 1936, and then continued to decline with the exception of 1937. Nevertheless, the home sheltered 8,645 babies left homeless during the 1930s, and out of this total only two infants died—a clear indication of improved conditions and hygiene.[8]

The lower abandonment rates at the foundling home did not mean, however, that parents did not abandon children, but rather that they sacrificed the older ones. Reduced numbers of abandoned infants testified to the welfare networks that had been established by ethnic and religious communities as well as to the success of public health education now available to parturient women. These efforts had been furthered by the creation in 1915 of the Asociación Cantinas Maternales de Buenos Aires [Association of Mothers' Canteens of Buenos Aires]. Founded by the elite matron Julia Elena Acevedo de Martínez de Hoz, the association strategically placed the canteens in urban areas with high-density housing for the poor. Canteen volunteers provided two nutritionally balanced meals a day for breastfeeding mothers. Members of the association also made house calls to registered mothers. Eventually canteens for school-age children opened alongside the maternal canteens where the youngsters received two meals a day and a toothbrush. By 1929 six mothers' canteens opened in Buenos Aires along with four canteens for schoolchildren, and all received government subsidies. Mothers' canteens also operated in other cities.[9]

These efforts, however, did not stop the flow of older children into institutional life. Indeed, the flow of destitute migrants did not end with the rise of Perón. The Society of Beneficence, as well as other government-operated institutions, continued to receive the bulk of the homeless as internal migrants did not have ties with immigrant communities. Archival documents note that mothers traveled with children, and children migrated on their own. In some cases, public authorities sent children to Buenos Aires. This human migration placed new strains on social policies and provided the backdrop for the welfare state.

A few examples, gleaned from the many files of the Consejo Nacional de Niñez, Adolescencia y Familia [National Council for Children, Adolescence, and the Family], confirm these stresses. "Clarissa B.," the child of a domestic servant and a day laborer from Tucumán, became one of the earliest migrant minors sent to the Society of Beneficence in 1930. The youngest of four children, Clarissa's parents sent her to the Society of Beneficence at the tender age of one because of her mother's ill health. During the subsequent years the family never visited her, and Clarissa went from one institution to another until 1947 when the Federal Intervener received a letter from a family in Mar del Plata seeking a domestic servant. A year later, the family returned Clarissa because of her headstrong temperament. She then went to work in another home. Many families tried, but few could put up with her insolence.[10] "Inés A." provided a later case. She went into the Society of Beneficence in January 1944 after her father's death. The family had lived in Santa Fe, but without the salary from the household head, and without dependable relatives, the mother moved with her children to Buenos Aires where she worked as a cook. Unable to care for the nine-year-old Inés, the mother petitioned for the admission of her daughter. After the daughter was placed, the mother visited her constantly.[11]

The Patronato Nacional de Menores received a petition from the father of "Julia" R., an eleven-year-old girl from Córdoba living with her aunt, asking the organization to take custody of the girl because of her mother's severe illness. Evidently the child demonstrated an adolescent temperament, and the aunt could no longer handle her, even though the child had never run away or stayed out too late. The real reason for the aunt's ire, as revealed in the documentation, was that her brother had abandoned the child and left her with the responsibility. Nevertheless, Julia paid the price at the Hogar "Santa Rosa."[12]

"Ana María" G., a domestic servant, arrived in Buenos Aires from Mendoza around 1945 after she could no longer deal with her day-laborer husband's irresponsible life and poor treatment of her. She had five children ranging from ten years old to newborn twins. Before migrating, she had lived with her brother in one room with two beds and one mattress for ten people. Ana María sent her twin infants to the foundling home, one of whom was sent to live with a wet nurse outside the institution while the other remained in the home.

In October 1948 Ana María retrieved one of the twins. The child only remained with her mother until 1954, however, because Ana María asked to readmit her because the family lived in a "pathetic" house made of wood and zinc siding. For food they lived from hand to mouth with the help of items donated by another daughter's employer. Eventually both of the younger daughters went back into institutions, although the former wet nurse took them out on vacations. The children remained institutionalized until the 1960s.[13]

In 1949 two juveniles ran away from the regional Patronato Nacional facilities in the territory of Río Negro. Once caught by authorities, the judge in Río Negro sent them to the Ricardo Gutiérrez facility, very far from the homes of their parents. At the Ricardo Gutiérrez facility, one boy's aunt visited him regularly, and he remained a ward of the court until he turned twenty-one in 1952.[14]

These stories indicate that the world depression severely disrupted the lives of many parents and children. When added to the tales of need by local residents of Buenos Aires, as well as those of victims of the 1944 earthquake in San Juan, these stories underscore the constant demand of Argentines for public welfare related to children. The situation could be remedied either by strengthening the Argentine family and the aid offered to mothers with young children, or by providing institutional care for the minors.

Biotypology, Eugenics, and Mother-Child Welfare

One conservative group, the Asociación Argentina de Biotipología, Eugenesia y Medicina Social [Argentine Biotypology, Eugenics, and Social Medicine Association], became both visible and vocal during the 1930s. The group advocated solutions to dysfunctional children and families based upon principles of eugenics, the science of good births, and biotypology— the science linking environmental, physical, and social family traits to individuals. The group was founded by prominent physician and scientist Dr. Arturo Rossi after he studied with the Italian biotypologist Nicolà Pendè. As early as September 1930, the organization Rossi founded had designed a program that initially focused more on the control of infectious diseases than on eugenics. Subsequently this entity described its new mission as shifting the discourse on children to mothers because "today with the advances of modern science it is indispensable to shift the focus from the child since, in infancy, *the child is nothing and the mother is everything.*"[15]

The Asociación de Biotipología, Eugenesia y Medicina Social, a collaboration of a number of distinguished Argentine scientists including the physicist Mariano R. Castex, the group's first president, was inaugurated in 1932 in the halls of the Faculty of Medicine of the University of Buenos Aires with many government officials attending. The organization's stated aim was to educate intellectuals and instruct the masses on issues affecting future generations of Argentines.[16]

The association published a magazine, but one of its first acts was to obtain permission from the mayor of Buenos Aires to broadcast a radio program. When it first aired in 1932 the program, eventually called *Eugenismo*, offered fifteen minutes of advice to families, mostly about the value of social workers. After complaints from the members of the Socialist Party that permission to broadcast had not been granted by the municipal council, the radio show disappeared. The main focus of the opposition by the socialists was the ability of a group they considered fascist to have access to the airwaves.[17]

Indeed many, but not all, members of the group supported fascist views that included strong support of motherhood. For example, in 1935 Dr. Alberto Peralta Ramos of the Society of Beneficence's Instituto Maternal and Dr. Josué Beruti gave a talk entitled "Eugenics and Maternity," in which they contended that having healthy mothers would solve the most pressing eugenic problems in Argentina. They even cited Joseph Goebbels, who wrote that "the mother and child constitute the mortgage of societies that defend their immortality," and who further argued that the key to this immortality was the opening of more maternal and infant clinics.[18] This was one of the very few direct statements lauding fascist governments published in the journal.

Yet most eugenists in Argentina, unlike those in North America and

Europe, concerned themselves less with specific racial causes of infant mortality and weakness than with economic misery and defective patriarchy as basic causes. In 1936 even the Spaniard Dr. Carlos Bernaldo de Quiros, one of the most fervent eugenics advocates, wrote that most governments and the public misunderstood eugenics because they believed it relied principally on racial degeneration theories. In contrast, he argued that approximately 70 percent of all the problems were due to economic circumstances.[19]

The association advocated many viewpoints. For example, in a 1933 radio program the teacher Celia Rimondi proposed the creation of the "Week of the Mother and Child" and "Mother and Child Day," without racial distinctions. In fact, these celebrations had been supported by feminists in many countries. To justify her plan, Rimondi made the following statement: "We believe that the eugenic guidance of mothers and children, according to the current state of science and sociology, is one of the cornerstones of Medicine and Social Assistance, and, for this reason, of the political sociology of nations."[20]

To further disseminate their ideas, members of the association, in collaboration with Dr. Tomás Amadeo, president of the Museo Social Argentino [Argentine Social Museum], published in April 1936 the first issue of a new monthly magazine called *Hijo mío* [My Son]. With the public support of the Boy Scouts, the Feminine Symphonic Association, and other educational groups, the first issue contained articles suggesting how to furnish a child's room, select washable dresses for girls, and identify appropriate sexual education for children. Other articles chided fathers for sending their children to boarding schools because they had no time to become involved with their education and presumed that parental authority should be given to mothers.[21] In a subsequent article, "Scientific Wet Nurses," *Hijo Mío* published pictures of women sitting in separate cubicles, expressing milk. Not only did they not feed the infants directly, but they also wore masks and headscarves during the procedure. After the women expressed their breast milk it was frozen in molds for later use.[22]

Despite the conservative ideological influences on some biotypologists, their child care recommendations often were neither unique nor conservative. Progressive mother-infant programs, including the use of milk extractors and the need to educate new mothers, had been widely accepted both inside and outside of Argentina. As Nancy Stepan has pointed out, both Argentine feminists and male politicians had been aware of the relationship of reproductive rates to the nation-state. Outside Argentina, mothers' pen-

nationalist eugenics

sions had been advocated in the United States since 1909, and in 1912 the nation established a Children's Bureau, funded by the national government and operated by feminists to empower mothers to help their children. Linked to the settlement-house movement, the Children's Bureau successfully promoted social welfare legislation in the 1920s, although it lost control of mother and child welfare with the passage of Social Security legislation in the 1930s. Great Britain and Germany also debated and implemented versions of mother-child welfare, often placing the costs of child welfare on mothers as was done in the Argentine Mothers' Caja de Maternidad.[23]

President Justo presided over the First National Conference on Social Assistance in 1933. In this conference, the biotypologists held sway. The emphasis on the family was so strong that the noted physicist Mariano Castex, along with several specialists, urged social workers to adopt the notion of biotypology. Castex defined biotypology to people who worked with children and pointed out that Pendè offered a way to understand developmental psychology by observing the individual within his or her environment. The author ended his discussion urging the collection of biotypical data on all individuals.[24]

While some members of the Concordancia might have been swayed by the fascist elements of groups like the biotypology organization, admiration did not result in government policies. Legislation supported conservative and progressive laws for children and mothers, but few proposals became law. In 1932, two Concordancia deputies, Ramón G. Loyarte and Benjamín S. González, even suggested creating a National Department for Child Social Assistance, based upon the recommendations of a 1930 conference in Washington that advocated free prenatal, natal, and postnatal care for working mothers and state employees. The Argentine plan would be financed through a series of taxes including a 2 percent tax on electricity consumption in Buenos Aires. In the legislator's accompanying message, they spoke of having met the directors of the Children's Bureau and of being persuaded by their actions, as well as by their advocacy of social workers. They also cited the literature on children's rights and the patriotic need to protect children. This measure, too, did not pass.[25]

Concordancia supporters even proposed legislation to combine social assistance and weaken patriarchal rights over juvenile delinquents. On September 22, 1933, Senator Ramón S. Castillo (who would go on to become president) presented a comprehensive law designed to protect orphans and children under the age of eighteen who had been "morally" abandoned by their parents and therefore deserving of state support. If enacted, parents would lose the ability to recirculate or privately place children without government permission, and judges could decide if children remained with parents or went to institutions. Furthermore, the new law permitted adoptions of such minors, even if their parents still lived, and the Society of Beneficence would only care for children under the age of ten. Again, this proposal never passed.[26]

Argentine socialists also defended child welfare, and curiously they had better luck with their legislative proposals. Although a section of the Socialist Party formed an alliance with the Concordancia, the most visible supporters of child welfare remained within the original party. On September 30, 1933, Angel Giménez and Enrique Dickmann fought unsuccessfully with the conservative Manuel Fresco to have a vote on the Castillo legislation introduced in the matter, when he insisted that the project be voted on according to the congressional schedule.[27] The opposing parties disagreed only on the timing of the vote rather than on the issue, which clearly had supporters within both progressive and conservative traditions.

Alfredo Palacios, the first Socialist Party deputy elected to the national Congress and the fervent enemy of the Concordancia's electoral fraud, joined the Argentine senate as a member of the Alianza Civil [Civil Alliance] in 1932. From that vantage point, he became the architect of legislation to establish the Caja de Maternidad. When Palacios submitted his own plan on September 7, 1933, he invoked national fears of degeneration, particularly among male military conscripts, as a justification to support his legislation. Before he cited his statistics, he noted that "the Argentine nation is degenerating, and it injures our national pride." Such a comment could as easily come from a biotypology or eugenics advocate as from a socialist.[28] Palacios then utilized a mixture of economic, patriotic, and eugenics arguments. As far as he was concerned, "the offspring of the poor degenerates suffer due to lack of food, and because of the fatigue and hunger of *their mothers*. I invoke in this chamber the name of the nation so that a law of social justice will be passed, one that protects the physical integrity and moral of the future citizens and cares for the workers who will become mothers as well as those who have already given birth."[29] Palacios concluded with lengthy statistics from medical specialists as well as with the observation that almost all European countries and Brazil and Chile had passed similar legislation.

The Caja de Maternidad promoted by Palacios guaranteed for parturient women a period of paid vacation for thirty days before giving birth and forty-five days after the event. Regardless of where they worked, mothers

role of ♀'s bodies in nation-bldg
+ common cause of otherwise
enemies

would receive a maximum benefit of two hundred pesos per month and the free care of a doctor or midwife, and they would not lose their jobs. To finance this benefit, working women had to contribute to the fund. Before the law passed in June 1934, Alicia Moreau de Justo, the most visible socialist feminist, sent an emphatic note to the senate urging support for the legislation, and the biotypologists also lauded the law's enactment. This mutual concern for maternal and child welfare and an understanding of the impact of economics on the poor by both the Argentine Right and the Left facilitated the passage of key laws during the 1930s. In addition, it reinforces Sandra McGee Deutsch's theory that the extreme Right and Left in Argentina and other Latin American countries aligned on the issue of creating a welfare state and promoting social reform. Their differences related more to the structure of democracy than to the creation of a welfare state.[30]

Socialist feminists in favor of mother and child welfare disseminated their ideas through the journal *Vida Femenina* [Feminine Life]. In 1935 the feminist Josefina Marpons lauded Palacios's various legislative efforts to defend working mothers as well as his 1934 Caja de Maternidad. She argued ironically that women needed to know that "it is only the socialist spirit after so many years of resistance that has imposed the sacred right of the infant to enjoy his mother's breast milk, as well as the equally sacred right of mothers to give birth to sons for the nation."[31]

The following year the feminist socialist Alicia Moreau de Justo, in an article called "The Child: The Hope of Humanity," supported groups advocating child welfare and took the opportunity to critique one view of patriarchy by chastising those who only viewed children as property or as beings who would care for them in their old age. And, once again, she defended state child welfare policies: "The State intervenes even more frequently as part of this new collective conscience to protect children even from their parents when they are incapable of raising and educating them."[32]

In 1937 Alfredo Palacios launched another major child welfare campaign, this time focused on the condition of children in the northern provinces of Argentina. Palacios declared that the pro-immigration sentiment "To govern is to populate," expressed by the Argentine jurist Juan Bautista Alberdi, needed to be modernized, and he corrected it to proclaim "Gobernar es fortalecer, instruir y educar al ciudadano" ["To govern is to strengthen, instruct, and educate our citizens"], thereby reflecting the significance of decreased foreign immigration and the need to help Argentine citizens whose poverty had been ignored.[33] At his own expense, Palacios traveled to several impoverished provinces including Tucumán, Salta, and Santiago del Estero in order to interview workers, children, and politicians. He later supported subsidies to hospitals and benevolent groups in these provinces. In this way the socialists relentlessly pursued their dreams of national government-sponsored welfare.

Just before Justo ended his presidential term, he authorized the creation of a Registry of Social Assistance under the supervision of the Ministry of Foreign Relations and Religion. The organization was established to "force the registration of all works of social assistance in the country to coordinate these services . . . nationally, provincially, municipally, and privately." The registry also issued identity cards to recipients of social aid. This act facilitated calculating the exact amount of subsidies received by each group, although few documents remain that substantiate the registry's activities.[34]

The 1938 election of the Concordancia candidate Roberto M. Ortiz gave even more incentive to promoting welfare legislation. Ortiz, a member of the Radical Party wing linked to the Concordancia, also committed his support to child welfare and welfare state reforms. In his inaugural speech to Congress he paid special note to the situation of poor, uneducated children and families in Argentina and the need to provide state aid for them, and he encouraged provincial welfare groups to petition for more subsidies while national legislators contemplated the form of the new welfare state.[35]

The Argentine Radical Party did not remain indifferent to child welfare. In 1941 the Radical Party deputy José A. Cabral introduced a massive project to reform all major national laws into what he called a children's code. The rights included protection by the state; the right to be born "normally" and to develop; the right to happiness and health; the right to be recognized by parents; the right to be educated; and the right to be fit for "the struggle for life." To achieve these goals, he proposed a new national board that would monitor the rights of children in every sense. Twenty-five pages of governmental reforms defined the functions of the board. In September Cabral and others then proposed the formation of a national social security system, which was to be funded by employee contributions to insure workers in the events of illness, maternity, accidents, unemployment, disabilities, old age, and death. Such an institution became a reality only after Juan Perón's election.[36]

These proposals were not the only ones prompted by concerns about mothers and children. The Caja de Maternidad indeed passed, most likely because the financing for it came from contributions by female workers. By 1939, the number of women workers covered by the fund reached 258,813, or 80 percent of those who lived in the city of Buenos Aires.[37] At the same time, it became clear that establishing a welfare state independent of private philanthropies would not proceed quickly. Therefore legislators decided to increase the subsidies for provincial mother-child institutions, particularly during the early 1940s. Indeed, a series of special requests came before the chamber of deputies to construct modern hospital facilities allied to local Societies of Beneficence throughout the Argentine interior. These requests continued throughout the 1940s and demonstrated how the politics of subsidies continued to dominate political interests, as well as the fact that subsidies to local groups conflicted with a top-down welfare state.

Measuring the Growth of the Welfare State and Subsidized Philanthropy

An examination of Annex M of the 1934 budget indicated that the Society of Beneficence received 8.6 million pesos for social assistance, while the total amount of private social assistance, including hospitals and schools, had climbed to 9.1 million pesos. In the thirty-six-page list of recipients the largest subventions allocated within greater Buenos Aires included 220,000 pesos for schools operated by the Conservation of the Faith; 200,000 pesos for the Conferences of San Vicente de Paul; 120,000 pesos for the Patronato de la Infancia of Buenos Aires; and 90,000 pesos for the installation of Mothers' Canteens in the city and province of Buenos Aires, and similar sums were allocated to the maternity hospital of Córdoba (119,000 pesos) and the tuberculosis hospital of Córdoba (107,200 pesos). Subsidy recipients among the immigrant community included 10,000 pesos for the Argentine Jewish Asylum for the Elderly and Boys, 15,800 pesos for the Argentine Asylum for Jewish Female Orphans, and 3,700 pesos for the high school of the Syrian-Argentine Protective Society. The vast majority of the recipients, however, were organizations headed by Catholic women.[38]

Over time, the subsidies for philanthropy soared. In the 1937 budget, under the category of "Cooperation for Private Social Assistance," more than 12 million pesos went mostly to provincial hospitals requesting funds to build more maternity clinics. Many organizations that had received subsidies in 1932 got even more money by 1937. After that date, the reorganization of the welfare state began, and budgeting became far less transparent, but surveys of requests for subsidies for philanthropic activities in the 1940s indicated that many more received funding.[39] The lack of transparency makes clear quantitative analysis impossible.

In 1940 Dr. Luis Siri, the subdirector of the Dirección de Maternidad e

Infancia, conducted an internal study of how welfare activities had been funded by the national government since the nineteenth century. Although Siri's study ignored the important efforts of municipal governments since the 1880s to finance social assistance, and it never defined what was meant by "welfare," its findings reiterated the reality that national subsidies, even to the Society of Beneficence, had been minimal prior to 1880. Thereafter, according to Siri's calculations, the total percentage of the national budget devoted to assistance programs rose to only 3.22 percent in the 1930s. This percentage represented 28 million pesos devoted mostly to subventions for philanthropic groups, but, as Siri put it, "often these subsidies were allocated by political concerns and frequently applied without any technical expertise, and thus were not used as efficiently as one might have suspected."[40] With these words Siri harked back to the complaints expressed by Emilio R. Coni in 1917. The state-administered welfare state remained a dream, but state-supported philanthropies flourished.

The Campaign to Remove Juvenile Delinquents from the Streets

With the strong state-supported anti-infant mortality, anti-abandonment, and pro-mothering campaigns now in place, renewed attention by the state focused on the behavior of older street children. This time, the real increase in the floating population caused by internal migration needed to be addressed. In the 1930s, in response to more and more children working on the streets, the municipality of Buenos Aires enacted tough anti-vagrancy edicts. For that reason, the number of children hauled before public authorities began to increase. In 1935, for example, 140 minor boys and girls went to jail for vagrancy. When added to other minor violations, 3,195 boys and 164 girls faced terms in reformatories or placement in private homes. The following year 503 boys and 17 girls were arrested for vagrancy, a number that soared to 849 boys and 23 girls in 1939. Altogether, 3,904 children faced reformatories or jail time, a number that in 1941 increased to 5,527 boys and 190 girls. In many ways the new anti-vagrancy edicts stigmatized a generation of children already impacted by the economic depression.[41] Where would all these children end up?

When the consequences of the world depression hit both the countryside and the city, the number of older street children became very visible. At this time the Argentine government was continuing to rely on its network of private institutions, most linked to religious groups, to educate and reform poor children adrift in the city. In 1930, Jorge Coll, the legal specialist who became the minister of public instruction and who drafted most of the proposals for new juvenile delinquency statutes after 1919, declared that such reformatories, where large numbers of children congregated, were operated by religious staff rather than by specialists in modern cottage-style reformatories. He then added the following statement: "Nevertheless, regardless of religious beliefs, I understand that it is essential for the authorities, the juvenile courts, the commissions of the Patronato (Nacional de Menores) and directors of institutions, to collaborate with the societies of beneficence. In fact, I think it is indispensable . . . as well to have a tutelary association to deal exclusively with children under the disposition of the juvenile courts [as the result of the Agote law] . . . because other institutions refuse to accept these kinds of minors in their establishment. They are prejudiced against the children because they believe that crime is an indication of dangerousness, when in fact the majority of cases are the result of being orphans."[42]

A number of publications also focused on juvenile delinquency. In the province of Córdoba one of the founders of non-Freudian Argentine psychiatry, Dr. Gregorio Bermann, published a study of juvenile delinquency in 1933. Significantly, the title of his two-volume work, *Needy and Delinquent Minors in Córdoba*, reflected the fact that the term *delincuencia juvenil*, or juvenile delinquency, still had not come into technical usage, and that he, too, continued the tradition of linking abandoned children with delinquents and immoral families.[43]

Bermann blamed child behavior not only on the dismal poverty that forced many poor families in Córdoba to live in huts with few amenities, and that kept many children from attending school on a regular basis, but also on the moral level of the family. Poor families could bring up virtuous children in moral home environments unaffected by alcoholism and the hereditary effects of syphilis, or even the consequences of hyperthyroidism. Furthermore, he argued that the working-class minors in the Argentine interior experienced even more precarious conditions than those in Buenos Aires, but fewer children ended up in jail. In 1925 and 1926, the majority of the children jailed in Córdoba for crimes and misdemeanors consisted of males over the age of sixteen. Police imprisoned only twenty-nine girls in 1925 and sixteen in 1926.[44] The smaller percentages of children in jail could have been due to disinterest on the part of the police.

In his own studies of delinquency, Bermann argued against a genetic explanation and a degeneration model in favor of psychological child development and a sociological analysis of the family. As he put it, "At times, it is possible to establish clearly that the child in question did not show any criminal tendency until he had survived some adverse situation such as a difficult puberty, the death of a parent, a disappointing new friendship, or some interior crisis."[45] Yet at the same time Bermann used sociological analysis to determine the impact of the economic situation, the absence of one or more parents, poor discipline, and an immoral family. The immoral family could consist of a poorly formed family structure; one whose male adults offered inappropriate role models; or one in which elders encouraged the child to adopt criminal behavior such as prostitution for the girls.

Bermann was deeply disturbed by the continuous presence of children working in the public space. He understood that the children's income could make a difference between survival and desperation for many poor families, but the street offered no alternative to education. Most of the girls held in the local Buen Pastor Asylum in Córdoba had been servants, and the boys in jail had generally worked as day laborers in the countryside or in some sort of domestic or industrial apprenticeship. Only small numbers worked in factories, as there were few industries in Córdoba before the development of the auto industry. And although only one or two of the incarcerated worked as newspaper boys, Bermann reiterated the findings of Ingenieros to prove the dangers of such jobs. As far as the girls were concerned Bermann did not want to link their work with criminality, but rather he felt that the girls came under bad influences or had friends who led them into trouble.[46]

As the men spoke out, female juvenile delinquency experts began to weigh in on these matters—not as representatives of philanthropies but rather as stewards of children and as mothers. The Argentine educational system was expanding and women obtained even more access to higher education and professional careers. Although initially they often pursued careers of public health physicians or teachers, increasingly they turned to social work and focused on juveniles. In the early twentieth century, hospitals, charities, and philanthropic organizations often trained their own nurses and social workers, but gradually women could study these careers in public schools such as the one for nurses founded in 1886 by Cecilia Grierson, the first female physician in Argentina.[47]

Argentine feminists had initially become involved in advocating policies to promote women's and children's issues through the Pan American Child Congresses which began to meet in Buenos Aires in 1916. However, disputes between female physicians and their male counterparts led the men to take control of the congresses in the 1920s, and the feminists turned to issues such as female suffrage and advocating reforms of the civil codes.[48]

As part of the reaction of male physicians to feminist physicians, the male doctors set up the first social workers' schools as an adjunct to their own plans. The doctors envisioned visiting semi-professionals who through education would help lower the incidence of chronic diseases such as tuberculosis. In 1922 Alberto Zwanck envisioned a school with this purpose, but no such public school existed until 1924 when the University of Buenos Aires set up a program within its Public Health Program, and the Museo Social Argentino opened its own program in 1930. The same physicians who set up the visiting social workers school also set up the course in social work established at the Museo. Over the years the courses, which were open to both males and females, graduated a modest number of students. The graduates did not have enough education to practice medicine, nor sufficient understanding of sociology to enable them to operate independently—but this was precisely the intention of the founding physicians (and unlike the nursing program envisioned by Grierson). Despite the male physicians' initial efforts, the social work profession, which was deeply influenced by U.S. female social workers involved in the Pan American Child Congress, became increasingly feminized.[49]

Although Latin American women did not hold positions of power within the structure of the congresses, within the career of social work they had the opportunity to demonstrate their expertise and their commitment to mothers and children. Equally important, by 1935 the Pan American Child Congress participants, both male and female, presented a variety of reports about the state of training for social workers in their respective countries. This profession offered new authority for Latin American females to speak about nation, region, and its impact on family dynamics.

Furthermore, during the 1920s Argentine male juvenile specialists began to meet with feminist U.S. social workers such as Katherine Lenroot of the U.S. Children's Bureau. Lenroot's 1927 presentation at the Pan American Child Congress in Havana on juvenile delinquency prevention focused directly on the need to incorporate parents—both fathers and mothers—into programs for children at risk. In her view, prevention was far more valuable than the subsequent treatment of social and medical ills. If nation-states wanted to decrease the incidence of juvenile delinquency, then they had to help instruct parents on how to monitor their children and not merely turn them over to state care as the male juvenile delinquency specialists had been proposing. Lenroot also recommended classes in child care for mothers of newborns, as well as more specialized activities for visiting nurses and scientific studies of juvenile delinquency.[50]

Until 1942 no program in Argentina offered social workers training in a system where they were not simple helpers to doctors. Dr. Blanca Azucena Cassagne Serres, a lawyer, used the Patronato de Recluídas y Liberadas [Protection of Incarcerated and Paroled Women], an organization promoted by the Justo government to provide mentoring for women leaving prisons, as her stepping stone to founding a new social workers' school. As an attorney who first became involved in juvenile delinquency efforts in the 1930s, Cassagne Serres initially spoke of mother-focused women aiding juveniles. In 1937 she argued that placing a child in a reformatory did not solve anything. Citing several authorities, she argued that children needed to be understood—starting from the origins of their personality disorders and on through to their eventual misconduct. This implied understanding daily life from a humane perspective, and mothers needed to be trained as well as institutional workers.[51]

In 1940 Cassagne Serres became president of the Patronato, and in 1941 the organization opened a program for social workers, the Escuela Argentina de Asistentes de Menores y Asistentes Penales [Argentine School for Assistants to Minors and the Imprisoned]. Four years later the school became independent of the Patronato, and in the following years it was taken over by the Buenos Aires School of Law and Social Sciences. Throughout this time, and until 1955, Cassagne Serres served as president of the social workers' school, which with its majority of female students enjoyed a much higher enrollment than that of the men's school. Further, out of the total of six topics, the courses in legislation, psychology, and pedagogy had female professors. Curiously, Cassagne Serres taught psychology (in which she often emphasized the emotional rather than intellectual aspects of mothers), while the feminist Dr. Lucila de Gregorio Lavié taught law. These women helped prepare professional women for life outside philanthropy.

Another female delinquency specialist, Telma Reca, confronted the male specialists from their own disciplines: pediatric medicine and psychology. From the 1930s until the 1970s she published a series of books and articles about juvenile delinquency and child development. Reca trained as a pediatric physician at the University of Buenos Aires Medical School, where she graduated with honors in 1928. In 1932 she won the prestigious Eduardo Wilde award for her book comparing child delinquency in the United States and in Argentina. In the book she boldly rejected moral reform as a means of solving children's problems. As she put it, "[t]he child is . . . an amoral not an immoral subject. Such children have the potential to become delinquents because they do not know the precepts of the society in which they live," usually because they come from incomplete and impoverished families. Furthermore, she cited the works of Freud to show how external events could affect a child's instinctive development, although she noted that Freudian views rarely advanced the study of child delinquency.[52]

Reca's comparison of juvenile statistics from Buenos Aires with those of U.S. cities showed that in Buenos Aires minors committed many more crimes against people relative to crimes against private property, which was opposite of the case in the United States. Her study further showed that in Buenos Aires the police arrested proportionately fewer minor girls for sexual infractions than in the United States, and far fewer girls ran away from home in Buenos Aires. She believed that these differences reflected significant differences in the nature of the family unit in each country, as well as the degree of urbanization. Nevertheless, in the 1920s in Buenos Aires 43 percent of children in jail came from dysfunctional or incomplete families. Reca also signaled the absence of juvenile courts in Argentina, as well as police harassment of children working in public places, as unique characteristics of Argentina's juvenile delinquency policies, and she suggested the legalization of jobs for boys like selling newspapers as part of the solution.[53]

Reca analyzed the role of patriarchy and philanthropy in juvenile reform. According to her conversations with children in reform schools, most preferred not to return to their families even though few complained about them. Rather, the children believed that if they returned to the same neighborhood they would be influenced by the friends who got them into trouble. Instead, children wanted to go to a place where they could receive both schooling and training for an occupation. From the perspective of the workshops of the Society of Beneficence, they would not have learned much because the society's workshops, in her opinion, offered little technical training. By the 1940s when public reformatories had opened for girls, moral reform and workshops continued to dominate treatment of minor girls. Nevertheless, it was precisely to these kinds of institutions or domestic service that judges and defenders sent minor girls because even the recently created state facilities used the same approach. Reca critiqued the reality that several different state entities each operated reformatories: "The Patronato Nacional de Menores is part of the Ministry of Justice and Public Instruction and operates the Colonia Hogar Ricardo Gutiérrez and the Instituto Tutelar de Menores; the Commission of Asylums and Regional

Hospitals, a dependency of the Ministry of Foreign Relations and Religion, administers the Colonia Olivera; the Alcaldía de Menores, as part of the Federal Police, is under the jurisdiction of the Ministry of the Interior."[54] In addition, she noted that many public officials sent many more children to numerous private charitable institutions.

In 1936, Susana Malbrán joined the debate. Her analysis of statistics supported the idea that working on the streets did not turn boys into delinquents. She claimed that out of 2,000 boys interviewed by officials of the jail for boys and the Medico-Legal Office of the National Prison, 423 boys had sold newspapers, of whom 47 percent had committed more than one crime. A total of 861 street children or those without a profession had similar rates of recidivism. Messenger boys or street hawkers formed slightly over 5 percent of the boys (116), and only 22 percent were recidivists. Finally, a total of 600 boys had other jobs or were students, but only 17.5 percent were recidivists. The statistics showed clearly that the poorest children, particularly those working in the streets, were most often picked up by the police, and that newspaper vendors were not commonly arrested.[55]

Three years later Clara de Altbáum joined the discussion on juvenile delinquency by publishing *Delincuencia infantil* [Infantile Delinquency]. Altbáum had studied the literature produced by social feminists like Florence Kelley and Ellen Key, and she enthusiastically adopted the developmental term juvenile offender even though the title of her book retained the traditional terminology and she clearly identified herself as a mother. She also disagreed with Césare Lombroso that children were innate delinquents. Like Reca, she believed that children had malleable personalities, and that specialists had to understand child development and the "magical attraction" of children to working on city streets.[56] Although Altbáum agreed that factory labor had deleterious effects on children, she believed that the issue needed to be studied. At the same time she still opposed children selling newspapers.

Despite the well-reasoned arguments of female delinquency specialists, by the end of the 1930s biotypology became a standard classification procedure in the *gabinetes pscicopedagógicos* [psycho-pedagogical offices] of the reform schools. The methods used did not involve phrenology, measuring height or body size, or even categorizing by race. Instead, specialists rated boys and girls on family background and behavior. For example, in a study by the Ricardo Gútiérrez facility 400 boys between the ages of eight and twenty were examined during the period from 1939 to 1941. The boys received ratings on a four-point scale (from good to bad) on the basis of education, intellectual faculties, affective qualities, disposition [*voluntad*], morality, character, family environment, and economic situation. The latter two criteria seem to have counted the most. The majority (308) lived in misery, had "deficient" or bad family environments (537), and were poorly educated (435). Specialists identified their personalities to be generally unstable (264) or sexually perverse (122). Only 76 had "apparently normal" personalities, and most came from families with defects such as neuroses or alcoholism (229) or that were incomplete (153). A total of 85 families were designated normal or complete, and these families tended to have more children.[57]

A similar study conducted in the Santa Rosa reformatory for girls in 1940 examined 200 girls, although the focus was largely on their "genital history." Child specialists carefully noted when the girls reached puberty and began menstruation, and data was kept regarding how many received treatment for vaginal discharges or irregular periods. Three of the girls were single mothers, three were pregnant, and four had had abortions. Curiously, the genital examinations mentioned nothing about virginity; it seems most likely that the specialists presumed all these girls had lost their virginity.

In terms of family situation, only 5 came from so-called normal families, and only 89 came from legitimate unions. Among the family problems encountered were mental illness (30), alcoholism (47), tuberculosis (28), syphilis (7), and immoral families (40). The case notes for child "Oriana" O. stated: "Mentally weak, several siblings, mother had several illegal unions before joining up with the father. The father was such a chronic alcoholic . . . that he wanted to rape one of his stepdaughters. Eight members of the family lived in a room occupied by a 'maternal uncle' of O.O. . . . After the mother died. . . . the three youngest daughters were raped by the cousin and father of the young girls, and the girls were obliged to beg to support the adult men, because the father had lost a position in the police."[58] The statisticians found that 14 girls had mothers or fathers serving prison time, some of whom were habitual offenders. In general, they only found 4 families that they considered normal, and only 9 in good economic conditions, while 78 came from "miserable" circumstances. The specialists expressed dismay upon discovering that the girls did not live in separate bedrooms and often suffered from sexual abuse.[59]

The people who examined the girls found that 41 had either been brought up in orphanages or as servants in the houses of strangers, or they had been transported by strangers from elsewhere to the national capital, which to the specialists indicated "the kind of miserable people who give up their children at a very early age," although it is more likely that many girls had migrated to the capital city. In addition, they found up to 4 siblings interned in the Santa Rosa facility among 53 who had sisters there, which could have been avoided by providing monetary assistance to the families. However, since the families had no relatives to turn to, they sent the children to reform school.[60]

The analysis of mental abilities revealed equally depressing statistics. Specialists identified 121 girls with low mental abilities, or more than 60 percent of all the girls. Similar statistics categorized the girls' emotional stability, disposition, character, and morality. Several girls were characterized as hysterics. The records of 144 girls led to the conclusion that they had deficient educations. Like the boys, many lived on the streets and earned their living there, although a few had worked in the needle trade. The officials at the Santa Rosa facility refused to qualify the following occupations as work: prostitution, vagrancy, ballet dancing, and selling stamps on the street. Eventually, only 6 girls were released without parole (mostly to get married), 16 were released to their homes under parole, and the rest to other institutions. A total of 17 girls remained because they were defined as "difficult" children—most likely unruly or unwilling to marry.[61]

In both of the studies, the specialists made no attempt to differentiate youths and adolescents, nor did they give any age-appropriate explanation for perceived difficult or unruly behavior. In effect, these poor and undereducated children from incomplete or impoverished homes did not have the luxury of developing their individual identities through adolescence.

Although the desire to categorize and study all of the inhabitants through classification and biotypology marked the Mariano Castex proposal as extreme, the origins of such classifications clearly stemmed from the concerns about dysfunctional families, particularly errant fathers and street children. Indeed, the study of family situations that served as a hallmark of progressive studies of juvenile delinquency and street children since the early twentieth century favored studying poor children as a group, rather than individuals, and family conditions instead of personal development. From this perspective middle-class children should be spared group analysis, and thus biotypology remained a technology of classification only for the poor, the street children, and the juvenile delinquent.

Did children fare better under the increased supervision of the state, juvenile delinquency specialists, and biotypologists than they did under the female philanthropists? No institution, according to contemporary experts, could repair the damage done by parental abandonment. "Juan" P., for example, entered the Society of Beneficence as a baby. Prior to that time, he had been in the Casa Correccional de Mujeres with his mother. Not until 1939 did officials try to find out his exact birth date and the whereabouts of his parents. They discovered that both parents had died and that he had eight siblings, none of whom knew their own birth dates. Juan's brothers and sisters began to visit him and tried to obtain custody of Juan and a sister also interned in an orphanage. Despite their efforts, the damas refused to accede to their request because the older siblings were single. Juan's godmother wrote him letters urging him to behave, but she also indicated that she knew he received good treatment. In 1941 she advised Juan that she and her husband were too old to care for him during vacations, although she finally obtained custody of him in 1943.[62]

"Isaac" S. went to live at the Society of Beneficence in 1931 as a newborn whose nineteen-year-old mother resided in the girls' orphanage. Until the age of five he lived at the home of an external wet nurse, and then the damas sent him to various institutions. In 1937 the damas finally tried to locate his birth mother, but to no avail. Instead, Isaac's wet nurse became a frequent visitor and took him out for vacations. He did not see his mother until 1948 when she asked that he be released to her. By that time, according to the records, the impact of being rejected as a baby and abandoned by his family had taken its toll. He had a bad reputation and was considered "impulsive, bad company, and when he has unjustified temper tantrums he is capable of committing any kind of crime."[63]

In 1937 "Ramona" L., at the tender age of nine, had already been abandoned by her father and mother. The mother abandoned her at the age of four in 1932. Her father was a gardener whose employer turned the girl over to the defender of minors because she shouted and cried all the time, which led the employer to believe that the father mistreated her. In 1938 Ramona came under the tutelage of the Patronato Nacional de Menores where social workers noted that she had been crippled by osteomyletis but was intelligent and had no "bad habits." According to the father's employer, Ramona's mother had been "a woman with few morals and had little affection for her children." The father kept only his son, and then disappeared.[64]

Ramona stayed in institutions for many years. According to evaluation reports, she could not be sent into private care because of her precarious health, and in 1947 she traveled to Córdoba to live in an institution operated by the Asociación de Niños Débiles [Association for Weak Children]. Alone and almost incarcerated in a hospital environment, she begged to return to Buenos Aires. In a letter directed to a member of the Patronato Nacional, she implored the official to let her return and attend a regular school: "As the kindly and good father of the minor girls in your care, I hope you help me fulfill my wish to return quickly to Buenos Aires. I know that you have always been a protector and a help to all of us who are under your tutelage."[65] Although the tutor tried to get Ramona released from the hospital, the mother superior who served as director opposed his wishes. Ramona returned to Buenos Aires in 1948 only because she suffered from appendicitis and needed an operation. At that point, the nuns categorized her as mentally handicapped and she remained in institutions of the Patronato Nacional de Menores. Finally, a year after Ramona had reached the age of majority her older sister obtained custody after questioning the earlier evaluation that Ramona be institutionalized forever.

The story of Ramona shows that even though the Patronato Nacional de Menores operated the majority of the residential facilities for female juveniles, particularly after the opening of the Santa Rita facility in 1938, the organization still depended upon female religious workers to staff institutions, and girls like Ramona had to deal with the authority of the mother superior. Nevertheless, Ramona clearly saw the male representative of the Patronato Nacional de Menores as her defender, and she felt comfortable writing to him about her plight.

The number of older children entering the state-controlled Patronato Nacional de Menores soared. In 1931, when it began, 1,250 minors were under its supervision—a clear indication that state institutions had begun to replace philanthropic ones. Seven years later the number of children increased to 1,800, and by 1943 the organization controlled 2,900 children. In turn, although the Patronato Nacional sent the children to its own establishments, most were sent to private institutions that received subsidies for each child they admitted. These institutions included the schools operated by the Salesian Brothers and the nuns of Don Bosco, and similar institutions located in the territories of Misiones, La Pampa, Chubut, Neuquén, Río Negro, Santa Cruz, and Tierra del Fuego. Most girls initially went to the two Patronato Nacional Santa Rosa and Santa Rita facilities, but one third of them went either to the Society of Beneficence's girls' orphanage or to other institutions. Within these entities children constantly moved from one place to another, but rarely did they return to their parents and home. Furthermore, the members of the Patronato openly admitted that it was very difficult to place in private settings minor males between the ages of eight and twelve and female minors over the age of sixteen. During these years children began to assert their independence, thus making it difficult for biological parents to accept them, and intolerably so for foster parents. Children with physical or intellectual handicaps were deemed impossible to place.[66] By the end of the 1940s institutional care had increased, but it could neither completely replace private institutions nor solve some of the thornier issues associated with child welfare.

The growth of these institutions and the number of children under their control, however, reinforced state commitment to child welfare reform. Like many other aspects of the welfare state, child welfare remained underfunded, but the increase in institutions operated by the government provided disturbing signals to female philanthropic groups that their relationship to the national government could change dramatically.

Efforts by Provinces to Promote Child Welfare

During the 1930s urban governments also directed their scarce resources toward helping mothers and removing older children from the streets. Once again the expansion of secular and nonimmigrant group programs increasingly signaled the end of traditional philanthropic groups. Provincial governments also showed themselves capable of organizing conferences and promoting discourses regarding mothers, children, and social policies. Between 1929 and 1938, the province of Santa Fe held three child congresses. Attended mostly by male specialists, the meetings promoted legislation that would advance child welfare within the province.

Provincial specialists advocated restricting child labor so that minors could attend school. Attendees urged support for indigent children, encouraged families to limit the amount of time that boys played football so that they could attend to their studies, promoted more artistic endeavors within the public schools, urged teachers to deal with children with limited intelligence, and suggested the creation of juvenile courts. Provincial officials faced the same reality seen in the national capital: religious communities associated with philanthropic movements operated most of the existing facilities for abandoned children. Therefore the growth of new institutions meant that public authorities would have more direct control over needy children.[67]

To help families, the province of Santa Fe in 1941 enacted Law 2994, which established a fund to help the elderly, the infirm, mothers, and orphans residing in that province. The fund provided a monthly pension to qualified people, and the amount that a mother received depended upon the age of the child and whether the child was orphaned. Complete orphans received a bit more than the others. To be eligible, immigrants had to have resided in the country for at least fifteen years, and mothers could not earn more than fifty pesos per month. José L. Araya, a juvenile judge from Rosario, Santa Fe, considered the pensions far too meager to support a family with more than two children, and he argued that mothers needed to earn more money to supplement the pension.[68]

In 1945 Judge Araya made comments that are reminiscent of those of the Córdoba psychiatrist and delinquency specialist Gregorio Bermann. Araya considered provincial children generally poorer and at greater risk for delinquency. As he put it, "In general, all the interior cities, from the perspective of the visitor, present a picture of numerous children who live from charity, minor theft, or part-time work. Street children wander about in search of bread, . . . with neither orientation nor hopes of ending that painful situation." He predicted that they would end up spending their adult lives in hospitals and in jails. He partially attributed this problem to the low rates of school attendance, and he noted that a study conducted in Rosario in 1934 indicated that 14 percent of children never attended school and that 74.12 percent had formally abandoned it—mostly due to work, lack of resources, and illness.[69]

In the province of Buenos Aires, the arch-conservative governor Manuel Fresco implemented a modern program of child welfare. Inspired by both of the 1933 congresses, Fresco began his administration in 1936 with a survey of child abandonment that disclosed that more than 9,000 children had been taken off the streets in recent years, most of whom were taken in by private families, that is, as domestic servants. Only 2,900 children had been sent to institutions. As part of his reorganization of the child welfare programs, in 1937 Fresco unified all jurisdictions under the Dirección General de Protección a la Infancia [General Bureau for Child Protection], as recommended by the 1933 National Conference on Abandoned and Delinquent Children. Then he sent a specialist to Paris to attend the First International Congress on Child Psychiatry.[70]

Fresco also devoted resources to juvenile delinquency, nurseries for abandoned infants, and help for hearing- and speaking-impaired children. By 1938 he reported that 9,583 minors remained under the protection of the province. Ironically this represented 400 percent more children than were covered by the Patronato Nacional de Menores. Furthermore, Fresco claimed to coordinate the activities of public and philanthropic groups. And along with repressing communism and advocating fascism, he had also implemented police and judicial reforms to keep children off the streets as well as preventing adults from exercising patria potestad over nonbiological children without governmental permission. The provincial government financed most of these programs with gaming taxes. Domingo Mercante, another Buenos Aires governor, expanded these facilities from 1946 to 1952.[71]

From Social Policies to a Welfare State

The new national bureaucratic entities confronted extensive opposition from the philanthropic community. From the perspective of the philanthropists, the rationalization of social policies through the expansion of state intervention directly endangered the autonomy of a variety of groups and institutions, both secular and religious. Clearly the philanthropists preferred subsidies to a welfare state.

For the Society of Beneficence, the damas viewed governmental requests for information regarding the care of their wards, as well as data on how they spent their money, as potential threats to the organization's "special" relationship with the Argentine government. The damas also believed that they had the right to spend private legacies and donations according to the wishes of the donors, not the government. While they still saw themselves as carrying the mantle of authority provided by the liberal Rivadavia, the damas increasingly identified with the more conservative Catholic community that supplied not only their labor force but also their upper-class private donors.

During this period of transition the national government twice offered— in 1931 and in 1940—female philanthropists an expanded role in the provision of welfare. National leaders actually offered the Society of Beneficence the opportunity to direct all public asylums and regional hospitals. In December 1940, for example, Minister of Finance Federico Pinedo wanted to transfer all of the hospitals and institutions in the province of Buenos Aires to the Society of Beneficence, and the budget for 1941 was to be amended to provide adequate funds. The president of the Society at that moment recounted to her colleagues that the same offer had been made to the Society in 1931, and both times it was turned down because it involved too much work. In addition she ironically reminded the minister of finance that "it should not be forgotten that the [society] created by Rivadavia was called 'the Society of Beneficence of the Capital,' which meant that the group was only responsible for institutions in the national capital."[72]

At the same time, right-wing supporters of the Concordancia did not spare the Society of Beneficence from criticism because they believed in a national welfare state. Indeed, in 1936 Dr. Carlos Bernaldo de Quiros, one of the strongest supporters of eugenics, supported the reorganization of the National Department of Hygiene to include an agency to oversee mother-child issues, and he saw no reason to exclude the Society from its surveillance.[73] Other battles weakened the Society. Subsequent efforts to create a National Tuberculosis Commission, a National Department of Social Assistance, and a National Institute of Nutrition had the ability to challenge the Society's policies in various institutions. Each time, the damas met to devise a strategy to deal with these efforts, occasionally calling upon their legal advisors for help. On those occasions prior to the election of Juan Perón they managed to have themselves exempted from inclusion in the system.[74]

Other challenges confronted female philanthropic groups. The immigrant-based groups simply continued to expand their establishments and provide sustenance to needy children. This did not seem to be a risky venture at a time when increased immigration loomed as a possibility once Europe went to war. The immigrant associations wanted to be ready, but they had no way to calculate future needs. Non-Catholic religious organizations faced similar dilemmas. Their only interaction with the state consisted of petitions for subsidies.

Those groups operating the reform schools found the funding changes most disruptive. All of these organizations had to figure out how they would be affected by the recognition by the Argentine Senate in September 1942 of the Confederación de Beneficencia de la República Argentina [Confederation of Beneficent Societies of the Argentine Republic]. The entity had been given legal recognition earlier by President Yrigoyen as a group of institutions outside the Society of Beneficence. Organized by provinces and by the national capital, the Confederation consisted of fourteen "circles" of charities. The group appealed to socialists such as Alfredo Palacios who believed that the group could serve as a counterweight to the Society of Beneficence, and he cited a 1941 article from *La Nación* indicating that over 4,452 children had been helped by the group that consisted of 324 philanthropic societies. The proposal passed, and it served as yet another threat to the Society of Beneficence and philanthropic groups outside the Confederation. However, the Confederation never received the same political scrutiny and funding as did the Society of Beneficence. Furthermore, in the

1940s the Confederation could not impede the increased subsidies to philanthropic groups outside it.[75]

The 1942 Conference on Abandoned Children

During the Concordancia, the political differences between the extreme Right and Left in Argentina over the issues of the role of the military, the future of democratic governments, and the increased importance of the Catholic Church in state politics appeared insurmountable. In contrast, the battle over child welfare politics resonated less for the public than did the absence of democracy. The November 1942 Conference on Abandoned Children in many ways provided publicity and new ammunition for the philanthropic community. The consequences of the conference indicated that the future of philanthropy and private solutions for welfare was not about to disappear.

The conference took place just before the military coup of 1943. Once again, the highest government officials including President Ramón Castillo and former president Agustín P. Justo publicly endorsed the meeting. According to its organizational plan, not only would government officials and the president or delegate of the Society of Beneficence be eligible to attend, but conference organizers also invited a delegate from every private child welfare society in the country. This meant that the presence of philanthropists would overwhelm the number of other attendees.

In contrast with the meetings of the 1930s, the 1942 conference began with an extended study in support of legal adoption. The decision to emphasize adoption placed the meeting in a position that opposed the philosophy of socialists and feminists who championed strong state funding to help biological children. Rather than have the state bear the burden of caring for abandoned children, private childless families would be given the legal right to have both an heir and a child. The child rights specialist and attorney Jorge Coll supported this position as did the president of the meeting, Dr. Gregorio Aráoz Alfaro, a noted pediatrician from Tucumán. The next presentation, on the role of social assistance in helping families cope with children, both delinquent and adoptive, reinforced the idea that all kinds of families in need deserved help.[76]

Adoption had long been advocated by the Society of Beneficence and had been incorporated into recommendations of the Pan American Child Congresses, an international child welfare group, at its most recent meeting in Washington, D.C., in May 1942. Influenced by U.S. feminists who advocated a greater role for social workers and less emphasis on large institutions for children, the 1942 Argentine conference argued that such ideas should also be extended to terms of orphans or abandoned children.

In a similar feminist vein, Dr. José Araya of Santa Fe put in a report on the possible beneficial effects of having a corps of women police to specialize in juvenile court cases.[77] Both the Washington meeting and the one in Buenos Aires favored professionalizing women's participation in the welfare state, just as feminists had long argued. Araya remained silent regarding the future of large reform schools and orphanages. In many ways the debates over adoption and the role of social workers exemplified the main policy differences between female philanthropists and feminists regarding child welfare.

The 1942 Buenos Aires conference indicated that specialists had accepted the reality that a comprehensive welfare state was unlikely to be funded by the Argentine government, although they discussed its merits. Rather than demand a state-funded welfare state, the delegates, particularly the female philanthropists, advocated social work as a piecemeal approach of social policies along with adoption. By the time the 1942 conference adjourned, it was also evident that the female philanthropists would rally against a modern welfare state, and that many preferred financial support from their colectividades rather than complete support from the national government. Yet they still needed government subsidies not only to support their work but also to validate the social status of their members. The politics of the Concordancia had offered little solace to advocates of private philanthropy, as most of the legislation proposed would have expanded state intervention into issues related to mothers and children, and concerns about street children had eclipsed the earlier political concerns over abandoned infants. Under what conditions could the state consolidate the welfare state?

The 1942 meeting adjourned shortly before the 1943 military coup that led to the rise of Juan and Eva Perón. Indeed, few attending the meeting would have imagined that a supporter of both the military and the working class would have the legislative clout to finalize the welfare state contemplated for so long. Further, neither the complicated Peronist reaction to private philanthropy nor the gradual erosion of immigrant support for collective benevolence could have been predicted. Argentina, in many ways, stood at the crossroads of change.

CHAPTER 6

At the Crossroads of Change

PERONISM, THE WELFARE STATE, AND THE DECLINE

OF NON-PERONIST FEMALE AUTHORITY

Political repression in the 1930s took its toll on Argentine democratic politics, despite the lively discussions regarding child rescue and the need for a national welfare state. Periodic rigged elections in the midst of the world depression, accompanied by the rise of fascist governments in Spain and Italy (the origin of many Argentine immigrants), made it difficult to implement the expansion of political, social, and economic rights envisioned by feminists and female philanthropists. By the end of the Concordancia in 1943, tremendous interest had been raised regarding the need for social and political reform, but party differences prevented the passage of many laws, early welfare measures threatened philanthropic women, and the lack of an open democratic system seemed to cast a pall over everything.

The outbreak of the Second World War created the opportunity to sell Argentine wheat, cattle, and manufactured goods to European combatants, and thus provided the national government with funds to invest in social reform if consensus could lead to the enactment of new laws. Another military coup removed the Concordancia president Ramón Castillo from power in 1943—just before scheduled elections. Although Argentines expected the new military dictatorships to proceed as before, Juan Domingo Perón arose unexpectedly within the military clique's leadership ranks and eventually held three positions within General Edelmiro Farrell's 1944–1946 government, including minister of labor and welfare, vice president, and minister of war. Supported by his ties to the labor movement, Perón overcame efforts by military detractors to remove him from office on October 17, 1945, and he declared his candidacy for president. During Farrell's presidency Juan met and married an actress, María Eva Duarte (commonly known as Eva or Evita). Within a year of her husband's election to the presidency in 1946, Eva emerged as his key ally along with loyal representatives from the labor movement. Her presence enabled Perón to channel support for suffrage and child welfare into Peronism.

Throughout his first presidency from 1946 to 1955, Juan Perón argued that his political alliances would create a more just Argentina. Until inflation in the 1950s limited the benefits of government income derived from the Second World War, Perón had money to invest in reforms. His notable achievements included the passage of female suffrage in 1947, the enactment in 1949 of a new Argentine constitution that promised political and social rights, and a massive expansion of the Argentine welfare state. Even before the passage of the constitution, Perón claimed in May 1948 that "in social matters, no one in the world can make vain claims to have created anything equal to what we have achieved in the short time we have held political power. Today, before all the nations in the world, . . . Argentina figures in the vanguard of social justice."[1]

How did Peron manage to effect such change after years of fruitless deliberations of both individual rights and the welfare state? And were these changes novel? This chapter argues that Perón and Eva acknowledged the unfulfilled political demands of women and labor, as well as the critical need to resolve problems of limited social and political rights and social welfare. Juan co-opted key issues that had been supported by others and adopted them as his own, thereby assuming all of the glory for these reforms. This strategy also made it more difficult for his opponents initially to criticize his administration.

Peronism's success, however, inflicted important political costs to its enemies. Although women finally had the opportunity to vote in national elections after 1947, the way that suffrage passed in Argentina removed the political visibility that feminists had achieved in the 1930s, and Perón attributed the victory to his wife Eva. Similarly, the expansion of the national welfare state signaled the moment when female philanthropists lost an important source of social legitimacy—government subventions and access to policy making. The rights and benefits for women and children, along with families, workers, students, and other members of the Argentine public, became subsumed within Peronism. The welfare state also became intimately identified with the Perón regime. The precarious nature of this political strategy became only too clear after a military coup removed Perón from power in 1955. After that time, subsequent attacks against welfare structures became part of the anti-Peronist strategy. This chapter explores the loss of female authority of philanthropists and feminists and the formation of the masculine-dominated Peronist welfare state through four key examples of Peronist politics: female suffrage, the demise of the Society of Beneficence, the subsequent formation of the welfare state, and the passage of adoption laws. The success of one became entwined with the other, and all became embroiled in the mythology of Peronism.

The Triumph of Female Suffrage

The feminist dream of female suffrage, along with the political legitimacy that belonged to the victors, became an essential component of Peronist political strategy. As women increasingly mobilized to demand change, Perón needed to tap into this potential voters' pool, but first he had to wrest the women away from feminism and non-Peronist female philanthropy. Female suffrage, along with child welfare, had formed a fragile keystone to Argentine feminist campaigns. From the early twentieth century onward, feminists had debated the merits of suffrage as well as when and how to attain equal political rights. Resistance to suffrage within feminism coincided with an acceptance of gender difference at the same time that feminists advocated political equality and child welfare. Supporting suffrage made it difficult for feminists to ally themselves with philanthropists who advocated child welfare without supporting suffrage and political equality. Another thorny issue involved the linkage of political suffrage with military service in the Argentine constitution of 1853. The feminist Julieta Renshaw de Lantieri fought to separate suffrage from military service in the courts in order to clear the way for women's right to vote, and in the 1920s and 1930s several suffrage proposals arrived in Congress supported by the Socialist, Radical, and Conservative Parties. The only success of these proposals came in 1932 when the legislation passed the Chamber of Deputies, but eventually it withered in the Senate.[2]

Feminists and nonfeminists alike became even more active after 1932. Victoria Ocampo, the famous Argentine writer and journalist, presided over the Unión Argentina de Mujeres [Argentine Women's Union], which was specifically organized to promote suffrage. Members consisted of middle-class women belonging to many political affiliations, as well as previously apolitical women. The leading feminists Elvira Rawson de Dellepiane, Alicia Moreau de Justo, and Carmela Horne de Burmeister joined Ocampo, and the socialist feminist magazine *Vida Femenina* published articles supporting female suffrage while Ocampo also contributed with her own writings.[3] Each time legislators presented proposals, more Argentines became sensitized to the issue.

Suffrage constituted only one of the many issues that expanded women's political consciousness in the 1940s. The outbreak of the Second World War led many women, both immigrants and those born in Argentina, to support various war organizations. The Spanish Civil War (1936–1939) provoked outcries in Argentina. In September 1941, approximately forty-five thousand Argentine women, both native born and immigrant and from many walks of life, joined the Junta de la Victoria to fight against fascism. The struggle to create the state of Israel prompted many women in the Jewish collectivity to join Zionist organizations. This effort came as early as 1926 with the formation of the Argentine branch of the Women's International Zionist Organization, which was known as the Organización Sionista Femenina Argentina. By the 1940s women of Mediterranean origin became active within the Centro Sionista Seferadí [Sephardic Zionist Center], although it was originally created by women of Eastern European extraction.[4] Women's interest in political activities increasingly prompted them to take to the streets to demand changes or emphasize their advocacy of social issues. Yet corrupt Concordancia politics failed to take these changes into consideration.

The history of the final campaign to promote female suffrage has, like many other issues associated with Peronism, been embedded within Peronist mythology. Although new scholarship has come out regarding the campaign, the role of Peronist feminists never emerges.[5] Yet Peronism did have its feminist advocates, and both Peronist men and women took credit for the achievement.

Several of the most important suffrage advocates taught at the School of Social Work founded by Blanca Azucena Cassagne Serres, who formed a visible component of Peronism. In July 1945, just as Perón attempted to persuade President Farrell to enact suffrage through a decree, Cassagne Serres published an important pamphlet that she envisioned as a "program of action" to support female suffrage. Rather than speak of individual rights, she gave suffrage a motherist perspective by arguing that female suffrage supported both patriotism and the family: "I say to Argentine women that they must prepare themselves to educate their sons, brothers, and husbands in the true understanding of civics that the principles of May indicate, to maintain our tradition of liberty founded in Law and Justice." Her reference to "the principles of May" related to the declaration of Argen-

tine independence, and it followed a bold international discussion of female suffrage antecedents. In this way Cassagne Serres linked women's
civic responsibilities through suffrage to motherhood, because, as she mentioned earlier, "a woman . . . is always a potential mother."[6]

Lucila Gregorio de Lavié, a lawyer who taught social work with Cassagne
Serres, also joined the Peronist bandwagon; she was originally a staunch
member of the feminist movement. In 1944 then vice-president Juan Perón
appointed her head of the División de Trabajo y Asistencia a la Mujer
[Division of Work and Assistance to Women], under which his pro-suffrage
campaign developed. She directly supported Perón's call for a suffrage decree, and in so doing she was accused of being an opportunist by her former
colleagues.[7]

Gregorio de Lavié fought long and hard for female suffrage, and she
personally felt more loyalty toward Juan than toward Eva. In 1947, in an
article originally published in a journal of the Social Institute of the National University of the Litoral, she discussed the long history of legal rights
for women and the role of feminists who advocated such changes in Argentina. Then she discussed the meeting she organized on July 26, 1945, where
Vice-President Perón spoke at her invitation and promised to enact the law
proposed by Senator Soler on July 19, 1946. She only referred to Eva as
having a role after September 1947.[8] The following year Gregorio de Lavié
published a longer monograph for female citizens. She began on the frontispiece with the quote Perón made at the July 1945 meeting, as well as all of
the Peronist legislation that supported women. She also mapped out the
history and responsibilities of female citizens.[9]

Carmen Horne de Burmeister also angered feminists for supporting Perón. As another social worker and as founder of the Argentine Association
for Women's Suffrage, Horne de Burmeister along with her two compa-
triots formed part of the second generation of professional women who
benefited from their feminist predecessors but chose to expand the meanings of female suffrage to more working-class women and the public at
large.[10] Finally, male supporters of female suffrage became important at this
time. From 1943 onward Juan Perón sensed the possibility of expanding the
electorate in his favor by supporting female suffrage. He founded the division led by Gregorio de Lavié and supported the inter-American resolutions
made at Chapultepec Park, Mexico, in 1945, which advocated passage of
women's suffrage. But some men within his party took credit for the measure, especially Eduardo Colom.

As soon as the 1946 congressional sessions opened in May, several legislators once again submitted suffrage bills. Along with the journalists, Deputy Colom quickly joined those advocating expanded political rights for women, and in his address of June 27 he directly linked his proposal to the new "Peronist revolution." As he put it, "Authentic representative democracy was one of the principles of the national revolution of June 4, 1943, according to the most advanced principles of suffrage in world civilization." He blamed "the weight of oligarchy on the body dissolved by the revolution" for never passing female suffrage, just as it had opposed increasing workers' rights.[11] Despite this effort, a final vote continued to elude the Argentine Congress.

By September 3, 1947, supporters of female suffrage could wait no longer, and an estimated fifty thousand marchers assembled in the Congressional Plaza within earshot of legislators. Once again Colom urged his colleagues to take a stand and vote for the Senate's female suffrage bill, not only because of the women marchers but also for women who could not march because they needed to work. As Colom describes, these were women from "Santiago del Estero, of Catamarca, of San Luis, who labor in primitive factories and workshops to make the country greater; for the women who work in the sugar harvests in Tucumán, Salta, and Jujuy; for the women in Santa Fe, Buenos Aires, Corrientes, and Entre Ríos who share the agricultural and ranching labors at the side of their fathers, sons, and husbands; for the women of labor of workshops; for the Argentine women who taught us our first letters."[12] In other words, after lauding working women from all walks of life and everywhere in Argentina, Colom asked legislators to grant suffrage to the much larger female working class, not just the middle-class women marchers. He concluded his discussion by advising his fellow deputies that the Peronist bloc alone had enough votes to enact the law, but he invited the other deputies to join in. Within a week, the long-standing feminist battle for suffrage had been sanctioned as a Peronist plan to honor the place of working women. Victory did not empower feminists; rather they disappeared as the rationale for passing the legislation.

In Colom's oral history from 1972, transcribed by the eminent historian Luis Alberto Romero, he takes full credit for the law. Although several deputies presented similar pieces of legislation, each from different parties, Colom claimed that all the legislation sat in committee for the next few months because Eva asked him to delay the vote until she had returned from Europe. After returning, she then asked him to get it out of committee so that it could be discussed, to which he agreed. In other words, Colom declared that through his efforts he managed to give the spotlight to Eva

Perón during the final moment of passage and that he had been the person who arranged it all.[13]

Eva Perón played her first public political role in the battle for female suffrage. Before her trip to Europe, Eva delivered in January 1947 a series of radio speeches advocating suffrage, but not from a feminist perspective. Instead she described herself as Perón's most dedicated servant. In March Eva exhorted women to take to the streets to demand their rights and defend their homes, thereby providing a Peronist underpinning for the women's march to the congressional building on September 3. Furthermore, she explicitly identified herself with the mass of working-class women admired by Colom.[14]

Juan Perón quickly identified the passage of female suffrage as a Peronist achievement. He gave a speech that very evening honoring the women who received voting rights. The following day *El Laborista*, the Peronist newspaper operated by Domingo Mercante, elaborated further on the nonfeminist Peronist understanding of female suffrage. As the newspaper commented: "Now we cannot forget that with these rights come responsibilities. Each woman should believe that in our land it is her obligation to have healthy children and raise virtuous men who know how to sacrifice themselves and fight for the real interests of the Nation. Each woman should think how her obligations have increased because the State has given them rights which bring with them the obligation that each woman teach her children that their house has constructed an altar of virtue and respect."[15] This interpretation clearly linked suffrage and child welfare issues and placed them in a Peronist context. To secure this vision, the Peronists had to eliminate the influence of female philanthropists on child welfare. Such began the symbolic campaign against the Society of Beneficence.

The Creation of a National Welfare State

The attack against the Society began even before Perón came to power. Shortly after the 1943 coup, the military president Pedro Ramírez created a commission to study private philanthropy, and he moved subsidies from the control of the Ministry of Foreign Relations and Religion to the Ministry of the Interior. From the perspective of gendered power, this meant that the realm of philanthropy dominated by women would be subsumed by a masculine welfare state rather than being run by male friends and acquaintances. Thus the military governments began the confrontation with the formidable Society of Beneficence.

Initially, the generals simply wanted to rationalize the Society's role and integrate it more fully into the welfare state. By Perón's election in 1946, Juan envisioned limiting the damas' influence at the same time that his supporters demanded the demise of the Society. Theoretically, if Perón succeeded, the fate of the Society of Beneficence would provide a template for dealing with other private philanthropies. Indeed, early interventionist plans included integrating both the Society and other philanthropic groups into a rational welfare state.[16]

Intervention as conceived by the Peronist government would incorporate the Society of Beneficence as the basis of "Integral Social Assistance for the Entire Country." However, Peronists in Congress had other plans. Rather than keep the Society of Beneficence they wanted to close it down while they subsequently voted subsidies to other philanthropies, including the future Eva Perón Foundation. Perón refused to release the expanded funds in 1948, and as a result collective philanthropy suffered a major identity and funding crisis. Some groups survived despite the disappearance of government subsidies, while others simply withered away. In their place the Eva Perón Foundation threatened to take over all private philanthropy and thus symbolically integrate philanthropy into Eva's private charitable foundation.

The immediate impact of the military's first bureaucratic reshuffling in 1943 placed the Society of Beneficence under the control of the Ministry of the Interior, along with all other subsidized philanthropies. This shift meant that for the first time the damas would not be treated differently from other philanthropic groups. Their plight became even more tenuous that year when two new entities were created—namely, the Dirección Nacional de Salud Pública y Asistencia Social [National Agency for Public Health and Social Assistance] and the Secretaría de Trabajo y Previsión [Secretariat of Labor and Social Security]. Subsidized philanthropies moved, this time to the Secretariat of Labor and Social Security, while hospitals were placed under the National Agency for Public Health. The Society of Beneficence now reported to two different agencies.[17]

Although Juan Perón's first major effort to reform child welfare clearly targeted the Society of Beneficence, history has accorded him little credit for its demise. This story has been wrapped in mythology since 1948, in a version that attributed the Society's demise to Eva Perón. It pitted the wife of the recently elected president against some of the most powerful women in the country, and it became a classic parable about Eva's ability to end class discrimination. It also explained how some Peronists planned to replace the symbolism of the Society of Benevolence with the Eva Perón Foundation.

The myth began with Mary Main (under the pseudonym of María Flores). In 1952 Main argued that Eva had taken revenge against the Society's matrons after they refused to name her president of the Society despite the presumed custom of extending an invitation to the wife of the president to assume this role. According to Main, Eva went to Cardinal Copello to intervene in the matter, but even he could not deter the damas from their decision. For this reason, Main states that "Eva set out to destroy both [the damas] and their Society, and out of this fury of destruction there rose the plan for her own charitable organization. . . . the Eva Perón Foundation."[18] Other early versions of the confrontation reiterated that Eva wanted to be honorary president, although over the years—like rumors in a comic opera —the story changed from honorary president to president, and from indirect negotiations to a direct meeting between Eva and the damas.

In a biography of Eva Perón published in 1995, Alicia Dujovne Ortiz comes closer to the truth. She argued that Senator Diego Luis Molinari, author of the intervention request and a right-wing nacionalista [a group of extreme nationalists] turned Peronista, claimed that the action was based on the need to fulfill a government mission that the Society had been unable to accomplish. Henceforth, as Dujovne Ortiz pointed out, "the numerous hospitals operated by [the Society] would become part of the Ministry of Public Health. The measure can be explained, in great part, by the fact that the Society of Beneficence was subsidized by the State." At the same time Dujovne Ortiz recognized that a campaign had been mounted accusing the Society of misusing the government lottery funds allocated to it. "It was rumored that the orphans and the unmarried mothers made money for the damas."[19] Mariano Plotkin in his *Mañana es San Perón* [Tomorrow is St. Perón Day], published in 1993, took the position that the closing of the Society was part of the formation of the modern welfare state, but he, too, did not examine all the relevant documents.[20]

Because the incident has been seen as a successful act of Eva's vengeance, few have bothered to sort fact from fiction. For example, wives of presidents neither became head of the Society nor honorary president as an automatic procedure, and there has been no verification that the famed meeting between Eva and the Society took place. An examination of extant documents in fact reveals at least two stories about the closure of the organization. The first sorts out what actually happened in 1946 and what role Eva played. The second points to a power struggle within Peronism after

Juan Perón took office—a struggle that necessitated the demise of the Society of Beneficence. Both show how female philanthropic power had decreased, but not how Eva benefited.[21]

Documents available in the Argentine National Archives and in the newspaper archives of the Argentine and U.S. congressional libraries all conclude that the political process began in June 1946. Neither Juan nor Eva prompted the confrontation; rather it commenced when a group of former students and employees of the Society wrote to Congress complaining they had been bypassed for promotion. Even worse, they accused the Society of withholding legislated pay raises and threatening supporters of Juan Perón.[22] In response, the damas fired the two men who submitted the congressional petition, consulted their attorneys, and formally complained to authorities. Subsequently other accusations appeared in the press. On June 24, 1946, the head of the Society had an interview with the minister of the interior, advising him of its legal actions. That same day she also met with Argentine Vice President Quijano. Two days later the damas' president also conferred with the president of the Chamber of Deputies, the vice president of the chamber, and the acting president of the Senate and made two telephone calls to President Juan Perón requesting an interview.[23] Only after all of these events occurred did the former students of the Society's orphanages meet with Eva Perón in early July to ask for her help.[24]

On July 19 the damas received word that their request for an interview with Perón had been granted. However, the opportunity to meet with him arrived too late for the women. They found out on July 25 that the Senate had urged the president to declare a federal intervention of the Society of Beneficence. This turn of events meant that the government could dissolve or reorganize the Society. The damas had always taken pride in the fact that the Society had been authorized by Bernadino Rivadavia, and they often brought students to see his statue and to celebrate his birthday. However, Senator Diego Luis Molinari had found a document in the Argentine National Archives written by Rivadavia that stated: "Unity cannot exist without order, and without order, unity is impossible." Molinari argued that the phrase exemplified the modern nature of Rivadavian political thought. In contrast, Rivadavia's decree empowering the Society of Beneficence had been a throwback to the colonial period. The words used by Molinari must have caused shivers up and down the spines of these resolute women. He claimed that the damas represented an outmoded idea of charity that was even less acceptable in the modern world because its leadership had deteriorated into an oligarchical circle of incompetent women who mismanaged millions of pesos of government money each year.[25]

During the Society's darkest hour, Juan Perón continued to evade his meeting with the damas. The best the women could do was an interview with the minister of the interior on July 25, at which time he told the damas' president that "they didn't need to worry yet because the Senate proposal had not yet been delivered and it was still up to the President to make a final decision."[26] The president of the Society responded that they were not worried because the Society in its 123 years had been valued and supported by governments. Even General Perón had done all he could to intercede in various matters when he headed the Ministry of War and Secretariat of Labor and Social Welfare. Nevertheless, on September 6 the Society's president informed her board that the president had indeed ordered the intervention and had named Dr. Armando Méndez San Martín as intervener. They did not meet with the president until September 18 when forty of the women went to the Casa Rosada to meet with him. At that time, according to *La Prensa* in the official file on the intervention, President Perón "expressed that the Society of Beneficence was necessary for the country," and he promised not to remove from their offices the physicians who worked for the entity.[27]

According to the recollection by the damas, the 1946 events portrayed the Society as the victim of a scurrilous and anonymous campaign to defame its character. The women also viewed themselves as experienced political actors who had tried their best to outwit their enemies. At no time did anyone in the Society ever mention Eva Perón as the cause of the Society's problems.[28]

In fact, Juan had been a thorn in the side of the Society since 1943. The gravest threat to the Society's political status had come with the military coup of 1943—the one that brought Juan Perón to power. Decree No. 12,311 of October 21, 1943, created the Dirección Nacional de Salud Pública y Asistencia Social [National Directorate of Public Health and Social Assistance], which meant that the Society's hospitals would be under its jurisdiction. In response, the damas wrote a memorandum that they handed to the head of the military government, President Farrell, on November 16, 1943. At that time, according to their report, the president promised that "he would never touch an institution created by Rivadavia and he would respect their leadership and autonomy, and if its autonomy was threatened, he would place the group under the control of the national president."[29] Nev-

ertheless, the damas could not obtain a written confirmation of this conversation. The lack of documentation became a problem when they met with
the minister of the interior, General Perlinger, who had no prior knowledge
of the presidential conversation. Eventually these wily women were beaten
at the game they had perfected because they underestimated Juan Perón's
desire to establish a welfare state.

The future of the group became clearer six months later when the president of the Society met again with General Perlinger. While he maintained
cordial relations with the group and even attended their ceremony to reward virtuous women [Premios a la Virtud], Perlinger warned that once the
statutes for the National Directorate of Public Health and Social Assistance
became public, the group could not continue to operate independently. In
response the Society's president commented that she understood completely and could accept subordination to the National Directorate as long
as the damas maintained their autonomy.[30]

Anxious to resolve the issue, the damas launched their most powerful
weapon: a visit to President Farrell. They did this with the confidence of
knowing it had always been impossible for an Argentine president to deny
the damas a request during a face-to-face meeting. President Farrell promised to help the group with this matter, but he mentioned that the government planned to "intensify its efforts related to public assistance and it was
hoped that the Society of Beneficence would collaborate."[31] In response, the
Society's president informed him that she had already met with the minister of the interior. As far as Farrell was concerned, it was a matter for
Perón's ministry to decide.

Once Perón became president he kept the damas of the Society on a
short leash by promising to meet them, but it was not until September 17,
1946, that he set a date. At that time, according to the report of the president
of the Society, Perón tried to calm the fears of the damas. According to their
offical notes on the meeting, "government efforts were not intended to
weaken the Society of Beneficence. Rather they were intended to restructure the group under the supervision of the intervener in order to expand
the institution at the same time that it added a more democratic leadership.
The statutes mandated that the Society coordinate its activities with government services. However, the basic elements of the organization would
remain so that the group could continue its social function with the same
sense of responsibility that had always guided the group. The President also
added that the Society formed part of an Argentine tradition that should be
maintained."[32]

Had Juan Perón lied to the women? Had he really intended to keep the Society intact and allow the women to participate in the activities of its institutions? According to the organizational diagram, "Integral Social Assistance for the Entire Country," he had not, but the Peronist Domingo Mercante, governor of the province of Buenos Aires, and his newspaper *El Laborista* had other plans. Particularly sensitive to social welfare issues, and long before Eva Perón became the champion of the poor and disenfranchised, Mercante expressed a clear vision of an ideal welfare state society and used his position both as governor and as editor to promote his ideas. *El Laborista* envisioned working-class women who raised their children to be patriotic citizens, and it saw Argentina as a country where these women and their families would have the right to affordable housing.[33] The paper published a variety of editorials and articles supportive of a caring welfare state. In May 1946 the newspaper defended the creation of the Secretariat of Public Health and the efforts by legislators to promote a child adoption law in Argentina.[34]

Through his newspaper, Mercante fueled working-class anger against the Society. On July 11, *El Laborista* claimed that many former inmates of the Society's institutions had bitter memories of their experiences and accused the members of having little tenderness for them.[35] On August 3, the newspaper continued its critique with a picture of a poor woman sitting in the street with a baby in her arms and a barefoot boy of about four years of age by her side. Peronists accused the Society of ignoring such women and children. Even more revealing, they claimed that the anti-Society campaign was attributed to *El Laborista*'s publishers, not Eva Perón. As they put it, "La Sra. María Eva Duarte de Perón, whose support we have solicited, has recognized our claims in this anxious clamor, assuring us that she will exert all her influence in this matter as soon as possible."[36] Either this effort was done to minimize the role of Eva Perón or it was a reflection of the sincere belief of Domingo Mercante that, among Peronists, he was the most committed to closing down the Society. In fact, when the decree closing down the Society passed, the newspaper directly took credit for it with headlines that proclaimed a victory for the journal and also mentioned that Eva Perón was ill and unable to be seen in public.

The intervener Méndez San Martín continued to meet with the damas, and his original plan included an expanded board that included the damas along with female representatives of labor unions and other groups. The new board would then elect its own president.[37] While this plan proved satisfactory to Méndez San Martín, and might have even been approved of by Juan Perón, others like Mercante wanted to punish the Society and close it down. As an unfavorable report on the Méndez San Martín's document explained, "the main problem with the [Méndez San Martín] proposal is the fact that the governance of the Society would practically be handed over to the damas who have been running it since it was intervened."[38] Clearly multiple and antagonistic opinions circulated among Peronists regarding the Society and whether the damas of the Society, as well as the philanthropic entity, would be of use to Peronism or a hindrance.

The damas recorded the Society's last days. They met with the intervener throughout 1946 and 1947, beginning on October 4, 1946. He urged the women to collaborate with him, and he consulted with them to name the Society's representatives to various hospitals.[39] He asked that the women prepare reports on the situation in their various institutions, and on December 7, 1946, the women delivered the reports. In return the women asked what specific role would be played by the newly named Junta de Damas [Women's Board]. As reported in the Society's minutes, the intervener and other government delegates "planned to keep the women in charge of the direction, administration, and supervision of all the dependencies of the institution, with broad powers to inspect according to current statutes. The statements were absolutely clear, leaving the impression that the Advisory Commissions will evaluate the work accomplished by the Society."[40] Perón then invited the women to organize a special exposition to show the contribution the group had made to Argentina, and he offered the services of the government petroleum monopoly building. The women took him seriously, and on December 23 they opened the exposition in the lobby of the building. The opening function was attended by Perón along with other dignitaries.

While Méndez San Martín tried to work with the women, he continued to make major reforms in the organization's institutions. In the orphanages, for example, children could have last names instead of matriculation numbers. Further, he changed the names of institutions to denote a less pejorative situation for the inmates; and he provided more culture events and recreation opportunities for inmates. In an annual report made during the intervention, the organization controlled fifteen institutions that cared for 4,251 boys and girls.[41] The situation of the Society of Beneficence remained in this limbo for most of 1947. Initially the institutions operated by the Society became subordinated to the Secretariat of Public Health, and in May an expanded commission had been named to govern them.

Perón remained polite to the women and invited several of them to attend a gala celebration in the Teatro Colón.[42] The women continued to meet until April 30, 1947, when they vainly hoped that the new plans to reorganize the Society of Beneficence could be altered by presidential influence. They recorded their last meeting in pencil.

The Society, however, did not remain as either Perón or the damas had imagined. The early commission that had incorporated the damas into the intervened organization dissolved in September 18, 1947 by Decree 28752. The decree placed the Society's various organizations under direct control of the Argentine government.[43] Hospitals, schools, and orphanages went to various government agencies and not to the Eva Perón Foundation, which did not exist legally until late 1948. Instead, much of the Society became absorbed first into the Secretariat of Public Health through Decree 13414 and then into the National Directorate of Social Assistance, created on October 13, 1948. This entity had control over the blind and over minors, and it covered a wide variety of social welfare activities whose institutions Eva Perón might have visited but did not control.[44]

The Eva Perón Foundation

While the damas of the Society struggled to retain control of their orphanages, two aspects of Peronist child welfare policies threatened all benevolent groups. The first involved Juan's desire to stop funding private philanthropies, and the second was the goal of the Eva Perón Foundation to absorb all private philanthropies. The desire by the legislators to continue funding private philanthropies complicated these two aims. As the Society of Beneficence suffered government intervention, Peronist and non-Peronist legislators launched plans to expand state subsidies to the agencies, almost entirely Catholic, that provided child welfare in the interior of the country. It must have been a very confusing moment for female philanthropists.

In the meantime the Eva Perón Foundation enjoyed tremendous public approval, and it too received generous government funding. Initially created in 1947 with a contribution by the president's wife, the foundation soon increased its ability to help the poor through so-called voluntary contributions from workers and businesses, as well as government subsidies. During Eva's lifetime the foundation accounted only to her, and she quickly used resources provided both by government funding and by subsidies from labor unions and other groups to construct welfare facilities such as the Hogares de Tránsito [Transit Homes], hospitals, old age homes, and schools throughout the country.

Mariano Plotkin has analyzed the foundation as a counterweight to the growing power of labor unions and Perón's desire to develop a welfare state. He notes that the organization also "presented in Peronist rhetoric... one more piece of the rupture with the past that Peronism represented. The work of the Fundación had substituted Peronist social justice for the old charity of the ancient régime. Although beneficence was portrayed as an entirely oligarchic enterprise, social justice was carried out by the people and for the people. In addition, unlike the old beneficence, social justice had scientific foundations."[45] Although Peronist social justice was supposed to be different, Plotkin also recognized the traditional nature of Eva's funding and the personal links between the donors and the recipient. In many ways her foundation represented the contradictions of the Peronist welfare state.

In 1948, just as Perón began to restrict funding for other philanthropies, conservative legislators contested the degree of control that a new national public welfare board would have over the private institutions receiving state subsidies. In September, legislators debated the National Public Welfare Board at the same time that Radical Party members had hoped to take up their project of a Children's Code, and partisans hoped to force a discussion of both issues since they dealt directly with mothers and children. In response, the Peronist Eduardo Barretta defended the Peronist strategy: "All [provincial] governments talk about children and their representatives and have come to this chamber to express them . . . They have always said that it is a grave problem that necessitates a solution; but this government identified . . . the true cause of child abandonment . . . the lower classes who live in poverty."[46] He maintained that the government contributed to the solution by raising salaries, and the better wages reduced the material and moral misery of fathers and mothers. Baretta informed legislators that the government had no plans to confiscate private organizations. The Society of Beneficence was an exceptional case because it had always been considered by the government to be a "part of public administration" and thus fell directly under the control of the Board. Curiously, the Eva Perón Foundation, recently founded, remained beyond the reach of board supervision even though it relied principally on government subsidies.[47]

The relationship between the Eva Perón Foundation and the government became even murkier in 1948 when Peronist legislators proposed to add fifty million pesos to the twenty million pesos already allocated to the Eva Perón Foundation to maintain the services established under its direction. At this point it became public that the Argentine government had also withheld the payment of subsidies to other philanthropic organizations that had been authorized by Congress. Radical Party legislators debated with great emotion whether the Eva Perón Foundation had the appropriate legal standing to receive such subsidies from the government.

Arturo Illia, future president of Argentina from the Radical Party (1963–1966), fervently opposed the idea of expanding the Eva Perón Foundation through large public subsidies. The foundation increasingly challenged the National Public Welfare Board and returned Argentina to the traditional state subsidies of private institutions. As late as 1948, as Illia pointed out, 3,052 private institutions had not received promised subsidies, and the National Public Welfare Board had suspended payments for the entire year. In response to fears that such organizations would have to close down, the Peronist deputy José Emilio Visca stated in August 1949 that all child welfare philanthropies should be taken over by the Eva Perón Foundation because "social welfare should only be controlled by one person."[48]

Clearly the structure of the welfare state had not been resolved by the Peronists, and congressional supporters of Eva Perón eagerly sought her control of immigrant and religious welfare organizations. The very thought of this uncertainty, coupled with the tug of war between the National Public Welfare Board and the Eva Perón Foundation, made the situation of these groups even more tenuous. Alberto Benegas Lynch (h) and Martín Krause have argued that "many Societies of Beneficence literally were 'silenced' during the Peronist regime. The fear of being intervened by the Eva Perón Foundation obliged them to survive without any publicity regarding their activities including their fund raising campaigns."[49] Other researchers have confirmed in interviews that immigrant groups were fearful of intervention although they continued their activities.

The rowdy 1948 debate indeed ended with increased funding for the Eva Perón Foundation, although Eva never did absorb other child welfare groups into her organization. In the long run, state bureaucracy won out and the Eva Perón Foundation as well as the Society of Beneficence's institutions ultimately became integrated into the welfare state. In the short run, however, this dispute among the Peronists brought only more uncertainty to philanthropists.

Peronist and non-Peronist legislators continued to present plans for expanding state subsidies after 1948 to private philanthropies. Amid chaotic welfare strategies, collective beneficence began to wane on its own, just as Congress began to reward their work with higher subsidies. The dwindling stream of immigrants, also a hallmark of Peronist politics, made the impressive immigrant orphanages and facilities irrelevant and expensive to maintain.

Peronism and Collective Benevolence

So what happened to other charitable institutions? Perhaps those most at risk for funding shortages were the many Catholic establishments that had taken on the burden of juvenile delinquency reform. Heavily subsidized for each child sent by defenders of minors or the Patronato Nacional de Menores, the establishments also received lump sum subsidies as well as subventions for the construction or repair of facilities. According to the testimony of national legislators these facilities, often in Buenos Aires or the surrounding province, along with the regional hospitals and orphanages truly suffered from the blockage of funds and government demands that the institutions provide at least 25 percent of their own funding.[50]

A glance through the debates from 1946 onward indicates that subsidies to the Society of Beneficence as well as to non-Catholic and immigrant-based philanthropic institutions had ceased. This was not exactly the case, however. Scheduled to receive annual subsidies, many institutions never got them. Yet the annual reports of philanthropies rarely indicated this dilemma, since they reported subsidies even when payments never arrived. Possibly some groups did receive government subsidies; nevertheless, a blanket of silence obscured the process until some of the most dependent organizations, unable to replace the subsidies with private contributions, began to complain in 1948.

The demise of elite women's control of the Society of Beneficence thus did little to resolve the question of how welfare institutions should be funded. In the early years of Peronism, petitions for subsidies to workers' organizations, as well as traditional philanthropies, particularly Catholic organizations, had been warmly received by Congress. In sprees of good will, both supporters and detractors of Peronism defended requests to double, triple, and even quadruple earlier subventions as well as provide massive one-time grants to benevolent groups. Politicians of all political affiliations tended to lump subsidies of different groups and categorize them as provincial requests—evidence of another political characteristic of the period. They envisioned wresting the power to distribute welfare from the provinces and from the president and to increase direct national subsidies.

This strategy did not always work, as some wealthy provinces such as Buenos Aires also expanded their own services under the support of both conservative and Peronist governors.

By the end of his first presidency, however, Juan Perón had transformed the basic definitions of child welfare. For the first time, family rights appeared in the 1949 constitution, and social security and social welfare became definitions of worker protections. Within constitutional provisions related to the family, the new constitution stated that "mother and child assistance will receive privileged treatment by the State."[51] During the debates preceding the passage of the constitution, the Peronist Arturo Sampay noted that the family never appeared in liberal constitutions, which led to the disintegration of the working-class family by forcing wives to go out to work. Therefore the constitution had to protect maternity and infancy. Other members of the constitutional convention noted that the most recent Latin American constitutions of Brazil, Ecuador, Uruguay, Venezuela, Cuba, Guatemala, and Nicaragua included provisions to protect the family, and that these sentiments reflected Latin American understandings of family needs.[52]

By the time the constitution went into effect, the Perón administration had also enacted adoption laws, eliminated the legal and social distinctions between illegitimate and legitimate children, and expanded direct state involvement in social welfare programs. Perón created a new slogan: "In the new Argentina, the only privileged ones are the children." Welfare state expansion, under these circumstances, became a natural corollary, both facilitated and criticized by political opponents in Congress, specifically the Radical Party. Both groups relied on the complex and often contradictory traditions that characterized national welfare in the past. These traditions included, first, the trend to create national bureaucracies that, instead of distributing goods and services based on need, provided them to all on the basis of rights; and, second, the distributive politics that favored direct subsidies to groups that sent petitions to Congress.

How did anti-Peronists react to Perón's formation of the welfare state? Among the opponents to Peronism, the Radical Party held the most seats in the Chamber of Deputies, and the Socialist Party had no representatives. Marcela García Sebastiani's analysis of the Radical Party during the early years of Perón's administration emphasizes the competitive drive of the Radical Party through the Unión Democrática [Democratic Union], the alliance that opposed Perón and had expected to win the elections. Peronists were not alone in their desire to promote a welfare state, and the Radical Party constantly presented its own ideas while criticizing those of the Peronists.[53]

An example of Radical Party politics came from Arturo Frondizi, another future president of Argentina (1958–1962). Shortly after the Society of Beneficence had been intervened, Frondizi led a campaign to limit the influence of foreigners in Argentina. Although he is most well known for his efforts to limit the influence of foreign petroleum companies, Frondizi also led a campaign that threatened all the organizations representing religious and foreign communities. On March 5 and May 8, 1947, a group of some of the most famous Radical Party legislators, including Frondizi, Ricardo Balbín, and Luis Dellapiane, presented a resolution requesting that the president mandate a written declaration of all the wealth of religious and philosophical (*doctrinas filosóficas*) organizations in the country. This inventory had to include the value of all properties, subsidies, and investments between 1937 and 1942. Accompanied by an inquiry regarding the landholdings of foreign groups, this measure, if passed, would impose a whole new level of state scrutiny of all religious institutions that operated welfare facilities.[54] Radical Party members assailed religious philanthropies as well as Peronists, and the actions of the Radical Party helped legitimize the Peronist welfare state.

Peronist welfare plans, in general, enjoyed great success. They affected all private philanthropy groups by first increasing and then ending the massive program of subsidies. The Eva Perón Foundation offered the only opposition. Perón's efforts to reshape child welfare enraged some Argentines and surprised others.[55] Despite their success, Perón's early child welfare programs also cast doubts upon his commitment to a traditional welfare state. At the same time that he created bureaucracies, he supported Eva's Foundation. He also insisted that the government enact measures to ensure child adoption. Although this issue has rarely been identified as part of a welfare state, in Argentina adoption became integrated into Peronist plans in the context of how the government could cope with the San Juan earthquake of 1944. The earthquake forced the government to face the reality that long-standing foster parent practices needed to be modified.

The enactment of Peronist adoption laws in 1948 demonstrates another conservative aspect to Perón's strategies. Just as he hesitated to close down the Society of Beneficence and other philanthropies, he equally resisted the thought of challenging family law. Perón initially supported an adoption as charity resulting from the 1944 San Juan earthquake, just as the Society of

Beneficence had supported adoption for abandoned and orphaned children. Once proposed, however, Peronist legislators expanded the legislation to cover more children; at the same time they specifically argued that all men had the right to a son and heir, even priests. Once enacted, adoption laws enabled state-controlled orphanages to promote adoption to lower the number of children in foster families and orphanages.

Child Adoption

The San Juan earthquake in January 1944 completely destroyed the western provincial capital city, leaving thousands of children orphaned and injured. The event also had its liminal moments, for it provided the context for Juan and Eva's meeting as well as a purpose for Peronism. During a public charity event designed to raise money for the victims of the earthquake, Juan met his future wife, the radio actress Eva Duarte. Supposedly Eva and Juan visited the provincial city and the devastation made them sensitive to issues regarding child welfare, and Juan Perón met San Juan victims, who traveled by train to Buenos Aires; this has been confirmed by photographs.

It took a presidential election and an additional year before President Juan Perón sent a message to the Argentine Congress on August 29, 1947, urging legislators to modify the national civil code, which made no provisions for adoption. Perón wanted a limited adoption law for victims of the earthquake, and initially he refused to support a broad adoption law that interfered with the property rights accorded to biological children. Indeed, he specifically limited his proposal to orphans and abandoned children as a philanthropic measure "because they are the ones who most need this protection. . . . [Thus] adoption will be allowed as an essentially philanthropic and social institution." At the same time he reiterated his support for the law only if it remained limited to certain groups of children because "any modification of family law should be undertaken with extreme prudence."[56]

Perón designed his legislative proposal specifically to help children in crisis. In taking a conservative stand on who could adopt, it required adoptive parents to be at least forty-five years old, childless after ten years of marriage, or have no legal heirs at the time of adoption. Only orphans, illegitimate children not recognized by their parents, or minors whose parents had lost the right of patria potestad became eligible for adoption. The proposal did, however, allow relatives to adopt minors.

Although Perón made his own views clear, his version of the law did not emerge from the committee on legislation. Instead, the Peronist-dominated Chamber of Deputies released another proposal that was much broader because it allowed any child under eighteen years of age to be eligible for adoption. If their parents were still alive, then children could be adopted only with the written consent of biological parents. Only barren couples who were eighteen years older than the child could adopt, and religious clergy were excluded. Finally, although it allowed fathers to adopt their illegitimate children, it placed limits on the total number of children adopted by a family.[57]

Antonio Benítez, the Peronist head of the deputies' legislation committee, specifically mentioned two reasons why he supported the more encompassing legislation: the changing family structure in Argentina that led to abandoned children and the San Juan earthquake. He objected to Perón's limitation on who could be adopted, "because it would involve a public pronouncement of why a child was being adopted, and that would mark the minor with a permanent stigma."[58]

Members of the Radical Party proposed that prospective parents be over the age of thirty-five for women and forty for men. Like the Peronists, they too allowed a father to adopt his illegitimate child, but unlike their opponents, the Radical Party legislators did not limit the number of children each couple could adopt. Furthermore, the Radical Party plan allowed foster parents to petition for the right to exercise patria potestad.[59]

When the time came to debate the merits of the various proposals, the Peronist Eduardo Barretta, who supported the limited adoption laws defined by the president, stated that any measure that broadened adoption rights to illegitimate children threatened the basic unit of society—the legal, biological family: "We should . . . turn to the fictive family through adoption, but never weaken the biological family because we must strengthen, fortify, and reinforce it. For this reason I believe [adoption] . . . should be restricted only to abandoned, orphaned, and fatherless children."[60] Thus, according to Barretta, the rights of fathers should not supersede family order.

Other legislators argued that only infants should be eligible for adoption, while some maintained that juvenile delinquency could be curbed by finding homes for wayward adolescent boys. A few turned the question around and posited that children had inherent rights. This was the position of Deputy Zavala Ortiz from Córdoba. When it was his turn to speak he proclaimed the child rights position of the Radical Party that "the essence of adoption is to find a father for the child and not a child for the father."[61]

He therefore urged his colleagues to make sure that future laws protected children, not fathers.

None of these deputies managed to persuade colleagues to resist patriarchal privilege in the matter of adoption. The law that eventually passed on September 15, 1948, enabled an adult man without legally recognized offspring, even a priest, to adopt at most two children. If married, his wife had to give judicial consent. In return, the child would be able to inherit from his new father, but he had no legal claim to inheritance or kinship with anyone else in the family. Thus the 1948 law, identified as Peronist but not reflecting the president's initial plans, ensured that property could be transmitted from father to son. The Peronist legislators, all men, defied the president to ensure liberal access to adoption, and the masculine privilege of recognizing illegitimate children to create an heir.[62]

While the Peronist state never offered statistics on adoption, state welfare for children fundamentally changed. As a result of the new law, children who previously might have spent their entire lives in institutional settings now had the opportunity to live with adoptive parents. This meant that orphanages could be smaller, and the cost of child welfare privatized.

The preservation of the children's records of the Society of Beneficence and of those who entered other state facilities allows analyses of what happened to some children adopted after 1947. The success of adoption varied tremendously from case to case, and often adolescence soured what had been considered a permanent situation for youngsters. In some cases adoptive parents returned the children, and in other cases the children requested a change in their legal situation. Adoption was a lengthy process, often lasting as long as two years or more, and it involved the observation of the families by social workers. Many requests for adoption began before a law existed. Foster parents before 1947 usually sought to give children their last names. After the adoption law passed, these requests turned into formal adoption procedures. Those petitions that began before 1947 have even more years of observations and notations than do later ones. Take, for example, the case of "Rosaura" B., who was abandoned as an infant at the foundling home of the Society of Beneficence in 1937. In 1941, after a stay at another Society orphanage, she was sent into foster care with an older, childless Italian couple at the same time that the Society determined that Rosaura's biological mother had died. The foster parents were thrilled with the child, and they promised to educate and raise her well, although the child often made life difficult for them.

In 1948 the couple petitioned the Society to permit Rosaura to use their last name, the traditional method of recognizing adoptive children, and this request was granted in August. Subsequently the couple and Rosaura went to Italy, and from there, in October 1951, they authorized an attorney to proceed with formal adoption in Argentina. As late as 1959 the couple was still requesting permission to adopt, and in January 1960 the child reached the age of majority and no longer qualified.

This case demonstrates the lengthy legal circuits that parents had to endure in order to adopt, as well as the extensive visits by social workers from the Society. In this case, it had been easier for the couple to append their last name to Rosaura than to adopt, even under Peronism. Most likely the fact that the couple took her to Italy made adoption slower and more complicated, but it also reveals how a legal procedure originally designed as a quick solution to the problems of children confronted by tragedies could drag on forever.[63]

In 1951 a male baby was abandoned in a bathroom at the Hospital de Niños. While healthy, the baby had several birth defects in his hand. Sent to the former foundling home, by then called the Casa Cuna "Eva Perón," the child never became eligible for adoption. Although he had several operations, he lived with his former wet nurse until 1966 when she took in a two-month-old baby. The child then remained institutionalized until he reached the age of majority in 1971.[64] This case demonstrated that the Peronist governments continued to discriminate against handicapped children and refused to allow them the opportunity to be adopted.

Many healthy institutionalized children had great difficulty adapting to life as an adopted child. "José B." was born in 1939 and placed with a middle-class family in 1945. From the beginning the child's rowdy and difficult behavior concerned the family, but within a year specialists told the social worker of the Society of Beneficence that in time the boy would behave better. Throughout 1946, however, the social worker noted that the child broke things, wet his bed, and seemed very nervous. Despite all these problems, José's adoptive parents decided to accept their son's behavior, and in 1951 they began the process that finally concluded successfully in 1954. José was very lucky—many children placed in families with hopes of adoption went back to institutions if they behaved badly or if they indulged in behavior such as dating without permission of their parents.[65]

In June 1948, Sra. "Adela Cecilia Campo" wrote to Eva Perón requesting the opportunity to adopt a child. Because she was childless after seven years of marriage, she and her husband wanted a daughter under the age of two. As she put it, "I know that the orphanages are filled with these children without parents, and we would . . . educate her and raise her as if she were our daughter."[66] On July 6 Eva's representative told Adela to go to the Society of Beneficence. Adela brought several letters with her, one of which explained why the couple had been married only in a civil ceremony. This was particularly important, as the Society had favored couples married in a Catholic ceremony and the Peronists continued the tradition. By 1954 the couple wanted to adopt, and in this case it took less than a year. Most likely Eva's intervention ultimately paved the way to a speedier adoption.

In many cases adults who intended to adopt ultimately returned children who did not live up to their expectations. "Victoria Bonano" took care of "Norma Franco" from 1936 to 1940, but in March 1947 Norma was given to "Emilia Monsanto," a fifty-five-year-old widow who wanted a child of twelve to keep her company and be her *ahijada* [godchild]. Emilia came with excellent recommendations, and equally important she had a maid so that social workers did not have to worry that Norma would be treated as a servant. For several years social workers visited them and often got reports that Emilia disapproved of Norma's willful behavior. Nevertheless Emilia kept Norma under control by threatening to return her to the orphanage and securing another godchild. In 1949 doctors examined the girl to see if she suffered from nervous problems, but the physician indicated that she simply suffered from adolescence—an unusual commentary at the time given that most specialists did not use this terminology.

In 1949 Emilia began proceedings for Norma that stipulated she would adopt her as long as the girl behaved herself. Three years later Emilia returned Norma to the office of adoptions. At this point Victoria stepped in and promised to take Norma back within two months if her behavior improved. Evidently Victoria did not take her back, since in 1955 Emilia returned to find out what had happened to Norma. Although Emilia was unwilling to adopt the nineteen-year-old Norma, she still willingly took her in because she could support herself. The widow and her charge remained together, each complaining about each other until the young woman reached the age of majority and no longer received supervision from the state welfare system.[67]

Generally speaking, the majority of adoption cases found in the archives of the Consejo Nacional de Niñez, Adolescencia y la Familia between 1948 and 1955 involved young girls. One telling sign that adopted children were truly adored by their adoptive families can be seen in those situations in which young girls received piano lessons—a marker of middle-class training. The most successful cases involved demonstrative, submissive, and loving children who were appreciative of their newfound parents. Many parents, in turn, tried to keep secret the origins of the children, and they complained about the monthly visits from social workers who might reveal the truth to the child.

As noted above, adoption legislation promoted the redistribution of children without parents to new families or legalized the relationship of children born out of wedlock. Since it is impossible to know how many private adoptions took place, it is important to recognize that the welfare state took advantage of this law to regularize the situation of many minors in state care, just as the damas had hoped. This reality linked traditional child welfare ideas on the use of adoption to the Peronist welfare state in order to ensure that most children lived with parents, biological or adoptive.

Perón's Second Five-Year Plan

On December 1, 1952, President Perón presented his Second Five-Year Plan to Congress, and both chambers passed it in less than twenty days. This time, however, the plan was much more specific about social welfare, juvenile delinquency, and the role of the state in the family. In preparation for the proposal, Perón in 1951 actually invited the Argentine public to write letters to him with suggestions for the new plan. Some forty thousand individuals responded and sent suggestions on a wide variety of topics including social welfare.[68]

Carlos Alberto Rey, from Mercedes in the province of Buenos Aires, began his letter with the Peronist phrase "En la nueva Argentina los únicos privilegiados son los niños" [In the New Argentina the only people with privileges are children]. To Rey this goal could not be achieved until transients, both young and old, and mothers with children asking for alms no longer begged in the subways, on church patios, and in front of office buildings.[69] Neighbors, both male and female, of the Barrio Central of Córdoba asked for child care facilities so that youngsters did not wander around.[70] Teófilo Baidaff of Buenos Aires and Santa Fe suggested that new parks or patios be constructed so that children would not have to play in the streets, thereby keeping them from becoming delinquents.[71]

Peronist women from La Plata, capital of the province of Buenos Aires, had even more grandiose ideas. In addition to having day care centers for children, they envisioned places where mothers could receive breast milk for their children [*lactaria*]; kindergartens and schools run by specialists, pediatricians, and schoolteachers; and clinics offering free vaccinations for children and parents. They argued that the facility should be free for all unemployed mothers as well as widows and abandoned mothers. To make the expensive idea more attractive, they proposed that all homes should be named for Eva Perón.[72] And a man from the province of San Juan argued that poor women needed much more help to prevent their children from being left alone, and that all single mothers with children under the age of sixteen should benefit from such aid. These letters acknowledged the historic importance of performing charity, and they linked it to Peronism.

Raul Eduardo Aubone wrote from San Juan to let the president know that many destitute women ("widows, separated women, abandoned women, and single mothers") with minor children still needed the support of the government to free them and their families from danger.[73] A mothers' club from rural Tucumán province requested the construction of a national school that for two years had been promised to the locality. Mario Crenovich wanted a nursery school for domestic servants in Buenos Aires, while Silvia Mazzantini of Rosario, Santa Fe, requested a home for female state employees and elder orphans. Another letter from Santa Fe requested that a Cantina Maternal be installed near the writer's neighborhood.

Other letters asked specifically for a large sum of money for the Eva Perón Foundation to eliminate beggars and the homeless, while Rosa Famá Traci suggested that spinsters be added to the category of protected people in Peronist legislation. Gerónimo Gonzáles Sarandí took another approach. He suggested the creation of a new Ministry of Social Security to replace the existing Institute of Social Security so that the Eva Perón Foundation could be incorporated into the evolving Peronist welfare state. He wanted Eva's group to become the formal replacement for the female-headed Society of Beneficence, and in that way the memory of the Abanderada de los Humildes [Flag Bearer of the Humble] could be perpetuated. Some correspondents, particularly men, also advocated reopening houses of prostitution and allowing divorce. These and other letter writers clearly wanted the government to be much more explicit about social welfare than in 1946.[74] Letter writers wanted the inclusion of specific reforms to help their community.

What they received, however, was a general government plan. Nevertheless, the Second Five-Year Plan devoted more time and energy to children, mothers, and the family than did the first. The first chapter of the plan defined Peronist goals for social policies. The eight social policies included social organization, work, assistance, education, public health, scientific research, housing, and tourism. Social assistance became a state function, although private entities could "cooperate in these actions, as long as their mission respects the dignity of those assisted and carries out their functions within the humanitarian and Christian principles of national doctrine."[75] Social security included maternity protection, while complementary social assistance provided specialized courts for juveniles and the construction or remodeling of homes for juveniles.

The Eva Perón Foundation became an integral part of government resources. Until Perón managed to integrate the Eva Perón Foundation into the welfare state (Eva had died by the time the plan passed Congress), he continued to rely on private or quasi-private philanthropy in the midst of expanding state programs. It is this mix of programs that led critics to doubt Perón's dedication to a national welfare state.

What did Perón's welfare state promise philanthropies? The answer depended on the particular group. In the case of the Jewish orphanages and day care centers, the outbreak of the Second World War presented new challenges for the Jewish damas. As refugees began to arrive in Argentina, the Jewish damas, as well as the Jewish community in general, hoped that once again Argentina would provide a haven for displaced Jewish children. These dreams were thwarted, however, by Peron's immigration policies. In 1944 Argentine Jews planned to bring in one thousand refugee children, but the Peronist government admitted only sixty-five. Then, in 1947, members of the Jewish community approached the Peronist minister of foreign relations to urge the government to admit one thousand children. The Peronist government supported the request, but the children never received permission to enter. Under these conditions, it seemed unlikely that there would be a great postwar need for Jewish orphanages.

Nevertheless, the goal of serving the Jewish community by providing a refuge for war victims encouraged the damas to believe that there would always be a need for the orphanage.[76] Until the children arrived, the damas kept themselves busy. They purchased small businesses for indigent adults and obtained sewing machines and other work implements for them, they found employment for the poor, and they paid rent for those who lacked funds to do so. They had a social worker, Aída Cherniak, and two women, Sofía S. de Reinoff and Rosa R. de Goldfarb, who served as inspectors and distributed layettes and clothing for the women. Still believing that orphans would arrive in droves from Europe, they decided to construct a fifth dormitory, and they continued their fund-raising activities with annual collections, teas, and dances at the best hotels.[77]

According to the traditional historiography of Peronism, the 1943 revolution, along with the growing demands on the women's group, should have induced the damas to reduce their activities. But the prospects of admitting one thousand Jewish children to Argentina, along with Argentina's subsequent recognition of Israel, signaled to some that relations between Jewish charities and the government were not as strained as they were for the Society of Beneficence, which was intervened in 1946.

In 1943 the Asilo Israelita de Huérfanas celebrated its twenty-fifth anniversary, to which *El Mundo Israelita* devoted an entire page. For their part, the damas continued to expand their activities, even though they often experienced financial woes. In 1945, the women purchased a rural property in General Belgrano in the province of Córdoba, so that the orphaned girls could have summer vacations. The local committee in Córdoba took charge of the property. The damas also received inheritances from the community that had supported them for so long, and they continued to receive a national subsidy as well as occasional donations such as 2,500 pesos from the state petroleum monopoly.[78]

This trajectory continued under Peronism. The 1950–51 report of the Sociedad de Damas Israelitas de Beneficencia mentions that the women had distributed 27,835 pesos in subsidies to poor Jewish people in Argentina, with only 4,560 pesos going to support babies. They also donated money to pay rent and cover medical bills as well as donate clothing and shoes. Furthermore, in a direct imitation of the Eva Perón Foundation, the Jewish damas opened Hogares de Tránsito for homeless and/or unaccompanied Jewish women who migrated from the Argentine interior. These women also received adult education religious classes. Clearly the damas did not want Jewish women to enter Eva's homes for transient adult women.[79] In any case, the Asilo Argentino de Huérfanas Israelitas survived the war years and was neither intervened nor taken over by the government as in the case of the Society of Beneficence. Nevertheless the Asilo did not prosper, and by the 1950s the few female Jewish orphans did not justify maintaining the orphanage. To make ends meet, the damas rented rooms to Hebrew language schools that prepared children to follow their Zionist parents to Israel. By the 1970s the damas sent the remaining orphans to Israel or they went to live with relatives, and eventually the building was sold to a bus company.[80]

The day-care center that was operated by the Yiddish-speaking German Jewish women flourished during the 1930s and 1940s. In 1936 Ana de Gaversky became president of the Hogar Infantil Israelita. The institution cared for 100 to 130 children each day, and there were two buses that transported the children from the center to their homes. At that point the organization did not own buildings of its own, so a building campaign was initiated that continued into the 1940s and eventually a building at Monte 2150 was purchased. By 1946 the organization was swamped with requests to help children, and so it began to contemplate opening another institution.[81]

The different experiences of these Jewish organizations cannot be attributed to their fund-raising methods. To support their activities, the damas of the Hogar Infantil Israelita organized collections similar to the other Jewish child welfare charities in Buenos Aires. Each year they campaigned just before the Jewish New Year to pay for gifts of food, and the organization relied heavily on bridge tournaments, dances, and an annual dinner. Equally important, individual contributions by donors always appeared in extensive lists published in the Hogar Infantil Israelita's annual reports along with many pages of paid advertisements by members of the Jewish community—a tactic that also was pursued by the damas of the Jewish girls' orphanage. From time to time they also solicited contributions at synagogues during important holy days such as Yom Kippur. To pay off the debt on the new Monte Street property (subsequently renamed Baldomero F. Moreno 2150), they created local committees in the interior so that women there could organize fund-raisers. Evidently the Jewish community in the interior faithfully supported the charities in Buenos Aires.[82]

Perhaps the difference came from the relationship of the groups to the Peronist government. During those years, the women who ran the Hogar Infantil Israelita seemed to be on better terms with the Perón government than were the other Jewish damas. As testimony to their support, for several years the women of the Hogar ran a page dedicated to Perón's Second Five-Year Plan in the Jewish press. In 1955, they supported the creation of a forest in Israel named after Perón by "planting trees as a just homage and expression of the friendship between two nations that are fighting to achieve greatness: Argentina and Israel."[83] While these women evidently did not receive subsidies, they did not openly oppose the Perón government and, equally important, their activities were limited to kindergarten and preschool classes rather than running an expensive orphanage. Their kindergarten continued to operate all through the 1960s.

The Jewish boys' orphanage made the strategic mistake of expanding beyond its financial capacity just as Perón came to power. Through the years the boys had always lived along with elderly males and females in several buildings. By 1935, 400 youngsters and elders lived at Cabildo 3642. Always financially pressed, this orphanage did not operate any workshops, and thus placed youngsters in different establishments, usually related to printing, as apprentices. In the 1940 report, the trustees announced that they had more than 67,000 pesos of debts, including mortgages, resulting from the need to expand the facilities on Cabildo Street. By then, they had 260 boys in residence, an increase of more than fifty over the previous year.[84]

To meet what they, too, believed would be a postwar expansion of orphans, the male governing board decided to launch a plan to build a separate orphanage. By 1943 they estimated that the number of children would expand in three years to 720 at a cost of $345,600 pesos per year for their maintenance. The demand from European refugees would probably expand the need to cover 1,200 children. In a stroke of luck, on January 9, 1943, the non-Jewish philanthropist José Itiurrat donated twenty hectares of land in Burzaco, province of Buenos Aires, along with buildings and a contribution of $1,000 pesos to sustain the venture. The value of the property was estimated at $500,000 pesos.[85]

Despite all the excitement surrounding the gift and the construction of the buildings, the dream of a boys' orphanage proved to be simply too expensive. By 1946, the fixed costs of the establishment exceeded $50,000 pesos per month, and they continued to grow due to inflation. That year the male leaders of the boys' orphanage had collected $212,301 pesos, but they failed to reach their goals. Three years later the men in charge had insufficient funds to buy clothing and shoes for the five hundred residents, and monthly dues covered only half the $85,000 monthly fixed costs. The trustees ended up begging for additional funds from the Jewish community, and an undated album of photos of residents offered poems that rendered them pitiable.[86] Eventually these boys also went to Israel while the old age home remained abandoned and underfunded.

Other groups had to deal with the rise of Perón's welfare state and the changed conditions for private philanthropy. The Patronato de la Infancia, created by Buenos Aires elites in 1892, had expanded beyond Buenos Aires; as early as 1893, it purchased a property in Mar del Plata to establish a juvenile reform school. The Patronato received contributions from elites as well as subsidies from the municipality of Buenos Aires and from the national government. In addition, it opened an infants' nursery and schools for children at risk, including a School of Arts and Trades [Escuela Artes y Oficios]. In 1921 the Patronato opened up a mothers' school to teach women how to raise their children. By the 1930s they too had financial problems, and it was estimated that financial reserves would be exhausted in 1940. But these concerns went unheeded until the trustees were forced to close down free primary schooling, and they turned over to the province of Buenos Aires their vacation spot for children in Mar del Plata along with their agricultural station in Claypole.[87]

In the 1940s the Patronato, in part as a way to celebrate its fiftieth anniversary, sponsored the second conference on abandoned and delinquent children. The anniversary celebration was attended by the leading conservatives in power, including the national vice-president Ramón Castillo, the mayor of Buenos Aires, the president of the National Education Council, and the president of the Chamber of Deputies. The joyful occasion masked the fact that the Patronato was in debt for more than $200,000 pesos; indeed, the foundation was dipping into its endowments to stay afloat. Further, in spite of the fact that the women's committee solicited a special national subsidy for $100,000 pesos from the Senate, conditions eventually became even more desperate.[88]

The 1943 military coup only aggravated the situation of the Patronato, as decrees had augmented employees' salaries and the monthly deficit was expected to increase to $135,000 pesos in 1946. In response, the board members explained their situation to Domingo Mercante, secretary of labor and welfare before Perón. Their only hope was to ask for greater government subsidies and sell off some of their properties, as well as restrict the admission of minors into their facilities. When the expected subsidies did not appear, they were reduced to selling off properties. The group had taken on too many projects and had gotten into financial problems long before Perón took power. The nonpayment of national subsidies made the Patronato's dependence on government funding more palpable, and turning over two schools to the provincial government became the only solution for the organization. After the overthrow of the Peronist government the Patronato again received government funding, but by that time their facilities had been reduced just like other philanthropic works designed to help poor children.[89]

Among the collective groups able to deal with the financial crisis and the changing demographic conditions in Argentina was the Patronato Español. Due to its close links with Spain and the size of the Spanish immigrant community (the second largest in Argentina), the organization did not need to seek national subsidies. Indeed, a series of donations from the wills of wealthy benefactors enabled the Patronato to purchase their building on Olleros 29449, and in 1935 they created a permanent endowment fund to ensure that money would always be held in reserve or would be used to purchase real estate that brought in income from rent. They sold or rented out other properties left to the organization. In the 1940s when the cost of clothing soared, the mother superior in charge of the school and orphanage purchased a loom. She learned how to weave and then taught the skill to several students, thereby reducing the costs of clothing. In this way the Patronato avoided the mistake of overbuilding and the institution exists today as a private school.[90]

The Demise of the Eva Perón Foundation

Curiously, the Eva Perón Foundation, so feared by members of collective benevolence groups, barely survived the death of its founder in 1952. Its very strength—the dynamism of its leader and the fierce loyalty and fear she engendered in others—proved to be its most visible and most vulnerable quality. After Eva died, Perón took control over the foundation. Most of its personnel came from the Ministry of Finance, and Ramón Cereijo served as its general manager. The only women who attended the meetings served as secretaries, and this male-dominated board continued after Eva's death. At that time, the men attempted to quell the foundation's disorganization and its indebtedness by transferring some of its institutions to other government entities and borrowing money. One of the first decisions, however, involved a request for help from the Cuban Embassy to contribute to a relief fund. Perón and his advisors turned down the request and recommended that henceforth such requests be routed through his office. The Eva Perón Foundation no longer served the political plans of its founder.

The expansive spending of the foundation did not end, however, because Peronist legislators quickly proposed new subsidies to finance its activities. But even these efforts proved insufficient to expand the foundation beyond its institutions under construction, planned, or already functioning. As early as 1952 the Peronist government began canceling pensions for people who had written to Eva as well as those who continued to enjoy pensions granted by the Society of Beneficence. By September 1954, Perón and his associates began selling off twelve grocery stores that the foundation owned and operated. After Juan Perón was overthrown in 1955, the Eva Perón Foundation's properties became part of the welfare state, just like those of the Society of Beneficence. Nevertheless, during Juan's administration the Eva Perón Foundation undermined the president's own plans for the welfare state. And even though he occasionally vetoed subsidies for the foundation, he could neither close it down nor protect it from financial difficulties.[91]

With the demise of philanthropies, a new body of family and child welfare laws evolved. The heart of the welfare state reformed Argentine families by creating new alternatives to child abandonment. In addition to adoption, in 1949 the Peronists supported a project introduced by the president to punish fathers who failed to support their minor children, and the Radical Party got its child right's code enacted. The Eva Perón Foundation received extensive congressional subsidies for its good works, orphanages, and old age homes, as well as for the many child sports activities that it sponsored. New regulations changed inheritance laws, granted divorce, and eliminated the social and legal stigmas of illegitimate births. In effect, a new Peronist family had been created—one characterized by its social flexibility and its political debt to Peronism. These families were supposed to become the political and social backbone of the state, as well as help to prevent the problems of childhood. This new Peronist family in fact owed its origins to a composite of conservative, feminist, socialist, and radical plans to reform the civil code. Each Peronist law had been enacted after years of debate and discussion. Being labeled Peronist did not indicate that Perón invented the idea, but rather that the Peronists had mustered a sufficient number of positive votes to pass the legislation. In return, the Peronists wanted to identify the ideas with Peronism.

Could these family reforms actually eliminate family disorder? The Peronists certainly tried to prove it in the case of juvenile delinquency. A secret study of juvenile arrests in the national capital from 1943 to 1952, compiled by the Ministerio de Asuntos Técnicos [Ministry of Technical Issues], noted that the number of juveniles arrested had decreased from 1,034 to 772, although it began to increase again after 1952. The category of "crimes against the administration and public officials," or political crimes, comprised the principal category of juvenile offenses.[92] While this meant that young people had begun to oppose the Peronist government, the Peronists attributed the decrease in robberies to improved economic conditions in Buenos Aires. The government never made the report public—an indication that it felt that a strong link between family reform and reduced juvenile delinquency had not been made.

According to Perón's ideology, "in the New Argentina, the only privileged ones are the children." This slogan was repeated over and over again, often appearing in political campaigns and equally often invoked by people

seeing state aid to improve child welfare facilities. It must have been dis-
heartening for ministry officials to find that juveniles resisted Peronist laws
in such great numbers. Perhaps they needed other ways to measure success,
but that was an onerous task. Juvenile delinquency arrests were as politi-
cized as any other statistic, and they depended upon the priorities established by the police or by other government officials. The number of children offered in adoption, whether through public or private means, did not
appear in Peronist documents. The number of children involved in state
welfare programs of one kind or another continued to increase, as seen by
the numbers of case files in the Consejo Nacional del Menor, Adolecencia y
la Familia that soared from approximately fifty thousand cases in the late
1940s to more than five hundred thousand cases by the end of the century.
Did this indicate the success of Perón's family politics, or perhaps its failure? Was it a measurement of the growth of the welfare state, or was it
perhaps the failure of other family and economic agencies associated with
the national government? If anti-Peronists dismantled the welfare state,
why did people continue to demand and receive child welfare? This conundrum has been ignored by welfare state specialists in Argentina and
elsewhere.

Conclusion

By engaging in child welfare campaigns, female philanthropists and feminists helped shape the contours of the welfare state in twentieth-century Argentina. Social policies regarding child welfare began at the community and municipal level during the era of massive immigration in the nineteenth century. Members of the immigrant community, along with female philanthropists as well as religious groups, met children's needs by performing works of charity and using their child welfare institutions to convey their communities' support as well as legitimate their own authority. Feminists aided this project by advocating legislation to augment maternal authority over children and provide working women with a fair wage.

The imposing child welfare institutions found in the capital cities of most provinces as well as in the national capital validated women's status within their communities. Their orphanages enabled the women to perform charitable acts and assured immigrant and religious collectivities that future immigrants could avail themselves of these services. The philanthropists' legitimacy as well as their hopes to continue providing services turned out to be wishful thinking, because their primary clients after the Second World War were migrants from the interior provinces, and the national government modernized social policies by creating a welfare state. The cyclical nature of child welfare and its ever-changing constituency meant that community-based child welfare programs only lasted as long as the specific target population existed. In contrast a national welfare system offered more flexibility, and perhaps a longer life, but it gave women more limited voices as professionals rather than philanthropists. Furthermore, the Peronist solution to child assistance, based upon increasing the salary of heads of households and forcing men to acknowledge their economic responsibilities to the family, further diminished female authority, and not all family and child welfare problems could be solved in this way.

National social policies toward children in Argentina initially built upon existing community infrastructures through the politics of subsidies. From 1900 to 1930 congressional subsidies for existing institutions outside the control of the Society of Beneficence facilitated the public commitment to child welfare at a modest cost, along with the creation of national bureaucracies (which ultimately were underfunded) to deal with juvenile delinquents. The definitive shift from reliance almost completely on municipal and private subsidized philanthropies to a more centralized welfare state took place during the world depression and the Concordancia era from 1930 to 1943.

The shift began with a motherist approach—the creation of mothers' pensions, the reexamination of the need for adoption, the promotion of child welfare congresses, the cessation of the detention of minors in prisons, and the authorization of construction of new national reformatories for female minors. Feminists supported this legislation. These strategies acknowledged the focus of philanthropic work, and yet they potentially endangered the subsidies that child welfare organizations depended upon, Still, this threat did not deter philanthropists from petitioning for even more subsidies.

By the 1930s, efforts by distinct political groups, along with their combined debates regarding child welfare, inflamed the passions of Argentine legislators. Pork barrel legislation doled out more subsidies to private entities and created a maternalist support network, but spent little on that bureaucracy. Years of discussion, legislation, and minimal funding ended in the 1940s and served as a catalyst in the creation of the Peronist family and welfare state in the 1950s, just as the move of women from the house to street protests fomented support for female suffrage.

In the meantime, Argentine feminists fought for the rights of biological mothers to have greater legal power over their children. From the feminist-socialist perspective, poor women and children became the responsibility of the national government. At the same time, women demanded equal access to education (something only realized in the 1940s). Suffrage was also demanded, but when it was won in 1947 it was only to have the Peronists claim the vote as their victory, and it identified women workers and Eva Perón as the recipients of Peronist largesse. The role of feminist Peronists, their contributions to the suffrage campaign, and their transformation of feminist rhetoric became hidden under layers of Peronist mythology that reified Eva Perón.

The more state-driven welfare bureaucracy based upon notions of rights

never completely replaced the earlier welfare state based upon philanthropic views of need. This proved especially true for women, who were still
regarded primarily as housewives and mothers even while they entered the
university faculties in droves. The Peronist welfare state, utilizing adoption
as a key child welfare tactic, further attempted to reduce the costs of this
aspect of the welfare state. Child-focused social policies indicate that a
welfare state did develop, but until 1955 subsidized philanthropy continued
—whether from damas or from Eva Perón. This welfare state became increasingly directed by men, not women, especially after the death of Eva
Perón.

Was Argentina unique? Most likely it was not. This study provides clear
evidence that welfare states evolved all over the world and modernized
aspects of philanthropy. Equally important, the welfare histories of other
non-European countries should not be based upon an ideal system that
rarely served all needs even in large and well-industrialized societies. Instead it should rest upon the evaluation of social policies and their implementation not only by male-controlled governmental agencies but also
by private groups, just like those that functioned in the United States
and Europe. Such analysis must include the role that both philanthropic
and feminist women played in the formation of the welfare state in local
and national areas, and it must acknowledge the value of performative
philanthropy.

What did the new welfare state mean for Argentines? Rhetorically, in the
new Peronist family the welfare state did not imply massive payments to
dysfunctional parents or children with problems. Instead, it offered a series of options. For the first time parents had the possibility of staying
together or filing for divorce. Fathers protected and supported their children whether biological or adoptive, and children honored not only their
own parents but also the paternal and maternal figures of Juan and Eva
Perón. The Catholic Church, canon law, philanthropic organizations other
than the Eva Perón Foundation, demands by feminists, and concerns about
child inheritance were denied as forces that previously necessitated child
welfare. Last names became available to all, husbands treated their wives
more civilly, complete divorce finally became available, and street children
simply did not exist in the new Argentina.

During the early years of Peronism, the Peronists claimed that efforts to
improve working-class life, along with the creation of all kinds of pension
plans and welfare schemes and the replacement of philanthropic charity by
Eva Perón's version of social justice, augured the simultaneous maturation

of the welfare state and the end of class-based poverty and economic distress in Argentina. This so-called new Peronist world lumped together the poor and the working class, and all solutions stemmed not only from improving the lot of male workers but also by their increasing ability to cope with family problems. Women gained rights through suffrage and equal access to higher education in return for their subordination to the government, at the same time that they received more or less similar pay for the same work as done by men.

From the Peronist perspective (which was uncomfortably similar to the views of their enemies—the communists), improved economic conditions for workers, as well as a better understanding of family dynamics, guaranteed ideal conditions for the new Argentine family. The Peronist propaganda film *Fin de semana* [The Weekend] exemplified the rosy dream world of the Peronist future. Like the family-based television shows of the 1950s and 1960s in the United States such as "Ozzie and Harriet" and "Father Knows Best," in the Peronist ideal world all families owned a car and lived in clean and well-decorated homes (in the Argentine case, an apartment). Inhabiting this universe were conflict-free families, headed by a benevolent father with a mother who stayed at home and offspring who dutifully attended school. Class differences no longer divided Argentines, and children of different ethnicities and religions became fast friends.[1]

This movie's optimism, of course, ignored the real tensions caused by family reform, the legal and social repercussions of adoption and divorce, and state treatment of poor and abandoned children. It also underestimated the impact of changes in gendered philanthropy, family relations, economic conditions, and welfare that affected not only Argentina but also the rest of the world. And it presumed that these changes could not be reversed even though their implementation depended upon a steadily expanding national budget for child welfare, regardless of costs and inflation, as well as the masculinization of the welfare state.

Opponents to Peronism viewed its social politics as the destruction of traditional values. Enrique Medina's *Las tumbas* [The Tombs], a novel about juvenile delinquency published in 1972 and banned in Argentina during the military dictatorship, summed up the social destruction wrought by Peronism. Indeed the novel appeared to be an indictment of the Peronist social system. *The Tombs* depicts a male child wrenched from his mother without explanation and sent to a reform school. The title refers to the dormitories where both hardened criminals and children without a history of dysfunctional behavior are all thrown together, and there the young boy at the center of the novel [no girls inhabited the tombs] discovers violence and sodomitic sexual attacks. Medina's critique of taking children out of biological families and maternal authority and into state reformatories could have been written any time after the 1919 Agote law, and it had little to do with the specifics of Peronist reforms. In fact it displayed the same tropes regarding the sexuality of juvenile delinquents that had characterized the understanding by the Argentines of age-related class differences.

Perhaps Medina correctly believed that not much had changed for boys sent into state reformatories. Perón's promises and rhetoric, accompanied by the highly publicized pro-child activities performed by Eva Perón, led to heightened expectations that ignored the financial difficulties of providing massive state investments in children. The institutional changes in orphanages and reform schools, as well as efforts to modernize juvenile delinquency theories, changed little. Youngsters no longer suffered the ignominy of identification tags and they all received last names, but the cruelty of fickle prospective adoptive families along with the psychological costs of institutional living, in an atmosphere that continued to expect the patriarchal and submissive child values of the past, led to unrealistic expectations for both prospective parents and young people.[2]

Medina also chose to ignore the true changes in Argentine society from the 1940s onward—shifts that could be seen in other contemporary Western societies in the throes of urbanization and globalization. Demographic and occupational changes during the Perón years in Argentina noted by Susana Bianchi resulted from a combination of the impact of the world depression, patterns of decreased fertility among the increasingly native-born population, and the greater visibility of women on the streets and in paid employment.[3] The changes meant that women would no longer serve as unpaid representatives of their ethnic or religious groups, and the traditional methods of dealing with children could not be re-created. The same situation occurred in the United States and in European countries where nongovernmental organizations replaced philanthropy within their own countries and as part of foreign philanthropy in foreign aid.

Bianchi has argued that, according to the Catholic Church in Argentina, the family was already in a state of crisis in the 1940s. The church, concerned about the increased involvement of the state in family matters particularly related to children, echoed sentiments that also predated Peronism. Thus while Bianchi noted that the family was a significant element in the Argentine conflict between church and state, she limited her discussion to family values, the importance of young boys to the church, and the fears of destabilizing the family through new laws that enabled illegitimate and adopted children to inherit. Therefore she did not consider that the church had to be equally concerned with women's new roles, because without the volunteer services of philanthropic women many of the church-linked child welfare programs could not continue as before.

The impact of the Perón years on state childhood policies spread far beyond what Bianchi imagined, but not necessarily due to Perón. Rafael Gagliano has argued that Argentine adolescents in the 1940s, mainly second- and third-generation Argentines, became freed from the traditional immigrant expectations that emphasized obedience and patriarchy. Now children followed their own dreams. More boys went to school and had hopes for careers. Girls also attended school in greater numbers, although they were still advised by teachers that their future rested in hearth, home, and reproduction. This had little to do with Peronism. Yet women joined the professional labor force thanks to expanded and free enrollment in public universities—a fact that genuinely was a consequence of Perón's political politics as well as demands by feminists. In this way Perón's rhetoric about social justice had particularly liberating meanings for the young—meanings that by the 1960s were linked to revolution and governmental confrontation rather than charity.

While it is important to see how changes in Argentina during the Peronist era have been viewed as exceptional, we also need to examine these changes from international and contemporary perspectives, as well as from the viewpoint of historic social policies in Argentina. In fact, similar societal changes emancipated the children of the 1960s from parental and governmental authority all over the world. What happened in Argentina thus could not be attributed solely to Perón's social policies but rather to demography and an increased focus on postwar youth and on women.[4]

For children who had traditionally experienced discrimination due to inheritance laws and the traditional categories of illegitimacy, Peronism provided a new path. In this case change truly did relate specifically to governmental policies. Nevertheless, Juan Perón approached child welfare from female perspectives supporting child adoption that had long been articulated by the Society of Beneficence. Members of his own party opposed Perón's views, due to their desire to assert masculine privilege in adoption.

Nevertheless, Perón's personal beliefs did not dictate the formation of the Argentine welfare state. Isabella Cosse's work on Peronist laws eliminating stigmatic legal categories for children in the 1940s has pointed out that Peronism did not begin with a fixed ideology to restructure the family and that Perón was not the only Peronist advocating change. Just as adoption laws came as a response to an earthquake, Cosse argued that other laws that affected child welfare and women's rights regarding illegitimate children and property formed part of a male Peronist program proposed late in Perón's first presidency. Even the Second Five-Year Plan only included limited family reforms. She attributes the continued push to consider this legislation as partly an effort to separate Peronism from the Catholic Church and partly the consequence of the divergent views held by Peronist legislators, particularly former members of the Laborista Party, members of the political opposition, and Perón himself.[5] In this scenario, Perón appears much less powerful as an authoritarian leader bent upon imposing his will on Argentines. Instead he became an arbiter among distinct and powerful political interests that emerged from below as well as from above.

Nevertheless, the Peronist men ultimately proved far more successful in creating child welfare than did the wife of the president. Unlike the Society of Beneficence damas whom she hated, Eva Perón never controlled the elite institutions she often critiqued, nor did her own institutions survive the overthrow of her husband in 1955. Instead, they all became folded into a masculine-defined welfare state that has persisted regardless of political ideology. Furthermore, during the 1950s it was the workers rather than the elite who commonly funded her projects with "voluntary" contributions. Eva utilized the rhetoric of class conflict, but she offered few direct appropriations from the rich to provide social justice for the poor. Instead the working class "voluntarily contributed" to the Eva Perón Foundation. From these perspectives, the story of child welfare and the rise of the welfare state becomes far more complex and cannot be based on specific campaigns, but rather must be judged as a whole. The rise of the welfare state and its relationship to women and child welfare also need to be folded into political history as an important issue for members of all parties.[6]

The role of female philanthropists and feminists in the development of child welfare policies in Argentina offers a view of continuity from the late nineteenth century to the mid-twentieth that rarely appears in the general political histories of Argentina. Feminism thus had a continuous impact during these years. The founding of the feminist movement coincided with the expansion of female education championed by the Partido Autonomista Nacional, and the subsequent creation of new political parties after 1890 meant that feminists found male champions among members of the Socialist and Radical Parties. Furthermore, both political parties had women's branches long before female suffrage was promulgated during the Perón years. Their commitment to female equality and women's greater legal rights within the family became apparent in the many proposals to reform the civil code as well as in adoption debates that permitted women as well as men to adopt children. Equal control over children, however, as well as divorce eluded feminists until after the conclusion of the Dirty War (1976–1983). Then new laws finally granted shared custody of children to both the father and the mother, and complete divorce also became law.

This study suggests that the welfare state may, in fact, be one component of a constant effort to maintain sets of social policies, and that the exclusion of women as policymakers can be perilous to its success. To this day, women activists have continued to focus on child and family rights, although now the leaders come from the poor sectors rather than those of the rich. Have these poorer women fared as well as their middle-class predecessors?

In recent years many professional women have involved themselves in supporting social movements founded by poor women—including soup kitchens, the acquisition of neighborhood health clinics, and land seizures. Perhaps the modern incarnation of female philanthropy is the Federación Argentina de Apoyo Familiar [Argentine Federation for Family Aid]. Based upon the earlier Casas de Niño, the program developed when a middle-class woman began to organize a variety of programs for children of working-class families as well as for those living on the streets. According to the group's Web site, the founder, Ana Mon, "a lawyer and a middle-class mother of five boys," went shopping one day and found a waif looking for food in a garbage can. In July 1985 she opened the first Casa del Niño Esperanza [The Hope Children's House] in La Plata, the capital of the province of Buenos Aires. Eventually forty additional facilities were opened, and the group has expanded to other Latin American countries.

In 1994 the Federación Argentina de Apoyo Familiar operated 101 centers of different types to assist a total of 3,048 children nationally. By 2001 this organization had reached 10,000 children, mostly in Argentina. This is but one of the many woman-controlled NGOs that have taken up the job formerly defined as either a national or a collective responsibility. Yet, at the same time, the number of children under government surveillance also grows, sometimes with pernicious consequences.[7]

Another, better-known example of recent efforts by women to defend children is the Mothers of the Plaza de Mayo. Originally organized in the 1970s to demand government information about disappeared children, over time it has transformed into a human-rights focused university. Once again, institutional building by women of a cross-class alliance has led to both visibility and public authority. Through them, the legacy of the early female philanthropists and feminists continues in the twenty-first century, and child welfare issues continue to appear at the forefront of Argentine politics.

Even more recently, poor female picketers [*piqueteras*] have led demonstrations in which the piqueteras cut off highway access to protest the lack of jobs and poverty. Further, some have argued that if Evita had lived, she would be a piquetera. Yet the performances of power by Evita and by piqueteras are quite different; Evita used class solidarity to build new institutional facilities, while the piqueteras use class solidarity to confront not only the nation but all who enter and leave their province or city, and this act has often led to anger. In this case class leadership has not led to the same alliances, but the piquetera phenomenon points once again to women's resilience and efforts in political organizing to achieve social policies.

Thus the history of female philanthropy and feminism offers broad contours to both unite and nuance distinct periods of modern Argentine political history. And without the sense of female community and authority they have embodied, government efforts to maintain social welfare and child rights are imperiled.

Notes

Introduction

1. Parts of this introduction have appeared previously in Donna J. Guy, "Feminists, Philanthropists, the Rise of the Welfare State and Child Welfare Policies," *Brújula* 4.1 (2006): 45–60. The bibliography on this subject is extensive, so I will only mention a few works here: Rachel Fuchs, *Abandoned Children: Foundlings and Child Welfare in Nineteenth-Century France* (Albany: State University of New York Press, 1984); Gisela Bock and Pat Thane, eds., *Maternity and Gender Policies: Women and the Rise of the European Welfare States, 1880s–1950s* (London: Routledge, 1991); Valerie Fildes, Lara Marks, and Hilary Marland, eds., *Women and Children First: International Maternal and Infant Welfare, 1870–1945* (London: Routledge, 1992); Robert G. Moeller, *Protecting Motherhood: Women and the Family in the Politics of Postwar West Germany* (Berkeley: University of California Press, 1993); Seth Koven and Sonya Michel, eds., *Mothers of a New World: Maternalist Politics and the Origins of Welfare States* (New York: Routledge, 1993); Linda Gordon, *Pitied but Not Entitled: Single Mothers and History of Welfare, 1890–1935* (New York: Free Press, 1994); Diane Sainsbury, *Gender, Equality, and Welfare States* (London: Cambridge University Press, 1996); Sylvia Schaefer, *Children in Moral Danger and the Problem of Government in Third Republic France* (Princeton, N.J.: Princeton University Press, 1997); Joanne L. Goodwin, *Gender and the Politics of Welfare Reform: Mothers' Pensions in Chicago, 1911–1929* (Chicago: University of Chicago Press, 1997); Young-Sun Hong, *Welfare, Modernity, and the Weimar State, 1919–1933* (Princeton, N.J.: Princeton University Press, 1998); Sonya Michel, *Children's Interests/Mothers' Rights: The Shaping of America's Child Care Policy* (New Haven, Conn.: Yale University Press, 1999); Lynne Haney, *Inventing the Needy: Gender and the Politics of Welfare in Hungary* (Berkeley: University of California Press, 2002); Mine Ener, *Managing Egypt's Poor and the Politics of Benevolence, 1800–1952* (Princeton, N.J.: Princeton University Press, 2003); Michael Bonner, Mine Ener, and Amy Singer Bonner, eds., *Poverty and Charity in Middle Eastern Contexts* (Albany: State University of New York Press, 2003); Ann

Taylor Allen, *Feminism and Motherhood in Western Europe, 1890–1970: The Maternal Dilemma* (New York: Palgrave, 1995); Sherri Broder, *Tramps, Unfit Mothers, and Neglected Children: Negotiating the Family in Late Nineteenth-Century Philadelphia* (Philadelphia: University of Pennsylvania Press); Steven King, *Women, Welfare and Local Politics, 1880–1920: 'We Might be Trusted'* (Brighton, U.K.: University of Sussex Academic Press, 2006); Magda Fahrni, *Montreal Families and Postwar Reconstruction* (Toronto: University of Toronto Press, 2004); and Judith Fingard and Jane Guildford, eds. *Mothers of the Municipality: Women, Work, and Social Policy in Post-1945 Halifax* (Toronto: University of Toronto Press, 2005).

2. Michel, *Children's Interests/Mothers' Rights*, 43–44.

3. See also Linda Gordon, *The Great Arizona Abduction* (Cambridge, Mass.: Harvard University Press, 1999); Maureen Fitzgerald, *Habits of Compassion: Irish Catholic Nuns and the Origins of New York's Welfare System, 1830–1920* (Urbana: University of Illinois Press, 2006); Bernadette McCauley, *Who Shall Take Care of Our Sick? Roman Catholic Sisters and the Development of Catholic Hospitals in New York City* (Baltimore: Johns Hopkins University Press, 2005). For the Latin American colonial context, see Bianca Premo, *Children of the Father King: Youth, Authority, and Legal Minority in Colonial Lima* (Chapel Hill: University of North Carolina Press, 2005); María Ines Passanante, *Pobreza y acción social en la historia argentina* (Buenos Aires: Editorial Hvmanitas, 1987); "International Feminism," special issue of *Gender and History* 10.3 (fall 1998); Angela de Castro Gomes et al., *Estado, corporativismo y acción social . . . en Brasil, Argentina y Uruguay* (Buenos Aires: Fundación Simón Rodríguez, 1992); Héctor Recalde, *Beneficencia, asistencialismo estatal y previsión social*, 2 vols. (Buenos Aires: Centro Editor de América Latina, 1991); Néstor Feroli, *La Fundación Eva Perón*, 2 vols. (Buenos Aires: Centro Editor de América Latina, 1990); Mariano Plotkin, *Mañana es San Perón* (Buenos Aires: Ariel Historia Argentina, 1993); Marifran Carlson, *¡Feminismo! The Women's Movement in Argentina from Its Beginnings to Eva Perón* (Chicago: Academy Chicago Publishers, 1988); Asunción Lavrin, *Women, Feminism, and Social Change in Argentina, Chile, and Uruguay, 1890–1940* (Lincoln: University of Nebraska Press, 1995); Karen Mead, "Beneficent Maternalism: Argentine Motherhood in Comparative Perspective, 1880–1920," *Journal of Women's History* 12.3 (2000): 120–45; Donna J. Guy, *White Slavery and Mothers Alive and Dead: The Troubled Meeting of Sex, Gender, Public Health, and Progress in Latin America* (Lincoln: University of Nebraska Press, 2000); "Rise of the Welfare State in Latin America," special issue of the *Americas* (July 2001); Tobias Hecht, ed., *Minor Omissions: Children in Latin American History and Society* (Madison: University of Wisconsin Press, 2002); Donna J. Guy, "Women's Organizations and Jewish Orphanages in Buenos Aires, 1918–1955," *Jewish History* 18.1 (2004): 75–93; Karina Inés Ramacciotti and Adriana María Valobra, eds., *Generando el peronismo: Estudios de cultura, política y género (1946–1955)* (Buenos Aires: Editorial Proyecto, 2003),

21–64; and Isabella Cosse, *Estigmas de nacimiento: Peronismo y orden familiar 1946–1955* (Buenos Aires: Fondo de Cultura Económica, 2006). Christine Ehrick, in *The Shield of the Weak: Feminism and the State in Uruguay, 1903–1933* (Albuquerque: University of New Mexico Press, 2005), offers a picture of feminists, both progressive and conservative, who had a more passive role in the formation of welfare state policies than what I found to be the case in Argentina.

4. Young-Sun Hong, *Welfare, Modernity, and the Weimar State, 1919–1933* (Princeton, N.J.: Princeton University Press, 1998), 19.

5. Ibid., 5.

6. Haney, *Inventing the Needy*, 63.

7. Fitzgerald, *Habits of Compassion*.

8. Theda Skocpol, *Protecting Soldiers and Mothers: The Political Origins of Social Policy in the United States* (Cambridge, Mass.: Harvard University Press, 1992). Critiques have been offered by Paula Baker in her review in *American Historical Review* 98.2 (April, 1998): 458–60; by Ann Firor Scott in "Discovering Women," *Contemporary Sociology* 22.6 (1993): 777–79; and by Walter Korpi in "American Exceptionalism in Social Policy Development," *Contemporary Sociology*, 779–81. Other reviews include Nancy Folbre, "Protecting Soldiers and Mothers: The Political Origins of Social Policy in the United States," *Theory and Society* 24.6 (1995): 869–74; and Christopher Howard, "The American Welfare State or States," *Political Research Quarterly* 52.2 (1999): 421–22.

9. Lisa DiCaprio, *The Origins of the Welfare State: Women, Work, and the French Revolution* (Urbana: University of Illinois Press, 2007).

10. Carmelo Mesa Lago, *Social Security in Latin America: Pressure Groups, Stratification, and Inequality* (Pittsburgh: Pittsburgh University Press, 1978); Guillermo V. Alonso, *Política y seguridad social en la Argentina de los '90* (Buenos Aires: FLACSO, Miño y Dávila Editores, 2000).

11. José Luis Moreno, ed., *La política social antes de la política social (Caridad, beneficencia y política social en Buenos Aires, siglos xvii a xx)* (Buenos Aires: Trama Editorial / Promoteo Libros, 2000.)

12. The historiographical debate can be found in the essay by Karina Inés Ramacciotti and Adriana María Valobra, "Relaciones de género en la campaña sanitaria de la Secretaría de Salud Pública de la Argentina (1946–1949)" in their *Generando el peronismo*, 21–64.

13. Daniel M. Giménez, *Gender, Pensions, and Social Citizenship in Latin America* (Santiago: United Nations/ECLAC, 2005), 21.

1. Female Philanthropy and Feminism

1. Lavrin, *Women, Feminism, and Social Change in Argentina, Chile and Uruguay*, 201–5.

2. John Boswell's *The Kindness of Strangers: The Abandonment of Children in West-*

ern Europe from Late Antiquity to the Renaissance (New York: Pantheon Books, 1988) provides the classic history of this European practice.

3. José Arias, *Derecho de familia*, 2nd ed. (Buenos Aires: Editorial Kraft, 1952), 360.

4. Donna J. Guy, "Niños abandonados en Buenos Aires (1880–1914) y el desarrollo del concepto de la madre," in *Mujeres y cultura en la Argentina del siglo XIX*, ed. Lea Fletcher (Buenos Aires: Feminaria Editora, 1994), 219.

5. Archivo Consejo Nacional de Niñez, Adolescencia y Familia [hereafter referred to as ACNNAF], Expediente No. 14.122, Request made to Da. Magdalena de Harilaos, July 15, 1925. All names have been changed and placed in quotes to comply with the regulations of the ACNNAF.

6. Argentine Republic, *Código Civil de la República Argentina* (Buenos Aires: Pablo E. Coni, 1874), Art. 398, 64–65 (my emphasis).

7. Ibid., Artículos 491–494, 76.

8. Moreno, *La política social antes de la política social*, 6.

9. Argentine Republic, Congreso Nacional, Cámara de Diputados [hereafter referred to as Diputados], *Diario de sesiones*, 1910, Vol. 1, August 8, 1910, 909–10.

10. Eduardo J. Bullrich, *Asistencia social de menores* (Buenos Aires: Jesús Méndez, 1919), 399–407.

11. *La Prensa*, August 10, 1910, 12.

12. Fondo Ministerio de Justicia e Instrucción Pública [hereafter referred to as MJIP], *Memoria*, 1920, 68, J. S. Salinas to Agente Fiscal Jorge M. Coll, and *Memoria*, 1924, T. 1, 190, "Anexos a la Memoria, Departamento de Justicia, Informe de la Comisión Honoraria de Superintendencia de Marcos Paz, Instituto Tutelar de Menores, y Patronato de Menores."

13. Letter of the President to the Chamber of Deputies, Diputados, *Diario de sesiones*, 1919, Vol. 5, January 20, 1919, 214.

14. Diputados, *Diario de sesiones*, 1919, Vol. 2, 708–9.

15. Diputados, *Diario de sesiones*, 1918, T. 1, June 3, 1918, 262; *Diario de sesiones*, 1919, Vol. 5, January 20, 1919, 214.

16. Law no. 10.903, Diputados, *Diario de sesiones*, 1919, Vol. 7, 965–66.

17. Instructions of Ernesto Nelson to delegates, Cámara de Apelaciones en lo Criminal y Correccional de la Capital, *Los tribunales de menores en la República Argentina: Su organización en la Capital Federal por la Cámara de Apelaciones en lo Criminal y Correccional, de acuerdo con la ley No. 10.903 de Patronato de Menores* (Buenos Aires: L. J. Rossi y Cía., 1922), 102.

18. Ibid., 210.

19. Inter-American Commission of Women, "Report of the Inter-American Commission of Women to the Eight International Conference of American States on the Political and Civil Rights of Women, Lima, December 1938," U.S. Library of Congress, mimeograph, 98–99.

20. Archivo General de la Nación [hereafter referred to as AGN], División Poder Judicial, Tribunales Civiles, Letra S, Legajo 16135, 1886.

21. AGN, Tribunales Civil y Comercial, Departamento Judicial, La Plata, Año 1921–22, Legajo 31, fojas 5–7.

22. Note that here and elsewhere in text, names given in quotation marks are pseudonyms.

23. Archivo General de la Provincia de Tucumán [hereafter referred to as AGT], Sección Judicial, Juzgado en lo Civil, R. vs. R., Caja 2000, Expediente 10, 1938.

24. AGN, División Poder Judicial, Tribunales Civiles, Letra G, 1897, Legajo 31, Gontran, Doña Blanca, solicitando la entrega de su hija Julia Artemisa, fojas 12–13, quotation on foja 13.

25. Ibid., 34.

26. AGN, División Poder Judicial, Tribunales Civiles, Letra S, Legajo 16.33, Suffern de Smith, D. Margarita solicitando patria potestad, August 1886–March 27, 1888.

27. Archivo Histórico de La Pampa, Fondo Justicia, Juzgado Letrado Jaramillo, Legajo 243, Freire Casilda de Basilio, reclama ropas y una hijita de 1 año.

28. Julio J. López del Carril, *Patria Potestad, tutela y curatela* (Buenos Aires, Ediciones Depalma, 1993), 8–9.

29. See Alfredo L. Palacios, *El dolor argentino: Plan sanitario y educativo de protección a los niños* (Buenos Aires: Editorial Claridad, 1938); and Alfredo L. Palacios, *La defensa del valor humano: Legislación social argentina* (Buenos Aires: Editorial Claridad, 1939).

30. This documentary can be found in the film collection of the AGN.

31. ACNNAF, Legajo 44.085. The reason he left so soon was that his behavior led to his dismissal from the orphanage.

32. ACNNAF, Legajo 46.978. According to a social worker, the young girl seemed to be very happy by her mother's side.

33. ACNNAF, Legajo 51.870.

34. ACNNAF, Legajo 5.879.

35. AGN, Sociedad de Beneficencia, *Libro de Actas No. 17*, Acta, September 16, 1912, fojas 204–205.

36. The Chicago juvenile court system was specifically mentioned in many writings of Argentine child rights' legal specialists.

37. Benjamín Dupont, *Patronato y asistencia de la infancia: Consideraciones sobre la necesidad imprescindible de una ley de protección á la primera infancia y estudio sociológico sobre la necesidad de reformatorios para los niños moral y materialmente abandonados* (Buenos Aires: Tipo-Lito del Sport, de E. Sarniguet y Cía., 1894), 10.

38. MJIP, *Memoria*, 1932, "Establecimientos Penales de la Capital Federal y Territorios Nacionales," 1, 384.

39. "Patronato de Menores," *Boletín del Museo Social Argentino* 10.3 (August 10, 1921): 38–40. Judge Oribe penned the article.

40. The Marcos Paz facility was later renamed after Ricardo Gutiérrez.

41. *Infancia y Juventud* 2 (1937): 7.

42. MJIP, *Memoria*, 1924, 181, Anexos a la Memoria, Departamento de Justicia; Patronato de Menores, *Memoria de la Comisión Honoraria de Superintendencia de la Colonia Hogar Ricardo Gutiérrez, Instituto Tutelar de menores y Patronato de la Infancia* (Buenos Aires, 1925), 22–23.

43. Patronato de Menores, *Memoria*, 1925, 40–42.

44. Argentine Republic, Congreso Nacional, Senado, *Diario de sesiones*, 1921, Law 11.179, Títle V, Articles 37–39, 829–830; Argentine Republic, Ministry of Justice and Public Instruction, *The Prevention of Juvenile Delinquency in the Field of Legislation and Social Work in Argentina: A Survey Ordered by Dr. Antonio Sagarna, Secretary of Justice and Public Instruction on the Occasion of the First International Child's Congress at Geneva, August 24–28, 1925* (Buenos Aires: Cía. General de Fósforos, 1925), 4.

45. Juana María Begino, "El Congreso Nacional del Niño; La Liga para los derechos de la mujer y del niño y sus trabajos," *Cara y Caretas*, Nov. 16, 1912.

46. "Congreso Americano del Niño," *La Vanguardia*, July 14, 1916, 1.

47. For specifics on these meetings, see articles on Pan American feminism in Guy, *White Slavery and Mothers Alive and Dead*.

2. Benevolence and Female Volunteerism

1. Dinisio Petriella, *Los italianos en la historia del progreso argentino* (Buenos Aires: Asociación Dante Alighieri, 1985), 22.

2. James R. Scobie, *Buenos Aires: Plaza to Suburb, 1870–1910* (New York: Oxford University Press, 1974).

3. Buenos Aires Municipality, *Patronato y asistencia de la infancia en la capital de la república: Trabajos de la comisión especial* (Buenos Aires: El Censor, 1892), 7.

4. Alejandro Bunge, *Una nueva Argentina* (Buenos Aires: Hyspamérica, 1940), 174.

5. Emilio R. Coni, "Causas de la morbilidad y mortalidad infantiles," in Buenos Aires Municipality, *Patronato y asistencia de la infancia*, 105–6.

6. Fuchs, *Abandoned Children;* David Ransel, *Mothers of Misery: Child Abandonment in Russia* (Princeton, N.J.: Princeton University Press, 1988); and David I. Kertzer, "Gender Ideology and Infant Abandonment in Nineteenth-Century Italy," *Journal of Interdisciplinary History* 22.1 (1991): 1–25. See also Ann Twinam, *Public Lives, Private Secrets: Gender, Honor, Sexuality, and Illegitimacy in Colonial Latin America* (Stanford, Calif.: Stanford University Press, 1999).

7. Kristin Ruggiero, "Honor, Maternity, and the Disciplining of Women: Infanticide in Late Nineteenth-Century Buenos Aires," *Hispanic American Historical Review* 72.3 (1992): 353–73; Kristin Ruggiero, "Not Guilty: Abortion and Infanticide in Nineteenth-Century Argentina," in *Reconstructing Criminality in Latin America*, ed. Carlos A. Aguirre and Robert Buffington (Wilmington,

Del.: Scholarly Resources, 2000), 149–66; and María Celia Bravo and Vanesa Teitelbaum, "Entrega de niños, infanticidios y la construcción de una imagen de la maternidad en Tucumán (segunda mitad del siglo xix)," in *Temas de mujeres: Perspectivas de género* (Tucumán: Universidad Nacional de Tucumán, 1998), 81–96.

8. Angel Giménez, *El torno libre* (Buenos Aires: Juan H. Kidd, Cía., 1922), 8–9.

9. Enrique Bordot, *Un dispensario de lactantes de 1910 a 1921: Estadística y consideraciones sobre mortalidad infantil* (Buenos Aires: Las Ciencias, 1922), 13.

10. Buenos Aires Municipality, *Patronato y asistencia de la infancia*, 6–12; Buenos Aires Municipality, *Censo general de la población, edificación, comercio e industrias de la ciudad de Buenos Aires*, 3 vols., ed. Alberto B. Martínez (Buenos Aires: Cía. Sudamericana de Billetes de Banco, 1910), 2: 64.

11. María Rosa Lezica Alvear de Pirovano, "Profilaxis del abandono en la primera infancia," in *Patronato de la Infancia, Segunda Conferencia Nacional de la Infancia abandonada y delincuente* (Buenos Aires: Peuser, 1944), 371–72; and Adolfo S. Cianchetta Sivori, Antonio S. Cardillo, and Francisco Fernandez Rozas, "El abandono de la primera infancia en la República Argentina a través de la acción médico-social de la Casa Cuna," *Archivos de Salud Pública* 5.3 (March 1949): 308–10.

12. ACNNAF, Legajo 8.374, 1883; AGN, Tribunales Civil y Comercial, Departamento Judicial, La Plata, 1889–90, Legajo 20, La Plata, October 23, 1890, foja 1.

13. AGN, Defensoría de Menores, February 13, 1909, Legajo 182, foja 189.

14. AGN, Tribunales Civiles, T. 16.928, 1883, Letra T, Doña Bartola Tabares vs. Manuela Nadal.

15. ACNNAF, Legajo 50.225. Note that pseudonyms hereafter are enclosed in quotation marks.

16. ACNNAF, Legajo 48.668.

17. ACNNAF, Legajo 13.968, 3 September 1903; Legajo 8.519, 1912; Legajo 48.770.

18. MJIP, *Memoria*, 1898, Report of the Defender of Minors of the Southern District, 116.

19. AGN, Sociedad de Beneficencia, Casa de Huérfanas, Legajo 161, foja 138. Letter of Juan Osuna to Sociedad de Beneficencia, December 18, 1889. This one letter is typical of a series of letters encountered in the archives of the Sociedad de Beneficencia regarding the inability of relatives and legal guardians to support children.

20. AGN, Sociedad de Beneficencia, Casa de Huérfanas, Legajo 162, foja 72, Letter of Sara M. de Venn to the president of the Sociedad de Beneficencia, December 24, 1903.

21. Ricardo González Leandri, *Curar, persuadir, gobernar: La construcción histórica de la profesión médica en Buenos Aires, 1852–1886* (Madrid: Consejo Superior de Investigaciones Científicas, 1999).

22. José Penna and Horacio Madero, *La administración sanitaria y Asistencia Púb-*

lica de la ciudad de Buenos Aires, 2 vols. (Buenos Aires: Guillermo Kraft, 1910);
Ernest Crider, "Modernization and Human Welfare: The Asistencia Pública
and Buenos Aires, 1883–1910," Ph.D. diss., Ohio State University, 1976.

23. Decreto de la Intendencia Municipal, December 1890, in Buenos Aires Municipality, *Patronato y asistencia de la infancia,* xv-xvi.

24. Archivo Patronato de la Infancia, *Libro de Actas,* Acta, June 7, 1892; Acta,
March 10, 1893. Manuel Aguirre generously offered to pay for fifteeen beds;
Acta 25, April 1893. The discussion of congressional proposals can be found in
Acta, September 21, 1892, and June 6, 1894. The 1894 statutes are in Patronato
de la Infancia, *Protección á la infancia: Antecedentes para el estudio de una ley
reunidos por los doctores Faustino Jorge y Alberto Mayer Arana Vicepresidente 10 y
secretario del Patronato de la Infancia* (Buenos Aires: Imprenta Coni Hermanos,
1908).

25. Proyecto de reglamento, Archivo Patronato de la Infancia, *Libro de Actas,*
tomo 11, March 2, 1921, fojas 231–34. I would like to thank Dra. Noemí Girbal
de Blacha for this reference.

26. AGN, Sociedad de Beneficencia, Expediente 8523/1 "Sociedad de Beneficencia
de la Capital: Reseña sobre su organización y su obra 1823–1942," n.p., n.d.

27. "El Instituto de Maternidad de la Sociedad de Beneficencia," *Boletín del Museo
Social Argentina* 17.82 (April 1929): 168–71; and Alberto Peralta Ramos, "Concepto y organización del Instituto de Maternidad de la Sociedad de Beneficencia de Buenos Aires," in *Primer Congreso Médico, Hispano-Lusitano-Americano,
Sevilla Octubre de 1924* (Buenos Aires: El Policlínico, 1924), 9.

28. The correspondence regarding the June 18, 1891, resignation of the Sociedad
de Beneficencia from the Casa de Expósitos has been transcribed in Sociedad
de Beneficencia, *Origen y desenvolvimiento de la Sociedad de Beneficencia de la
Capital, 1823–1912* (Buenos Aires: Tipografía M. Rodríguez Giles, 1919), 280–
83. The correspondence from Wilde can be found in AGN, Casa de Expósitos,
Legajo 102, letter from Wilde to the president of the Sociedad de Beneficencia, fojas 223–29; the response from the Presidenta is at fojas 230–38. The
president noted that infant mortality in the foundling home was less than 20
percent. I would like to thank Karen Mead for facilitating some of these
documents.

29. Report of Dr. Pedro de Elizalde, Patronato de la Infancia, *Segunda Conferencia
Nacional de la Infancia abandonada y delincuente,* 1944, 368.

30. Estela Pagani and María Victoria Alcaraz, *Las nodrizas en Buenos Aires: Un
estudio histórico (1880–1940)* (Buenos Aires: Centro Editor de América Latina
14, 1988), esp. 12–19; Dr. Eugenio F. Ramírez, "Medidas para prevenir la morbilidad y mortalidad infantil: Inspección de la leche," in Buenos Aires Municipality, *Patronato y asistencia de la Infancia,* 219–24; Dr. Emilio R.Coni, *Higiene
social: Asistencia y previsión social. Buenos Aires caritativa y previsor* (Buenos
Aires: Imprenta de Emilio Spinelli, Editor, 1918), 82–96. A picture and expla-

nation of the lactarium can be found in Oscar Rodríguez, *La protección social del recien nacido: Bases para una legislación en la República Argentina* (Córdoba: Aniceto López, 1936), 153–63.

31. Alberto Meyer Arana, "La beneficencia en Buenos Aires," in Martínez, *Censo 1910*, 3: 671, 687.

32. José C. Moya, *Cousins and Strangers: Spanish Immigrants in Buenos Aires, 1850–1930* (Berkeley: University of California Press, 1998), chapter 6.

33. Passanante, *Pobreza y acción social*, 69, 72–75; Susana Belmartino, Carlos Bloch, Ana V. Persello, and Hugo Quiroga, *Las instituciones de salud en la Argentina, desarrollo y crisis* (Buenos Aires: Secretaría de Ciencia y Técnica, Area de Estudios e Investigacíon en Ciencias Sociales para la Salud, 1987), 17–22.

34. These comments are based upon the child registry of the Asilo Argentino de Huérfanos Israelitas from 1918 to 1933. The names for these children as well as for those who entered the Society of Beneficencia remain anonymous. I would like to thank Paul Armony for his willingness to lend me the photocopies of this volume.

35. Gloria Rut Lerner, "El Asilo de Huérfanas Israelitas," unpublished paper, Universidad Nacional de Luján, 23.

36. Archivo Centro de Documentación e Información sobre Judaísmo Argentino "Mark Turkow" [Archivo Turkow], *"Ezrah" Hospital Israelita* (January 1, 1914): 97–98, "La infancia abandonada: Necesidad de un asilo infantil en nuestro medio."

37. Gabriela Dalla Corte and Paola Piacenza, *A las puertas del Hogar: Madres, niños y Damas de caridad en el Hogar del Huérfano de Rosario (1870–1920)* (Rosario: Prohistoria Ediciones, 2006), 16–18.

38. Alberto Benegas Lynch (h) and Martín Krause, *En defensa de los más necesitados* (Buenos Aires: Editorial Atlántida, 1998), 72.

39. Passanante, *Pobreza y acción social*, 49.

40. Katherine A. Lynch, *Family, Class, and Ideology in Early Industrial France: Social Policy and the Working-Class Family* (Madison: University of Wisconsin Press, 1988), 46–47.

41. Karen Mead, "Gender, Welfare and the Catholic Church in Argentina: Conferencias de Señoras de San Vicente de Paul 1890–1916," *Americas* 58.1 (2001): 91–119.

42. Beatriz I. Moreyra, "La política social: Caridades, estado y sociedad civil en Córdoba (1900–1030)," paper presented at VI Jornadas de Historia de las Mujeres y I Congreso Latinoamericano de Estudios de las Mujeres y de Género, Buenos Aires, August 2–5, 2000.

43. Ana María T. Rodríguez, "Mujeres, estado y filantropía," Primer informe de avance, Beca de Iniciación, Consejo Nacional de Investigaciones Científicas y Técnicas (CONICET), July 1996, 62.

44. Coni, *Higiene social*, 21–24 (quotation on 25).

45. Emilio R. Coni, *Asistencia Pública Nacional: Proyecto de creación* (Buenos Aires: "La Semana Médica," 1917).

46. *Infancia y Juventud*, October-December 1937, 67–68.

47. "Nota explicativa sobre la finalidad del censo verificado por el Patronato Nacional de Menores. Algunas consideraciones acerca de la protección a la Infancia dentro de la Capital Federal, en relación con los establecimientos tutelares," *Infancia y Juventud*, October-December 1937, 64–71. I would like to thank Isabella Cosse for this information.

48. Buenos Aires Municipality, *Memorias*, 1908, 235–38.

49. I would like to thank Daniel Campi for this important information from his careful survey of the published compilation of laws of Tucumán.

50. Argentine Republic, Diputados, *Diario de Sesiones*, "Subsidios y subvenciones," 1910, tomo 1, and tomo 3, "Inciso 17 of the Budget," 394–404.

51. Argentine Republic, Diputados, *Diario de Sesiones*, "Subsidios y subvenciones," 1920, Anexo M, June 30, 1920, 2:800–23.

52. Argentine Republic, Diputados, *Diario de Sesiones*, "Subsidios y subvenciones," 1933, Leyes sancionadas, 6:452–68.

3. *Performing Child Welfare*

1. Natalie Zemon Davis, Conclusion, in Bonner, Ener, and Singer, eds., *Poverty and Charity*, 318.

2. Damas del Socorro, *Memorias de la Sociedad Damas del Socorro* (Buenos Aires: Martin Biedma, 1880). The quote is from the *Memoria* of the 5a sección norte, 103.

3. AGN, Archivo Fílmicos, Colección Max Glücksmann, Legajo 319, Tambor 296, 16. 1913, Reparto de Ropa a los niños Pobres.-Tigre Hotel. Other early film clips show the damas' horse-drawn carts sinking into the mud as the women traveled to suburbs to provide free meals.

4. *Caras y Caretas*, 1908, n.p. Compare the two photos of uniformed children of the Patronato with the incoming boys.

5. Patronato de la Infancia, *Cien años de amor: Centésimo aniversario, Patronato de la Infancia* (Buenos Aires: Privately printed, 1993).

6. These comments are based upon a sampling of files in the 1880s and 1890s found in the Sociedad de Beneficencia archives at the ACNNAF, Registro de Niños. Since making photocopies or taking photos of these archives is prohibited, it is not possible to reproduce the evidence used to make the statements.

7. See her address to the Congreso Católico Argentino-Uruguayo [Argentine-Uruguayan Catholic Conference], October 23, 1906, which later was published in Celia Lapalma de Emery, *Acción pública y privada en favor de la mujer y del niño en la República Argentina* (Buenos Aires: Alfa y Omega, 1910), 9–40.

8. Lapalma de Emery, "Fuerza victoriosa de la caridad," in *Acción pública y privada*, 45.

9. Lapalma de Emery, "Acción municipal a favor de la mujer y del niño," in *Acción pública y privada*, 86.

10. Cármen P. de Nelson y Angela S. de Cremata, "Hogar profesional de reeducación para niñas," in República Argentina, Ministerio de Relaciones Exteriores y Culto, Dirección de Administración, *Primera Conferencia Nacional de Asistencia Social*, 3 vols. (Buenos Aires: Enrique L. Frigerio e Hijo, 1934), 3: 64, 66.

11. Sociedad de Beneficencia, *Origen y desenvolvimiento de la Sociedad de Beneficencia de la Capital 1822–1912* (Buenos Aires: Tipografía M. Rodríguez Giles, 1919), 148.

12. AGN, Fondo Sociedad de Beneficencia, *Memoria*, 1927, n.p. These figures tended to be inconsistently reported because in the 1924 *Memoria*, 463, they claimed that they fostered 781 children between 1910 and 1924. The numbers do not add up to the sums indicated because there were other categories.

13. Patronato Nacional de Menores, *Primera Conferencia Nacional sobre Infancia abandonada y delincuente* (Buenos Aires: Imprenta Colonia Hogar Ricardo Gutiérrez, 1934), 220.

14. Ibid., 221–24.

15. Buenos Aires Municipality, *Censo general de población, edificación, comercio e industrias de la ciudad de Buenos Aires,* 2 vols. (Buenos Aires: Cía. Sudamericana de Billetes de Banco, 1889), 1:182.

16. Emilio Coni, *Higiene social*, 169–72.

17. Omar Acha, "Catolicismo social y feminidad en la década de 1930: de 'damas' a 'mujeres,'" in *Cuerpos, géneros, identidades: Estudios de historia de género en Argentina*, ed. Omar Acha and Paula Halperín (Buenos Aires: Ediciones del Signo, 2000), 195–228.

18. Donna J. Guy, "The Politics of Pan American Cooperation: Maternalist Feminism and the Child Rights Movement, 1916–1960," *Gender and History* 10.3 (fall 1998): 449–70.

19. See Marcela María Alejandra Nari, "El hogar, los niños, el esposo y la patria: La creación de la mujer-madres y el surgimiento del feminismo en la Argentina, 1890–1910" (Ph.D. dissertation, University of Buenos Aires, 1991), esp. chap. 4.

20. Lavrin, *Women, Feminism, and Social Change*, 97.

21. Elvira Rawson de Dellepiane, *Apuntes sobre higiene en la mujer* (Buenos Aires: Pablo E. Coni é Hijos, 1892), 9.

22. Ibid., 31–32.

23. Ibid., 33.

24. Ibid., 42.

25. Asociación "Universitarias Argentinas," *Primer congreso femenino internacional de la República Argentina* (Buenos Aires: A. Ceppi, 1911), 219, 304, 428–29.

26. Raquel Camaña, "Femeninidad," *Atlántida* 13 (1914), 109.

27. "Congreso del Niño," *La Prensa*, October 13, 1913, 9. The speeches of this meeting were never published in their entirety.

28. Ernestina A. López de Nelson, "Nuevos ideales filantrópicos," *Boletín Mensual del Museo Social Argentino* 3 (1914): 75–77.

29. Juana María Begino, "El Congreso Nacional del Niño: La Liga para los derechos de la mujer y del niño y sus trabajos," *Cara y Caretas* (November 16, 1916).

30. "Programa de las Secciones," in *Congreso Americano del Niño, Buenos Aires, Argentina, julio de 1916* (Washington: Unión Panamericana, División de Conferencias y Organismos, Departamento Jurídico y de Organismos Internacionales, Serie Sobre Congresos y Conferencias Número 62, 1950), 7–12.

31. Organización de Estados Americanos, Instituto Interamericano del Niño, *Congreso Panamericanos del Niño: Ordenación sistemática de sus recomendaciones, 1916–1963* (Montevideo: Organización de Estados Americanos, 1965), 73, 77, 232–33, 268; and Lavrin, *Women, Feminism, and Social Change*, 109.

32. Paulina Luisi, *Algunas ideas sobre eugenia: Trabajo presentado al 1er Congreso Americano del Niño, Buenos Aires, 1916* (Montevideo: El Siglo Ilustrado, 1916), 11–23. Luisi's speech in 1916 was preceded by an equally controversial address given by Dr. Emilio R. Coni in 1909. For Coni's speech, see Stepan, *"The Hour of Eugenics,"* 58.

33. Coni, *Higiene social*, 127–28; and Lavrin, *Women, Feminism, and Social Change*, 111.

34. Paula Halperín, "Mi mamá me mima: Mujeres, médicas y socialistas en *Unión y Labor*," in Acha and Halperín, eds., *Cuerpos, géneros e identidades*, 107–33.

35. "El Instituto de Maternidad de la Sociedad de Beneficencia," *Boletín Mensual del Museo Social Argentino* 17.82 (April 1929): 168–70.

36. Archivo Patronato Español, *Libro de Actas*, Libro 1, fojas 1–3. I would like to thank Sra. Elsa Insogna for her permission to photograph these books. Patronato Español, Instituto Nuestra Señora del Pilar, *"El pasado nos cuenta," 1912–2002: 90 Años al Servicio de la Comunidad* (Buenos Aires: Asociación Civil Patronato Español, 2002), 5.

37. Archivo Patronato Español, *Libro de Actas*, Libro 2, foja 5. The woman who donated the ticket came from Salamanca (fojas 13–15, 21).

38. Patronato Español, Instituto Nuestra Señora del Pilar, *"El pasado nos cuenta,"* 33.

39. Ibid., 16, 47.

40. Ibid., 658. Sociedad de Socorros de Damas Israelitas, *Reseña sobre la marcha de la Sociedad de Socorros de Damas Israelitas*, 1918–19, 11; 1920–21, 12–13. The Society changed its name to the Sociedad de Beneficencia de Damas Israelitas in 1927. In addition to helping parturient women, the Jewish community had already established an association to prevent young Jewish girls, particularly immigrants, from becoming entrapped in "white slavery" or the international traffic in women and children. See Donna J. Guy, *Sex and Danger in Buenos*

Aires: Prostitution, Family, and Nation in Argentina (Lincoln: University of Nebraska Press, 1991). The advertisement was published in *Mundo Israelita*, May 7, 1927, 4. It noted that the president of Argentina would be accompanied by his wife, members of the Argentine Congress, and ambassadors of foreign countries.

41. Gloria Rut Lerner, "El Asilo de Huérfanas Israelitas," unpublished paper, Universidad Nacional de Luján, 23.

42. There were earlier presidents of this women's group, but after 1919 they identified these two women as the first and second presidents. See Lerner, "El Asilo de Huérfanas Israelitas, 20.

43. A long controversy preoccupied the Buenos Aires Jewish community. It began in 1931 when *Mundo Israelita* urged the group to provide an alternate slate of candidates. Subsequently the newspaper realized that those opposing Rebecca R. de Glücksmann never bothered to organize their own slate, and that unfounded rumors existed in the capital accusing the women of forming a closed circle of aristocratic women. Although *Mundo Israelita* publicly refuted this accusation, the orphanage suffered by having many fewer patrons. See "La renovación en la Sociedad de Damas," *Mundo Israelita*, August 22, 1931.

44. Sociedad de Socorros de Damas Israelitas, *Reseña sobre la marcha de la Sociedad de Socorros de Damas Israelitas, 1921–22*, 11; 1922–23, 16.

45. "Asilo Israelita Argentino," *Mundo Israelita*, July 24, 1926, 4.

46. For example, the Sociedad de Damas Israelitas de Beneficencia sponsored a tea dance at the Imperial Salon of the Alvear Palace Hotel on July 22, 1941. The proceeds were intended to subsidize the girls' orphanage. Archivo Instituto Científico Judío [hereafter Archivo IWO], *Mundo Israelita*, July 14, 1941. Prior to the construction of Alvear Palace, the Damas held events in the Plaza Hotel and the Savoy Hotel, both considered fine upper-class city hotels. Sociedad de Socorros de Damas Israelitas, *Reseña sobre la marcha de la Sociedad*. 1920–1, 12–13.

47. Archivo IWO, Hogar Infantil Israelita Argentina, *Libro de Actas*, 1931, foja 141; *Mundo Israelita*, August 1, 1931. An advertisement for the Hogar Infantil Israelita Argentino invited members of the Jewish community to an open house. "El Hogar infantil en su primer aniversario," *Mundo Israelita*, November 21, 1931; Archivo IWO, Hogar Infantil Israelita Argentina, *Libro de Actas*, May 31, 1933, fojas 14–24; September 19, fojas 44–50; January 2, 1934, fojas 167–71.

48. See, for example, the articles critical of the Jewish damas in *Mundo Israelita*, November 23, 1931, and February 20, 1932.

49. Archivo IWO, Hogar Infantil Israelita Argentina, *Memoria y balance general*, 11 ejercicio 1938–39, 15–16.

50. Archivo IWO, Hogar Infantil Israelita Argentina, *Libro de actas*, August 22, 1938, foja 21; December 18, 1940, foja 27.

51. Archivo IWO, Hogar Infantil Israelita Argentina, *Memoria*, 11 ejercicio 1938–39, 15–16.

52. Sociedad de Socorros de Damas Israelitas de Beneficencia, *Asilo Argentino de Huérfanas Israelitas Memoria y Balance,* 1945–46, 31–32, contains a list of holidays both secular and religious celebrated at the orphanage, along with a long list of prominent Jewish families who attended Passover services there.

53. Sociedad de Socorros de Damas Israelita, *Reseña sobre la marcha de la Sociedad,* 1927, 24.

54. Sociedad de Socorros de Damas Israelitas, *Reseña sobre la marcha de la Sociedad, 1923–24,* 17. Immigrant women also worked there, but it was closed the following year. Archivo IWO, *Mundo Israelita,* June 26, 1943, 12, "Através del Asilo de Huérfanas se cumple una tarea de gran importancia."

55. Advertisement, *Mundo Israelita,* June 26, 1930. It was only toward the end of the ad that they mentioned that they still needed to raise 200,000 pesos for construction costs for the new asylum.

56. "El general Justo y los niños," *Infancia y Juventud* 2 (1937): n.p.

57. "Las primeras memorias de Juan Perón," *La Opinión,* July 2, 1974, 4. I would like to thank Laura Michelle Diener for providing this information. Most likely, Perón's recollection of Eva's trip to San Juan is a false recollection.

58. According to Mark Healey, neither Juan nor Eva went to San Juan (personal conversation and e-mail correspondence, June 2005).

59. Statement of February 15, 1947, published in Eva Perón, *La palabra y el pensamiento y la acción de Eva Perón* (Buenos Aires: Editorial Freeland, 1973), 54.

60. Ibid., speech of April 14, 1948, 56–57.

61. The exposition, "Los mil y un Evita," was held from June 26 to July 26, 1996, at the Buenos Aires Palais de Glace.

62. AGN, Sociedad de Beneficencia, Subsidios 1951, letter of July 19, 1950. The file does not indicate whether Eva ever saw the letter.

63. AGN, Sociedad de Beneficencia, Subsidios 1951, letter of July 21, 1951. Once again, it is unclear if Eva ever read the letter.

4. Juvenile Delinquency

Parts of this chapter were previously published in Donna J. Guy, "Girls in Prison: The Role of the Buenos Aires Casa Correccional de Mujeres as an Institution of Child Rescue, 1890–1940," in Ricardo D. Salvatore, Carlos Aguirre, and Gilbert M. Joseph, eds., *Crime and Punishment in Latin American Law and Society Since Late Colonial Times* (Durham: Duke University Press, 2001): 369–90.

1. Aníbal Ponce, *Ambición y angustia de los adolescentes: Psicología de la adolescencia* (Buenos Aires: L. J. Rosso, 1936), 12; Ismael Dulce, *Nociones de puericultura práctica* (Buenos Aires: Editorial Bibliográfica Argentina, 1952), 28–29.

2. Diputados, *Diario de Sesiones,* August 1, 1892, 524. The presence of orphans among these children was recognized in a later discussion on September 16, although no suggestions were discussed that would ameliorate this issue (918).

3. Buenos Aires Municipality, *Reglamento Provisorio de la Casa de Corrección de Menores Varones de la Capital* (Buenos Aires: La Defensa, 1899), 3; Art. 61–63, 19.

4. Lucila Larrandart, Verónica Guargnino, Sergio Rocamora, and Mary Ana Beloff, "Informe del Grupo de Investigación de Argentina," in *Infancia, adolescencia y control social en América Latina: Argentina, Colombia, Costa Rica, Uruguay, Venezuela,* ed. Emilio García Méndez and Elías Carranza (Buenos Aires: Ediciones Depalma, 1990), 73.

5. AGN, Fondo MJIP, Letra P, Legajo No. 365, November 4, 1903.

6. Gabriel Carrasco cited in Eduardo O. Ciafardo, *Los niños en la ciudad de Buenos Aires (1890–1910)* (Buenos Aires: Centro Editor de América Latina, 1992), 11–12.

7. Roberto Levillier, "La delincuencia en Buenos Aires," in *Censo general de la población, edificación, comercio e industrias de la ciudad de Buenos Aires,* 3 vols., ed. Alberto Martínez (Buenos Aires: Compañía Sudamericana de Billetes de Banco, 1910), 3: 395.

8. Argentine Republic, Ministerio de Justicia e Instrucción Pública [hereafter MJIP], *Memoria,* 1906, 110; 1910, 115–16; and speech of Carlos Broudeur in Patronato Nacional de la Infancia, *Primer conferencia nacional,* 157.

9. Roberto Gache, *La delincuencia precoz (niñez y adolescencia)* (Buenos Aires: J Lajouane, 1916), 97. The book was awarded the Florencio Varela Prize in 1916 by the Buenos Aires Facultad de Derecho y Ciencias Sociales.

10. Ibid., 100–1, 106, 107.

11. AGN, Fondo MJIP, Legajo 110, April 23, 1908, annual report of Defensor de Menores Dr. A. Cabal.

12. *Revista Penitenciaria* 1.1 (1905), 66–67.

13. *Caras y Caretas,* 1908, n.p.

14. ACNNAF, Legajo 48.563. The damas also turned them away because they suffered from scalp ringworm (*tiña*).

15. Sylvia Schafer, "Between Paternal Right and the Dangerous Mother: Reading Parental Responsibility in Nineteenth-Century French Civil Justice," *Journal of Family History* 23.2 (1998): 174.

16. MJIP, Buenos Aires Police, *Memoria, 1913–1914,* 13–14.

17. "Protección de la Infancia," *Revista de la Policía de la Capital* 1.4 (July 15, 1888): 37–39.

18. In the provinces of Argentina there already was a tradition of anti-vagrancy laws that forced children into jobs. See Guy, *White Slavery and Mothers Alive and Dead,* 108–21.

19. Alberto Meyer Arana, *Colonias para menores: Bases que han servido para la organización de la Colonia de Menores Varones (Márcos Paz)* (Buenos Aires: Talleres Gráficos de la Penitenciaría Nacional, 1906), v, 8–9, 14, 20.

20. The term "morally disinfected" is my interpretation.

21. Argentine Republic, MJIP, *Memoria,* 1913, 2:204–5; 1915, 1:286–89, 298–99.

22. See the reports of these institutions in Argentine Republic, MJIP, *Memoria*, 1916, 1:35–37, 279–82; 1918, 1:154–59; 1919, 1:276–77; 1920, 1:267–75; 1923: 1:299–305; 1926, 1:232–35.

23. Argentine Republic, MJIP, *Memoria*, 1923, 1:304–5.

24. Argentine Republic, Ministerio de Relaciones Exteriores y Culto, Reformatorio de Menores Abandonados y Delincuentes, *Memoria* (Buenos Aires: Ministerio de Relaciones Exteriores, 1924), 1923, iv, vi.

25. Argentine Republic, MJIP, *Memoria*, 1918, 1:32–34.

26. Lila Caimari, in "Whose Criminals Are These? Church, State, and Patronatos and the Rehabilitation of Female Convicts (Buenos Aires, 1890–1940)," *Americas* 54.2 (1997): 185–208, argues that Argentine liberals invited the nuns because they operated on very little money and already had a presence in Latin America (see esp. p. 195).

27. Argentine Republic, MJIP, *Memorias*, Report of the Defensores de Menores, 1886, 1:65; Larrandart et al., "Informe del Grupo de Investigación de Argentina," 63.

28. Argentine Republic, MJIP, *Resultados generales del Primer Censo Carcelario de la República Argentina* (Buenos Aires: Talleres Gráficos de la Penitenciaría Nacional, 1909), 94–95.

29. Buenos Aires Municipality, *Anuario estadístico de la ciudad de Buenos Aires*, 1897, 265, 509; 1903, 275; 1915–1923, 250.

30. AGN, Fondo MJIP, División Expedientes Generales, Letra D, Legajo 106, Letter from Defensor José M. Terrero, May 7, 1901.

31. AGN, Fondo MJIP, División Expedientes Generales, Letra C, Legajo 38, 1895, Expediente 308, foja 1, May 21, 1895, Mother Superior to President J. E. Uriburu.

32. AGN, Fondo MJIP, División Expedientes Generales, Letra C, Legajo 38, 1895, Expediente 308, foja 2, response of Defensores through the Departamento de Justicia, February 4, 1896.

33. AGN, Fondo MJIP, División Expedientes Generales, Letra C, Legajo 47, Expediente 314, Letter of Mother Superior, June 4, 1900. The following day the mother superior wrote to minister of justice Osvaldo Magnasco that after writing the first letter she received notice that the prison had been given 24,000 pesos to expand the existing building, a sum that was insufficient to construct the new building she had suggested.

34. Argentine Republic, MJIP, *Memoria*, 1904, 1:134–35.

35. Argentine Republic, MJIP, *Memoria*, 1904, 1:134–35.

36. Argentine Republic, MJIP, *Memoria*, 1911, 130.

37. AGN, Fondo MJIP, División Expedientes Generales, Letra A, 1910, Legajo 11, Expediente 46, Asilo Corrección de Mujeres, April 12, 1910.

38. AGN, Fondo MJIP, División Expedientes Generales, Letra A, 1915, Legajo 16, Expediente 40, "Asilo de Corrección de Mujeres. Cuadros demostrativos del movimiento habido . . . durante 1913."

39. Argentine Republic, MJIP, *Memoria*, 1920, 413.

40. Argentine Republic, MJIP, *Memoria*, 1914, 1:365.

41. Argentine Republic, MJIP, *Memoria*, 1921, Report of the Mother Superior, 1:500–1.

42. ACNNAF, Legajo 13.557. The child entered the Society of Beneficence in 1905, and the file was maintained until 1919.

43. AGN, División Poder Judicial, Fondo Tribunales Civiles, Letra G, 1920, Gigena de Saldaño, sobre reclusión de su hija menor Juana Isabel, fojas 1–5, August 23, 1920, to September 1, 1920. The judge ordered that Juana be admitted to the Asilo del Buen Pastor.

44. ACNNAF, Legajo 61.969.

45. ACNNAF, Legajo 62.592.

46. ACNNAF, Legajo 61.951.

47. ACNNAF, Legajo 60.257.

48. AGN, Fondo MJIP, Legajo 110, letter from Ramón Domínguez to Minister of Justice R. Naón, March 31, 1909. When officials found a place for Domingo, they discovered that the father had given an inaccurate address.

49. AGN, Fondo MJIP, Letra D, Dirección de Justicia, Legajo 112, Expediente 127, December 6, 1911.

50. AGN, Fondo Sociedad de Beneficencia, Legajo 160, foja 348, letter from Nicolasa P. de Serantes to President Emma V. de Napp, January 16, 1878.

51. AGN, Fondo Sociedad de Beneficencia, Legajo 160, Unión Telefónica to President of the Sociedad de Beneficencia, July 20, 1883; Legajo 160, fojas 96–98, annual report of Casa de Huérfanas, March 13, 1886.

52. Sociedad de Beneficencia, *Memorias*, 1900, 5.

53. AGN, Fondo Sociedad de Beneficencia, Casa de Huérfanas, Legajo 162, fojas 265–67, letter from Casa de Huérfanas to President, Sociedad de Beneficencia, January 19, 1910.

54. See AGN, Fondo Sociedad de Beneficencia, Casa de Huérfanas, Legajo 163, foja 194, Director General de Arsenales de Guerra to the Sociedad de Beneficencia, April 19, 1915, and foja 195, April 23, 1915.

55. Alberto Meyer Arana, *La caridad en Buenos Aires*, 2 vols. (Buenos Aires, Imprenta Sopena, 1911), 1:372–73.

56. Sociedad de Beneficencia, *Memorias*, 1900, 153–254. At that time the boys' orphanage was the only place in Buenos Aires where minors were instructed in military training.

57. See, for example, AGN, Fondo Sociedad de Beneficencia, Legajo 45, foja 107, Asilo de Huérfanos to Sociedad de Beneficencia, July 26, 1906, regarding the request for boys for a military band; foja 113, Escuela de Apréndices Marineros, Dársena Norte, to President, Sociedad de Beneficencia, September 24, 1906, returning naval recruits; and foja 118, Asilo de Huérfanos to Sociedad de Beneficencia, October 5, 1906, explaining the problems encountered by naval authorities.

58. AGN, Fondo Sociedad de Beneficencia, Legajo 43, fojas 99–101. Bernabe Per-derera to President, Sociedad de Beneficencia, June 8, 1899.

59. Sociedad de Beneficencia, *Memoria*, 1900, 5.

60. Sociedad de Beneficencia, *Memoria*, 1900, 202.

61. AGN, Fondo Sociedad de Beneficencia, Expediente 8523/1, "Sociedad de Bene-ficencia de la Capital: Reseña sobre su organización y su obra 1823–1942."

62. According to "Registro General de Niños," *Sociedad de Beneficencia de la Capi-tal, 1823–1936* (Buenos Aires: privately printed, 1936), 158, although 6,214 ba-bies under the age of one were admitted from 1926 to 1935, only 3,393 children of other ages were admitted, and 485 (394 of whom were female) left to be placed in families.

63. MJIP, *Memoria*, 1894, Report of Defensor, Sección Sud, 1:131–46. These prob-lems were further elaborated in J. M. Terrero, Defensor de Menores, to Os-valdo Magnasco, Ministro de Justicia, AGN, Fondo MJIP, Legajo 106.

64. AGN, Fondo MJIP, Legajo 112, Letra D, annual report of Defender Castellanos, April 9, 1912.

65. MJIP, *Memoria*, 1911, 95.

66. Patronato Nacional de Menores, *Primera Conferencia Nacional sobre Infancia*, 140, testimony of Sra. de Piñero Sorondo.

67. Ibid., report of Jorge Ortiz de Rosas, 167.

68. Patronato de la Infancia, Meeting Minutes, Libro 2, 1894–97, July 16, 1894, foja 3.

69. Patronato de la Infancia, Meeting Minutes, Libro 2, 1894–97, July 16, 1894, foja 3; October 10, 1894, foja 35; June 9, 1895, foja 85; September 18, 1895, foja 109; 1911–1914, Libro 8, January 31, 1912, fojas 26–27; June 3, 1896, foja 156; Libro 11, 1919–1921, June 2, 1919, foja 3; August 20, foja 45. Patronato de la Infancia, *Anales* 22.7–8 (July-August 1914): 130–32.

70. Patronato de la Infancia, Meeting Minutes, Libro 12, 1921–1924, December 28, 1919, foja 62 and foja 255.

71. The quote is found in Dr. José Ingegnieros [*sic*], "Los niños vendedores de diarios y la delincuencia precoz," *Archivos de Psiquiatría y Criminología apli-cadas a las Ciencias Afines* 7 (1908): 329–48. Jorge Salessi, in *Médicos maleantes y maricas: Higiene, criminología y homosexualidad en la construcción de la nacio-nalidad (Buenos Aires 1871–1914)* (Rosario: Beatriz Viterbo Editora, 1995), has examined this report to explain the medicalization of sexuality.

72. Larrandart et al., "Informe del Grupo de Investigación de Argentina," 68–69; Decree of May 20, 1905, *Revista Penitenciaria* 1.1 (1905): 16.

73. *Revista Penitenciaria* 1.1 (1905): 99.

74. *Revista Penitenciaria* 3.1 (1907): 93–103.

75. *Revista Penitenciaria* 1.2 (1905): 39–45.

76. *Revista Penitenciaria* 1.1 (1905): 55–61.

77. Juan Carlos Landó, "Menores delincuentes," *Infancia y Juventud* 2 (1937): 17.

78. Buenos Aires Municipality, *Anuario estadístico de la ciudad de Buenos Aires*, 1903, 278; 1913, 260; 1923, 240.

79. Cesar Viale, *Estadística de los menores de que "dispuso" el Juzgado Correccional entre los años 1923 a 1928* (Buenos Aires: Talleres Gráficos Colonia Hogar Ricard Gutiérrez, 1933), n.p.

80. Argentine Republic, Ministry of Justice and Public Instruction, *The Prevention of Juvenile Delinquency in the Field of Legislation and Social Work in Argentina: A Survey Ordered by Dr. Antonio Sagarna, Secretary of Justice and Public Instruction on the Occasion of the First International Child's Congress at Geneva, August 24–28, 1925* (Buenos Aires: Talleres Gráficos de la Cía. General de Fósforos, 1925), 6–8.

81. Ibid., 8–9.

82. Tucumán Province, *Anuario de estadística de la provincia de Tucumán*, 1907, cxxxviii; 1910, n.p., 1918, 143; 1919, 159; 1920, 155; 1923, 138–39.

83. ACNNAF, Legajo 60.259.

84. ACNNAF, Legajo 62.317.

85. Dr. Gregorio Bermann, "Estudio de menores abandonados y delincuentes," *Actas de la primera conferencia latino-americana de neurología, psiquiatría y medicina legal*, vol. 2 (Buenos Aires: Imprenta de la Universidad, 1929), 304.

86. Ibid., 335, 336.

5. The Depression and the Welfare State

1. *Bulletin of the Pan American Union* 63.3 (March 29, 1929): 304; 66.2 (February 1932): 141.

2. Speech of Minister Yriondo, September 25, 1933, reprinted in Argentine Republic, Patronato Nacional de Menores, *Primera Conferencia Nacional*, 35–39. For newspaper coverage of the sessions, see *La Prensa*, September 26, 1933, 12; September 27, 9; September 28, 7; September 30, 13.

3. Argentine Republic, Patronato Nacional de Menores, *Primera Conferencia Nacional*, 138–39.

4. Ibid., 140–42.

5. Decree of December 28, 1932, Diputados, *Diario de Sesiones*, 1932: 1:333.

6. Emilia Heussner, "Detención provisoria de menores sistemas y establecimientos," *Infancia y Juventud* 31 (April-September 1949): 37–38.

7. Noemí Girbal-Blacha, "El estado neoconservador, el intervencionismo económico y la sociedad de los años treinta," in *Estado, sociedad y economia en la Argentina 1930–1997*, ed. Noemí Girbal-Blacha (Quilmes: Universidad Nacional de Quilmes Ediciones, 2001), 53–55

8. AGN, Fondo Sociedad de Beneficencia, Expediente 8523/1, Sociedad de Beneficencia, "Sociedad de Beneficencia de la Capital, Reseña sobre su organización y su obra 1823–1942."

9. "La Asociación Cantinas Maternales de Buenos Aires," *Boletín del Museo Social Argentino* 28:91 (January 1930): 29–31.

10. ACNNAF, Legajo 44.086. The interventor federal or national intervener is an

official designated by the president to take over the positions of officials removed by the president.

11. ACNNAF, Legajo 55707.

12. ACNNAF, Legajo 61.906.

13. ACNNAF, Legajo 55.987.

14. ACNNAF, Legajo 63.626.

15. AGN, Sala 7–2–5–6 Archivo Ing. Felipe Senillosa, Legajo 159, "Plan orgánico de la creación de la 'Comisión Nacional de Eugenesia y Medicina Social,' por los Dres. Octavio B. López y Arturo R. Rossi," September 20, 1930 (my emphasis).

16. "La palabra de nuestro Presidente, el Dr. Nicolás Lezano, se dirige a los intelectuales del país, exponiendo los puntos de vista del H. Consejo Superior de la Asociación Argentina de Biotipología, Eugenesia y Medicina Social en la historia, plan de acción y desenvolvimiento de estas especulaciones científicas y socials en la República Argentina," *Anales Biotipología, Eugenesia y Medicina Social* 2.35 (December 1934). For a different interpretation, see Stepan, *"The Hour of Eugenics,"* 60–61.

17. AGN, Sala 7–2–5–6 Archivo Ing. Felipe Senillosa, Legajo 159, letter from Juan Senillosa to Mayor Mariano de Vedia y Mitre, February 3, 1933; letter of Dra. Mercedes Rodríguez, Sec. de Higiene, Museo Social Argentino, to Juan A. Senillosa, August 24, 1933, with list of talks by members of the Museo Social Argentino for the radio program; letter from the Grupo Socialista Vicente Russomano, Sec., to H. Consejo Deliberante de la Ciudad de Buenos Aires, November 29, 1933; letter from Juan Senillosa to Vicente Russomano, Sec. Grupo Socialista, December 18, 1933.

18. "Eugenesia y maternidad," *Anales Biotipología, Eugenesia y Medicina Social* 2.36 (January 1935): 2.

19. Carlos Bernaldo de Quiros, "El determinismo económico en la fenomenología eugénico-social," *Anales de Biotipología, Eugenesia y Medicina Social* 3.67 (October 1936): n.p.

20. Ibid., n.p.

21. "A pesar de sus ocupaciones Ud. puede ser un buen padre," *Hijo mío* 1.1 (April 1936): 76.

22. "Nodriza científica," *Hijo mío* 2.8 (November 1937): 494–95.

23. Stepan, *"The Hour of Eugenics."* See also Koven and Michel, eds., *Mothers of a New World.*

24. Patronato Nacional de la Infancia, *Segunda Conferencia Nacional de la Infancia,* 1:203–4.

25. Diputados, *Diario de Sesiones,* May 9, 1932, 1:120–27.

26. Senado, *Diario de Sesiones,* September 22, 1933, 2:350–52.

27. Diputados, *Diario de Sesiones,* September 30, 1933, 6:254–55.

28. Senado, *Diario de Sesiones,* September 7, 1933, 2:43. Ricardo Salvatore has examined the studies of conscripts in his "Stature, Nutrition and Regional

Convergence: The Argentine Northwest in the First Half of the Twentieth Century," *Social Science History* 28.2 (2004): 297–304.

29. Senado, *Diario de Sesiones,* September 7, 1933, 2:44 (my emphasis).

30. The attractiveness of the extreme Right for left-wing ideologues in the Southern Cone during the 1930s was brilliantly analyzed by Sandra McGee Deutsch in *Las Derechas: The Extreme Right in Argentina, Brazil, and Chile, 1890–1939* (Stanford, Calif.: Stanford University Press, 1999).

31. Josefina Marpons, "Protección a la Maternidad," *Vida Femenina* 2.21 (April 15, 1935): 8, 10. Her article was followed by another one on the same subject in May 1935.

32. Dra. Alicia Moreau de Justo, "El niño: Esperanza de la humanidad," *Vida Femenina* 3.30 (January 15, 1936): 4–5.

33. Palacios subsequently published all his speeches and photos in his *El dolor argentino: Plan sanitario y educativo de protección a los niños* (Buenos Aires: Editorial Claridad, 1938), the slogan appears on page 13.

34. Alberto Benegas Lynch (h) and Martín Krause, *En defensa de los más necesitados* (Buenos Aires: Editorial Atlántida, 1998), 121.

35. Roberto Ortiz, inaugural speech to Congress, 1938, available at the Web site of the Latin Americanist Research Resources Project (http://lanic.utexas.edu/).

36. Diputados, *Diario de Sesiones,* June 18, 1941, 1:550–76; September 24, 1941, 2:226–46.

37. *Boletín del Museo Social Argentino* 28.219–20 (September-October 1940): 294–96.

38. Diputados, *Diario de Sesiones,* Anexo M: Subsidios y Beneficencia, 1934, 8:278–312. This did not include subsidies for construction or for items included in other sections of the budget.

39. Diputados, *Diario de Sesiones,* 1937, 2:2a parte, 114–56.

40. Dr. Luis Siri, "Bases para la elaboración del plan general de protección a la infancia en la República Argentina," in *Actos y trabajos del Primer Congreso Nacional de la Puericultura 7–11 octubre de 1940* (Buenos Aires: Imprenta Alfredo Frascoli, 1941), 2:208.

41. Report of Comisario Juan Alejandro Re, Patronato de la Infancia, *Segunda Conferencia Nacional,* 477.

42. Coll, *Conferencias,* 1930, 31.

43. For Bermann's role in the development of Argentine psychiatry, see Mariano Ben Plotkin, *Freud in the Pampas: The Emergence and Development of a Psychoanalytic Culture in Argentina* (Stanford, Calif.: Stanford University Press, 2001), 25–26; and Gregorio Bermann, *Los menores desamparados y delincuentes en Córdoba* (Córdoba: Talleres Gráficos de la Penitenciaría, 1933).

44. Bermann, *Los menores desamparados,* 1:48, 64.

45. Ibid., 1:79. His bibliography cites the early work of Jean Piaget.

46. Ibid., 1:97–103.

47. Lavrin, *Women, Feminism, and Social Change,* 259.

48. Donna J. Guy, "The Pan American Child Congresses, 1916–1942: Pan Americanism, Child Reform, and the Welfare State in Latin America," *Journal of Family History* 23.3 (July 1998): 171–91.

49. Norberto Alayón, *Historia del trabajo social en Argentina*, 3rd ed. (Buenos Aires: Espacio Editorial, 1980), 60–61.

50. Katherine F. Lenroot, "Prevención de la delincuencia juvenil," *Boletín del Instituto Internacional Americano de Protección a la Infancia* 1.4 (April 1928): 470–78.

51. Blanca Cassagne Serres, untitled article, *Infancia y Juventud* 3 (1937): 39–42.

52. Telma Reca, *Delincuencia infantil: Delincuencia infantil en los Estados Unidos y en la Argentina* (Buenos Aires: Talleres Gráficos de la Penitenciaría Nacional, 1932), 8–12.

53. Ibid., 194–203.

54. Ibid., 212–13; quotation on page 214.

55. Susana Malbrán, "El trabajo de los menores en la vía pública: Sus peligros; su reglamentaciones," *Boletín del Museo Social Argentino* 24.167–68 (May-June 1930): 128–31.

56. Clara R. de Altbáum, *Delincuencia infantil* (Buenos Aires: Artes Gráficas Belgrano, 1939), 57 (the quotation refers to Jane Addams).

57. "Gabinete psicopedagógico, Estadística desde el 16 de junio de 1939 al 14 de noviembre de 1941," *Infancia y Juventud* 30 (January-March 1944), n.p.

58. "¿Herencia o ambiente?" *Infancia y juventud* (August-September 1940): 18.

59. Ibid., 19–21.

60. Ibid., 21.

61. Ibid., 21–24.

62. ACNNAF, Legajo 44.497.

63. ACNNAF, Legajo 44.954.

64. ACNNAF, Legajo 61.921.

65. ACNNAF, Legajo 61.921.

66. Diagram found in *Infancia y Juventud* 16–17 (1943): 24–27. See also page 24 for the private institutions authorized to house minors; pages 32–33 for the disposition of minors in 1942; and page 40 for the comments on placing children. The comments about juvenile behavior are based upon the examination of thousands of cases in the ACNNAF, and the comments on disabled children were mentioned specifically on page 40.

67. These comments are summaries of works presented in *Tercer Congreso Provincial del Niño y Conferencia Nacional de Psicotécnica: Actuaciones y Trabajos, Rosario, Agosto de 1938*, 3 vols. (Rosario: Talleres Gráficos R.T. Suárez, 1941).

68. Ibid., 188–89.

69. José L. Araya, *Asistencia social al menor* (Rosario: Editorial Rosario, 1945), 96.

70. See Ronald H. Dolkart, "Manuel A. Fresco, Governor of the Province of Buenos Aires 1936–1940: A Study of the Argentine Right and Its Response to

Economic and Social Change," Ph.D. dissertation, University of California, Los Angeles, 1969, 236–37; and *Infancia y Juventud* 3 (1937): 93–101.

71. Fresco gave detailed information on his program in his annual messages of 1937 and 1938. See Manuel A. Fresco, *Mis mensajes 1936–1940* (Buenos Aires: Talleres Gráficos "Damiano," 1941), esp. 109–13, 189–95, and 229–34. Domingo Mercante's accomplishments are presented in Adriana María Valobra, "Public Health Policies, Women's Organizations and Mothers in the Province of Buenos Aires, 1946–1952," *Studies in the Social Sciences* 38 (July, 2005): 79–113.

72. AGN, Fondo Sociedad de Beneficencia, *Libro de Actas*, tomo 31, December 19, 1940, fojas 73–74.

73. "Horizonte Socio-Eugénico-Jurídico," *Anales de Biotipología, Eugenesia y Medicina Social* 4.68 (November 15, 1936): 5.

74. AGN, Fondo Sociedad de Beneficencia, *Libro de Actas*, tomo 29, June 17, 1938, foja 199.

75. Senado, *Diario de Sesiones*, September 17, 1942, 320–21.

76. Patronato de la Infancia, *Segunda Conferencia Nacional de la Infancia*. See the program for the first plenary session, which was devoted mostly to social work and adoption.

77. Guy, *White Slavery and Mothers Alive and Dead*, 33–51.

6. At the Crossroads of Change

1. Quoted in Jerónimo Remorino, *La nueva legislación social argentina* (Buenos Aires: Ministerio de Relaciones Exteriores y Culto, 1953), 8.

2. Lavrin, *Women, Feminism, and Social Change*, chapter 8.

3. Verónica Giordano, "Los derechos civiles de las mujeres y el proyecto de reforma del Código Civil de 1936: El acontecimiento, la estructura, la coyuntura," available on the Web site of the Instituto de Investigaciones Gino Germani, University of Buenos Aries.

4. Sandra McGee Deutsch uses oral interviews to reconstruct this history in her "Changing the Landscape: The Study of Argentine Jewish Women and New Historical Vistas," *Jewish History* 18.1 (2004): 49–73.

5. Adriana Valobra has written extensively on the suffrage campaign, although most of her work remains unpublished. The essay, "Creíamos demasiado en los hombres . . . No creíamos en la mujer," is available on the Internet. See also Gregory Sowles Hammond, "Women Can Vote Now: Feminism and the Women's Suffrage Movement in Argentina, 1900–1955," Ph.D. dissertation, University of Texas, Austin, 2004.

6. Blanca Azucena Cassagne Serres, *¿Debe votar la mujer? Cultura Cívica femenina: Constitución Nacional, division de poderes y sufragio femenino: Un programa de acción* (Buenos Aires: Editorial Licurgo, 1945), 41, 42.

7. Marifran, Carlson, *¡Feminismo! The Woman's Movement in Argentina from Its Beginnings to Eva Perón* (Chicago: Academy Publishers of Chicago, 1988), 187.

8. Lucila de Gregorio Lavié, *Trayectoria de la condición social de las mujeres Argentinas* (Santa Fe: Universidad Nacional del Litoral, Instituto Social, 1945), 18–19.

9. Lucila de Gregorio Lavié, *La ciudadana: Para las mujeres que votan* (Buenos Aires: Macagno, Landa and Cía., 1948).

10. Carlson, *¡Feminismo!* 173–87.

11. Eduardo Colom, Diputados, *Diario de sesiones*, June 27, 1947, 1:105.

12. Eduardo Colom, Diputados, *Diario de sesiones*, September 3, 1947, 4:73–74.

13. Recollections of Eduardo Colom, taken at the Instituto de Tella, Buenos Aires, March 27, April 12 and 20, and May 24, 1972. Used with permission from the Columbia University Oral Archive.

14. I am indebted to Adriana Valobra who generously shared with me her unpublished thesis on the 1946 female suffrage campaign. Her essay "¿Del hogar a las urnas? Una aproximación a los discursos de Eva Perón sobre los derechos politicos de las mujeres en el contexto de debate, promulgación y aplicación de la ley 13010/47" constitutes an important contribution to the historiography of Eva Perón.

15. *El Laborista*, September 24, 1947, 10.

16. AGN, Archivo Intermedio, Society of Beneficence Ministerio del Interior, remite copia autenticada del decreto no 9414 dictado el 4 de Setiembre de 1946, por el cual se declara Intervenida la Sociedad de Beneficencia de la Capital, nombrandose Interventor de la misma al Dr. Armando Mendez San Martin, "Plan Integral de Desarrolar," n.d.

17. Benegas Lynch (h) and Krause, *En defensa de los más necesitados*, 22; and Norberto Alayón, *La historia del trabajo social en Argentina*, 16.

18. María Flores [Mary Main], *The Woman with the Whip: Eva Perón* (New York: Doubleday, 1952), 102. Fleur Cowles, in another anti-Evita book, also claimed the meeting was conducted through intermediaries and dealt with the position of honorary president. Fleur Cowles, *Bloody Precedent* (New York: Random House, 1951), 187. John Barnes, in his compilation of anti-Evita stories titled *Evita, First Lady: A Biography of Eva Perón* (New York: Grove Press, 1978), 67, claimed that Evita wanted to be president of the Sociedad de Beneficencia. The debunking of the Evita myths began with Julie M. Taylor, *Eva Perón: The Myths of a Woman* (Chicago: University of Chicago Press, 1979); and Marysa Navarro and Nicolas Fraser, *Eva Perón* (London: André Deutsch, 1980). Neither book, however, explored this myth in depth. One unpublished source in which it is discussed is Peter Ross, "Policy Formation and Implementation of Social Welfare in Peronist Argentina, 1943–55," Ph.D. dissertation, University of New South Wales, Sydney, 1988. I thank Marta Goldberg for her comments about comic opera.

19. Alicia Dujovne Ortiz, *Eva Perón: La biografía* (Buenos Aires: Aguilar, 1995), 150.

20. Mariano Plotkin, *Mañana es San Perón* (Buenos Aires: Ariel Historia Argentina, 1993).

21. An earlier version of this story can be found in Donna J. Guy, "La 'verdadera historia' de la Sociedad de Beneficencia," in *La política social antes de la política social (Caridad, beneficencia y política social en Buenos Aires, siglos XVII a XX)*, ed. José Luis Moreno (Buenos Aires: Trama Editorial/Promoteo Libros, 2000), 321–41.

22. *La Tribuna*, June 13, 1946. I thank Barbara Tenenbaum and Noelle Villafuerte for their help retrieving this information.

23. *La Tribuna*, 24 June 1946, recounts the recriminations taken against the authors of the petition to Congress. In retaliation, on June 26 *La Tribuna* included a copy of the original petition.

24. *La Tribuna*, July 11, 1946.

25. Senadores, *Diario de Sesiones*, July 25, 1946, 1: 472–73.

26. AGN, Fondo Sociedad de Beneficencia, *Libro de Actas*, T. 35, July 26, 1946, foja 309.

27. AGN, Fondo Sociedad de Beneficencia, *Libro de Actas*, tomo 35, July 26, 1946, fojas 305–10; the quote is on foja 310. For the *La Prensa* clipping, see AGN, Archivo Intermedio, Society of Beneficence Ministerio del Interior.

28. For the historiographical controversy, see Guy, "La 'verdadera' historia de la Sociedad de Beneficencia," in Moreno, *La política social*, 321–41.

29. AGN, Fondo Sociedad de Beneficencia, *Libro de Actas*, tomo 33, December 10, 1943, fojas 199–200.

30. AGN, Fondo Sociedad de Beneficencia, *Libro de Actas*, tomo 33, June 30, 1944, foja 370.

31. AGN, Fondo Sociedad de Beneficencia, *Libro de Actas*, tomo 34, August 20, 1944, fojas 65–66.

32. AGN, Fondo Sociedad de Beneficencia, *Libro de Actas*, tomo 36, 30 December, 1946, foja 2. Compare this to Perón's statement in the *La Prensa* clipping cited above.

33. "A las madres laboristas: Debe cuidarse a los hijos porque son el futuro de la patria," *El Laborista*, March 2, 1946, 7; "Al pobre le está vedado tener hijos: No le alquilan habitación a un matrimonio porque tiene dos niñitos de corta edad," *El Laborista*, April 23, 1946, 6.

34. "Créose la Secretaría de Salud Pública: Designóse al Dr. Ramón Carrillo," *El Laborista*, May 30, 1946, 3; "Estudiase la adopción legal en la Argentina," *El Laborista*, June 11, 1946, 7.

35. "La Sociedad de Beneficencia no cumple con su verdadera misión," *El Laborista*, July 11, 1946, 8.

36. " 'No debe ser' Sociedad de Beneficencia," *El Laborista*, August 3, 1948, 6.

37. AGN, Fondo Perón, Ministerio de Asuntos Técnicos, Legajo 677, Sociedad de Beneficencia de la Capital, Proyecto de Estatuto elevado por esta intervención al Sr. Secretario de Salud Pública, January 10, 1947, Cap. III, art. 7, 9. "La intervención a la Sociedad de Beneficencia debe ser urgentemente llevada a cabo con rigor: Queremos colegios, no cárceles, es lo que piden los ex-alumnos," *El Laborista*, August 4, 1946, 9; "Llegó la hora de justicia: Fue intervenida la Sociedad de Beneficencia. Rotundo Triunfo de EL LABORISTA," *El Laborista*, September 7, 1946, 1.

38. AGN, Fondo Perón, Ministerio de Asuntos Técnicos, Legajo 677, Sociedad de Beneficencia de la Capital, Proyecto de Estatuto elevado por esta intervención al Sr. Secretario de Salud Pública. 1947. Informe del Sr. Osorio desfavorable al proyecto presentado por la Secretaría de Salud Pública.

39. AGN, Fondo Sociedad de Beneficencia, *Libro de Actas*, tomo 35, October 4, 1946, fojas 364–66.

40. AGN, Fondo Sociedad de Beneficencia, *Libro de Actas*, tomo 36, foja 22, December 7, 1946.

41. Sociedad de Beneficencia, *Reseña de la obra realizada por la intervención en la Sociedad de Beneficencia de la Capital, en su primer año, 1946 setiembre 1947* (Buenos Aires, privately printed, 1947), 41–42, 123.

42. AGN, Fondo Sociedad de Beneficencia, *Libro de Actas*, tomo 36, December 7, 1946, foja 21.

43. I thank Sra. Liliana Crespi of the Archivo General de la Nación for information provided in e-mail correspondence.

44. See the *La Prensa* clipping, May 17, 1947, in AGN, Archivo Intermedio, Society of Beneficence Ministerio del Interior.

45. Mariano Ben Plotkin, *Mañana es San Perón: A Cultural History of Perón's Argentina*, trans. Keith Zahniser (Wilmington, Del.: Scholarly Resources, 2003), 203.

46. Diputados, *Diario de Sesiones*, September 22 and 23, 1948, 5:3891.

47. Diputados, *Diario de Sesiones*, September 22 and 23, 1948, 5:3891; speech of Oscar Albrieu of La Rioja, September 22–23, 1948, 5:3894, 3896.

48. Diputados, *Diario de Sesiones*, September 22 and 23, 1948, 5:3891; August 4, 1949, 3:2182, 2193.

49. Benegas Lynch (h) and Krause, *En defensa de los más necesitados*, 140n. Sandra Deutsch's research on Jewish women's organizations has revealed similar anxieties among groups not necessarily involved with welfare activities (telephone conversation with the author, July 2, 2005).

50. Peter Ross, "Policy Formation," 248–49.

51. Presidencia de la Nación, Subsecretaria de Informes, Dirección General del Registro Nacional, *Reforma de la Constitución Nacional sancionada por la Convención Nacional Constituyente, el 11 de marzo de 1949, en la ciudad de Buenos Aires*, 2 vols. (Buenos Aires: n.p., 1950), 2:648.

52. *La Constitución de 1949 comentada por sus autores* (Buenos Aires: Editorial El Coloquio, 1975), 222–25.

53. Marcela García Sebastiani, "The Other Side of Peronist Argentina: Radicals and Socialists in the Political Opposition to Perón (1946–1955)," *Journal of Latin American Studies* 35.2 (2003): 311–29.

54. Diputados, *Diario de Sesiones*, March 5, 1947, 1946, 10:497–501; May 8–9, 1947, 1:386–88.

55. The plan dealt much more specifically with issues related to workers. República Argentina, Secretaría Técnica, *Plan de gobierno, 1947–51*, 2 vols. (Buenos Aires: n.p., 1946). An examination of Perón's early speeches reveals similar characteristics. See the Latin American Network Information Center collection, available at the Web site of the University of Texas.

56. Senadores, *Diario de Sesiones*, August 29, 1947, 2:243.

57. Diputados, *Diario de Sesiones*, June 23, 1948, 2:1181–87.

58. Diputados, *Diario de Sesiones*, June 23, 1948, 2:1188.

59. Diputados, *Diario de Sesiones*, June 23, 1948, 2:1181–87.

60. Diputados, *Diario de Sesiones*, June 24–25, 1948, 2:1200.

61. Diputados, *Diario de Sesiones*, June 24–25, 1948, 2:1213.

62. Law No. 13.252, Senadores, *Diario de Sesiones*, 1948, 4:3302–4.

63. ACNNAF, Legajo 50.163.

64. ACNNAF, Legajo 64.590.

65. ACNNAF, Legajo 51.895.

66. ACNNAF, Legajo 58.386.

67. ACNNAF, Legajo 48.638.

68. Eduardo Elena, "What the People Want: State Planning and Political Participation in Peronist Argentina, 1946–1955," *Journal of Latin American Studies* 37.1 (2005): 81–108, explores the topic of public works.

69. AGN, Fondo Perón, Ministerio de Asuntos Técnicos, Legajo 341, Letter of Carlos Alberto Rey, Mercedes, January 28, 1952.

70. AGN, Fondo Perón, Ministerio de Asuntos Técnicos, Legajo 445, December 1951, Córdoba, letter from Vecinas del Barrio Central asking for a house where children could stay while parents are at work.

71. AGN, Fondo Perón, Ministerio de Asuntos Técnicos, Legajo 341, letter of Teófilo Baidaff, Buenos Aires and Santa Fe, December 7, 1951.

72. AGN, Fondo Perón, Ministerio de Asuntos Técnicos, Legajo 341, letter from Peronista Mujeres que traban en la provincia de Buenos Aires, La Plata, December 27, 1951.

73. AGN, Fondo Perón, Ministerio de Asuntos Técnicos, Legajo 341, letter from Raul Eduardo Aubone, January 30, 1952.

74. AGN, Fondo Perón, Ministerio de Asuntos Técnicos, Legajo 341, letter from President María A. Side Zagni, Asesora, El Club de Madres de la Escuela Nacional #256 [Mothers' Club of the National School #256] Tucumán, El

Colmenar, January 1951; letter from Mario Crenovich, Buenos Aires, December 5, 1951; letter from Silvia Argentina Mazzantini, Rosario, December 18, 1951; letter from E. M. de Echeverría, Santa Fe, n.d.; letter from Guillermo Garvio, December 31, 1951; letter from Rosa Famá Traci, Córdoba, January 25, 1952.

75. *Segundo Plan Quinquenal de la Nación Argentina*, Ley 14.184 (Buenos Aires: Ediciones Hechos e Ideas, 1954), 485.

76. Archivo IWO, "Informe de la 'Soroptomis' por el año 1944," manuscript, 14; *Mundo Israelita*, January 18, 1947, "Han tenido éxito las gestiones de la DAIA para lograr que mil niños judíos ingresen al país," 7.

77. Sociedad de Damas Israelitas de Beneficencia, *Memoria*, 1941, 14–15, 30, 37.

78. Private inheritances that year reached 47,000 pesos out of 276,807.84 taken in, which was highly unusual. *Mundo Israelita*, June 26, 1943, 12.

79. Sociedad de Damas Israelitas de Beneficencia, *Memoria*, 1950–51, 15–16, 42.

80. Bertha Bairach, for example, still had a father, uncle, and disabled brother living in Buenos Aires. As an adolescent she finally went to live with her father and worked in his garment factory, eventually taking it over until it closed. Bairach interview with the author, September 23, 2001.

81. *Mundo Israelita*, October 4, 1941, 8. Hogar Infantil Israelita Argentina, *Memoria y balance general*, 1946–47, 48–49.

82. Archivo IWO, Hogar Infantil Israelita Argentina, *Memoria y balance general*, 1946–47, 39. *Memoria, 1985–86*, unpublished document.

83. Hogar Infantil Israelita Argentina, *Memoria y balance general*, 27 ejercicio, 1954–55, 33.

84. Archivo Turkow, *Judaica* 8.85 (July 1935): 282; Archivo IWO, Asilo Israelita Argentino de Ancianos y Huérfanos, *Memoria y balance general*, 1938–39, 16, and *Memoria y balance general*, 1940, 11.

85. Archivo IWO, *Mundo Israelita*, January 9, 1943, 7; Archivo IWO, Caja Hogar Israelita Burzaco, Asilo Israelita de Ancianos y Huérfanos, *Informe presentado por la Comisión Honoraria de Arquitectos*, 1943, n.p.

86. Archivo IWO, letter from President Moses Kleinman, Hogar Israelita Argentino para Ancianos y Huérfanos to Feige Gavinoser, March 1952; Archivo IWO, *Mundo Israelita*, September 27, 1952, advertisement for Hogar entitled "A Call from the Homes of Burzaco that All Jews should Heed," 2; Archivo IWO, Caja Hogar Israelita Burzaco, *Album-Asilo Israelita Argentino*, n.d. See, for example, the poem on page 6: "We are sad orphans, pariahs, weak leaves that the wind has tossed / We are everyone's brothers, we are weak children / In time we have forgotten the mother with her caresses.

87. Patronato de la Infancia, *Libro de Actas*, Vol. 12, 1921–24, Session 24, foja 255; Vol. 15, 1931–34, Session 36, June 20, 1934, foja 333; Vol. 16, Session 5, August 4, 1937, foja 285–86.

88. Patronato de la Infancia, *Libro de Actas*, Vol. 18, Session 30, May 13, 1942, foja 58; Session 33, June 3, 1942, foja 71; Session 3, July 2, 1942, foja 84.

89. Patronato de la Infancia, *Libro de Actas*, Vol. 19, December 26, 1945, fojas 228–29; May 22, 1946, foja 249; May 29, 1946, fojas 52–253; Dec. 11, 1946, fojas 368–69; Vol. 20, May 12, 1948, foja 153; August 4, 1948, foja 185; 4, June 20, 1949, foja 315; Vol. 22, April 13, 1955, foja 13.

90. Patronato Español, *1912–2002 90 años al servicio de la comunidad*, 27–33.

91. Ibid., 149; AGN, Archivo Intermedio, Fundación Eva Perón, Consejo de Administración, *Libro de Actas*, August 25, 1952, foja 10; September 22, fojas 25–27; November 16, 1952, foja 46; *Libro de Actas*, September 13, 1954, foja 1.

92. AGN, Fondo Perón, Ministerio de Asuntos Técnicos, Presidencia de la Nación, Ministerio de Asuntos Técnicos, *Servicio Estadístico Oficial de la República Argentina, La delincuencia infantil en la Capital Federal. Boletín Diario Secreto*, No. 608, August 8, 1952, 2–3.

Conclusion

1. AGN, Archivo Fílmico, *Fin de semana*.

2. Enrique Medina, *Las tumbas* (Buenos Aires: Ediciones de la Flor, 1972). See also Lila Caimari's indictment of the prison system in her *Apenas un delincuente*.

3. Susana Bianchi, *Catolicismo y peronismo: Religión y política en la Argentina, 1943–1955* (Buenos Aires: Trama Editorial/Promoteo Libros, 2001), 149–58.

4. Rafael Gagliano, "Consideraciones sobre la adolescencia en el período," in *Discursos pedagógicos e imaginario social en el peronismo (1945–1955)*, ed. Adriana Puiggrós (Buenos Aires: Editorial Galerna, 1995), 183.

5. Isabella Cosse, "Él orden familiar en tiempos de cambio político: Familia y filiación ilegítima durante el primer peronismo (1946–1955)," in *Generando el peronismo: Estudios de cultura, política y género (1946–1955)*, ed. Karina Inés Ramacciotti and Adriana María Valobra (Buenos Aires: Editorial Proyecto, 2003), 190–95; Isabella Cosse, *Estigmas de nacimiento: Peronismo y orden familiar, 1946–1955* (Buenos Aires: Fondo de Cultura Económica, 2006).

6. Ross, "Policy Formation and Implementation of Social Welfare in Peronist Argentina," 266.

7. Federación Argentina de Apoyo Familiar, 1994 newsletter. See also the information provided at the Web site of the Federación Argentina de Apoyo Familiar.

Bibliography

Archives

Archivo Centro de Documentación e Información sobre Judaísmo Argentina "Mark Turkow," AMIA (Archivo Turkow)

Archivo Consejo Nacional de Niñez, Adolescencia y Familia (ACNNAF)

Archivo General de la Nación (AGN)

    Archivo Fílmico

    Archivo Intermedio: Ministerio del Interior; Fondo Fundación Eva Perón

    Defensoría de Menores

    División Poder Judicial, Tribunales Civiles, La Plata

    Fondo Ministerio de Justicia e Instrucción Pública (MJIP)

    Fondo Perón

    Fondo Sociedad de Beneficencia

Archivo General de la Provincia de Tucumán (AGT)

    Sección Judicial

Archivo Histórico de la Pampa

    Fondo Justicia

Archivo Instituto Científico Judío (IWO)

    Asilo Israelita Argentino para Ancianos y Huérfanos: *Libro de Actas*; Child Registry

    Hogar Infantil Israelita Argentina: *Libro de Actas*; Registration Book

    Sociedad de Socorros de Damas Israelitas: *Libro de Actas*

Archivo Patronato de la Infancia

    Libro de Actas; *Memorias*

Archivo Patronato Español

    Libro de Actas; *Memorias*

Archivo Templo Libertad

    Sociedad de Socorros de Damas Israelitas de Beneficencia: *Reseña sobre la marcha de la Sociedad de Socorros de Damas Israelitas*, published under different names, 1948–1952.

Asilo Argentino de Huérfanas Israelitas: *Memoria y balance general*, published under different names, 1918–1952.
Columbia University Oral History Archive
  Eduardo Colom interview, 1972

Public Documents

Argentine Republic. *Código Civil de la República Argentina*. Buenos Aires: Pablo E. Coni, 1874.

——. Congreso Nacional. Cámara de Diputados. *Diario de Sesiones*, 1880–1955. Buenos Aires.

——. Dirección Nacional de Asistencia Social. *Reglamentaciones*. Buenos Aires.

——. Ministerio del Interior. Departamento Nacional de Higiene. *Guía oficial. Datos para la historia. Organización actual. División y funcionamiento. Legislación sanitaria argentina. Nóminas de profesionales y establecimientos de toda la nación.* Buenos Aires: Luis J. Maisonnave, 1913.

——. Ministerio de Justicia e Instrucción Pública. *Resultados generales del Primero Censo Carcelario de la República Argentina*. Buenos Aires: Talleres Gráficos de la Penitenciaría Nacional, 1909.

——. Ministry of Justice and Public Instruction. *The Prevention of Juvenile Delinquency in the Field of Legislation and Social Work in Argentina. A Survey Ordered by Dr. Antonio Sagarna, Secretary of Justice and Public Instruction on the Occasion of the First International Child's Congress at Geneva, August 24–28, 1925.* Buenos Aires: Cía General de Fósforos, 1925.

——. Ministerio de Relaciones Exteriores y Culto. Reformatorio de Menores Abandonados y Delincuetes. *Memoria*. Buenos Aires: Ministerio de Relaciones Exteriores y Culto, 1924.

——. Ministerio de Relaciones Exteriores y Culto. Dirección de Administración. *Primera Conferencia Nacional de Asistencia Social*. 3 vols. Buenos Aires: Enrique L. Frigerio e Hijo, 1934.

——. Ministerio de Salud Pública. *Memoria correspondiente al período junio 1946 a mayo 1952*. Buenos Aires: Departamento de Talleres Gráficos, 1952.

——. Ministerio de Trabajo y Previsión. Dirección Nacional de Asistencia Social. Ley 13.341. *Decreto Reglamentario 20492/49. Reglamentaciones*. Buenos Aires, 1950.

——. Patronato Nacional de Menores. *Primera Conferencia Nacional Sobre Infancia Abandonada y Delincuente*. Buenos Aires: Imprenta Colonia Hogar "Ricardo Gutiérrez," 1933.

——. Secretaría Técnica. *Plan de gobierno, 1947–51*. 2 vols. Buenos Aires, 1946.

——. *Segundo Plan Quinquenal de la Nación Argentina*, Ley 14.184. Buenos Aires: Ediciones Hechos e Ideas, 1954.

——. Policía de la Capital Federal. *Memorias*. N.p., 1880–1940.

Buenos Aires Municipality. *Anuario estadístico de la ciudad de Buenos Aires*. Buenos Aires, 1880–1930.

———. Asistencia Pública. Movimiento del Consultorio de Niños de la Asistencia Pública (Casa Central). Buenos Aires, 1899.

———. *Censo general de población, edificación, comercio e industrias de la ciudad de Buenos Aires*. 2 vols. Buenos Aires: Cía. Sudamericana de Billetes de Banco, 1889.

———. *Censo general de población, edificación, comercio e industrias de la ciudad de Buenos Aires,* 2 vols. Buenos Aires: Cía. Sudamericana de Billetes de Banco, 1889.

———. *Censo general de la población, edificación, comercio e industrias de la ciudad de Buenos Aires*. 3 vols., ed. Alberto Martínez. Buenos Aires: Compañía Sudamericana de Billetes de Banco, 1910.

———. *Memoria de la Dirección General de la Administración Sanitaria y Asistencia Pública correspondiente al año 1910*. Buenos Aires: La Semana Médica, 1911.

———. *Memorias de la Dirección General de la Administración Sanitaria y Asistencia Pública correspondiente a los años 1906, 1907, 1908, y 1909*. Buenos Aires: La Semana Médica, 1910.

———. *Patronato y Asistencia de la Infancia en la capital de la república: Trabajos de la comisión especial*. Buenos Aires: El Censor, 1892.

———. *Reglamento provisorio de la Casa de Corrección de Menores Varones de la Capital*. Buenos Aires: La Defensa, 1899.

———. *Statistical Annuary of the City of Buenos Aires*. Buenos Aires, 1912.

Buenos Aires Province. *Asistencia social y protección a la infancia en la provincia de Buenos Aires*. La Plata, 1937.

Córdoba Province. *Anuario de la dirección general de estadística de la provincia de Córdoba*. N.p., 1880–1950.

Mendoza Province. *Anuario de la dirección general de estadística de la provincia de Mendoza*. N.p., 1880–1950.

Tucumán Province. *Anuario de estadística de la provincia de Tucumán*. N.p., 1880–1950.

Journals and Newspapers

American Historical Review, 1998.

Americas, special issue: "Rise of the Welfare State in Latin America," 58.1 (July 2001).

Anales de Biotipología, Eugenesia y Medicina Social, 1933–1938.

Archivos de la Secretaría de Salud Pública, 1949.

Boletín del Instituto de Maternidad de la Sociedad de Beneficencia de la Capital, 1929–1944.

Boletín del Museo Social Argentino, 1912–1947.

Caras y Caretas, 1900–1910.
Contemporary Sociology, 1993.
Criterio, 1928–1948.
Gender and History, "International Feminisms," special issue, 10.3 (fall 1998).
Hijo Mío, 1936.
Infancia y Juventud, 1936–1942.
El Laborista, 1940–1948.
Mundo Israelita, 1924–1955.
La Opinión, 1974.
Political Research Quarterly, 1999.
La Prensa, 1880–1955.
Revista de la Policía de la Capital, 1905–1907.
Revista Penitenciaria, 1905.
La Semana Médica, 1880–1940.
Theory and Society, 1995.
La Tribuna, 1946.
La Vanguardia, 1880–1920.
Vida femenina, 1934–1937.

Published Sources

Acha, Omar, and Paula Halperín, eds. *Cuerpos, géneros, identidades: Estudios de historia de género en Argentina*. Buenos Aires: Ediciones del Signo, 2000.
Aguirre, Carlos A., and Robert Buffington, eds. *Reconstructing Criminality in Latin America*. Wilmington, Del.: Scholarly Resources, 2000.
Alayón, Norberto. *La historia del trabajo social en Argentina*. 3rd ed. Buenos Aires: Editorial Espacio, 1992.
Allen, Ann Taylor. *Feminism and Motherhood in Germany, 1800–1914: The Maternal Dilemma*. New Brunswick, N.J.: Rutgers University Press, 1991.
———. *Feminism and Motherhood in Western Europe, 1890–1970: The Maternal Dilemma*. New York: Palgrave, 1995.
Alonso, Guillermo V. *Política y seguridad social en la Argentina de los '90*. Buenos Aires: FLACSO, Miño y Dávila Editores, 2000.
Altbáum, Clara Ride. *Delincuencia infantil*. Buenos Aires: Artes Gráficas Belgrano, 1939.
Alvarez, José M. *La lucha por la salud: Su estado actual en la ciudad de Córdoba*. Buenos Aires: M. Biedma é Hijo, 1896.
Alvarez, Sonia. "Lo social asistencial en Salta: Convergencias y divergencias, Beneficencia laica, filantropía, higienistas y asistencial estatal (1900–1945)." Paper presented at the seventeenth Jornadas de Historia Económica, Tucumán, Argentina, 2000.
Anderson, Benedict R. *Imagined Communities: Reflections on the Origin and Spread of Nationalism*. London: Verso.

Anselmi, Jorge. *La prevención en la delincuencia prematura*. Buenos Aires: Editorial GLEM, 1938.

Arana, Alberto Meyer. *Colonias para menores: Bases que han servido para la organización de la Colonia de Menores Varones (Márcos Paz)*. Buenos Aires: Talleres Gráficos de la Penitenciaría Nacional, 1906.

Aráoz Alfaro, Gregorio. *Bosquejo de plan de profilaxis y otros trabajos sobre lucha contra la tuberculosis*. Buenos Aires: "Las Ciencias," 1918.

———. *El libro de las madres*. Buenos Aires: Cabaut y Cía., 1922.

———. *Nuestros males sociales: Como proteger eficazmente mujeres y niños*. Rosario: El Círculo, 1925.

———. *Política demográfica: Natalidad y mortalidad*. Buenos Aires: Imprenta Coni, 1940.

———. *Profilaxis de abandono del niño*. Buenos Aires: Talleres Gráficos A. Flaiban, 1919.

———. *Sobre la organización de la protección y asistencia de la infancia*. Buenos Aires: Talleres Gráficos del Ministerio de Agricultura de la Nación, 1919.

Araya, José L. *Asistencia social al menor*. Rosario: Editorial Rosario, 1945.

Archetti, Eduardo P. *Football, Polo and the Tango in Argentina*. Oxford: Berg, 1999.

Arenaza, Dr. Carlos de. *La infancia abandonada y delincuente y la Ley Agote: Conferencia leída en el Instituto Popular de Conferencias (agosto 19 de 1932)*. Buenos Aires: privately printed, 1932.

Arias, José. *Derecho de le familia*. Buenos Aires: Editorial Kraft, 1952.

Asociación "Universitarias Argentinas." *Primer Congreso Femenino Internacional de la República Argentina*. Buenos Aires: A. Ceppi, 1911.

Atkinson, Clarissa W. *The Oldest Vocation: Christian Motherhood in the Middle Ages*. Ithaca, N.Y.: Cornell University Press, 1991.

Augustine-Adams, Kif. "'She Consents Implicitly': Women's Citizenship, Marriage, and Liberal Political Theory in Late-Nineteenth- and Early-Twentieth-Century Argentina." *Journal of Women's History* 13.4 (2002): 8–30.

Baily, Samuel. *Immigrants in the Lands of Promise: Italians in Buenos Aires and New York City, 1870–1914*. Ithaca, N.Y.: Cornell University Press, 1999.

Barnes, John. *Evita, First Lady: A Biography of Eva Perón*. New York: Grove Press, 1978.

Barrera, Jaime. "¿Es un delito el aborto?" In *Primer Congreso Latino-Americano de Criminología: Realizado en la ciudad de Buenos Aires (R.A.) el 25 al 31 de Julio de 1938*. Vol. 3. Buenos Aires: Talleres Gráficos de la Penitenciaría Nacional, 1951.

Begino, Juana María. "El Congreso Nacional del Niño: La 'Liga para Los Derechos de la Mujer y del Niño y sus trabajos.'" *Cara y Caretas* (1912): n.p.

Belmartino, Susana, Carlos Bloch, Ana V. Persello, and Hugo Quiroga. *Las instituciones de salud en la Argentina, desarrollo y crisis*. Buenos Aires: Secretaría de Ciencia y Técnica, Area de Estudios e Investigacíon en Ciencias Sociales para la Salud, 1987.

Benegas Lynch (h), Alberto, and Martín Krause. *En defensa de los más necesitados*. Buenos Aires: Editorial Atlántida, 1998.

Benítez, Miguel. *Vagancia infantil.* Buenos Aires: n.p., 1929.

Bermann, Gregorio. *Los menores desamparados y delincuentes en Córdoba: Informe presentado al Poder Ejecutivo de la provincia de Córdoba sobre el estado antropológico, médico-social y criminológico de los menores delincuentes y desválidos.* Córdoba: Talleres de la Penitenciaría Nacional, 1933.

——. "Estudio de menores abandonados y delincuentes." In *Actas de la Primera Conferencia Latino-Americana de Neurología, Psiquiatría, y Medicina Legal.* Vol. 2. Buenos Aires: Imprenta de la Universidad, 1929.

Bialet Massé, Juan. *El estado de las clases obreras argentinas a comienzos del siglo.* Córdoba: Universidad Nacional de Córdoba, 1904.

Bianchi, Susana. *Catolicismo y peronismo: Religión y política en la Argentina, 1943–1955.* Buenos Aires: Trama Editorial/Promoteo Libros, 2001.

Blackwilder, Julia Kirk, and Lyman L. Johnson. "Changing Criminal Patterns in Buenos Aires, 1890–1914." *Journal of Latin American Studies* 14.2 (1982): 359–79.

Bock, Gisela, and Pat Thane, eds. *Maternity and Gender Policies: Women and the Rise of the European Welfare States, 1880s–1950s.* London: Routledge, 1991.

Bonner, Michael, Mine Ener, and Amy Singer Bonner, eds. *Poverty and Charity in Middle Eastern Contexts.* Albany: State University of New York, 2003.

Bordot, Enrique. *Un dispensario de lactantes de 1910 a 1921: Estadística y consideraciones sobre mortalidad infantil* (Buenos Aires: Las Ciencias, 1922).

Boswell, John. *The Kindness of Strangers: The Abandonment of Children in Western Europe from Late Antiquity to the Renaissance.* New York: Pantheon Press, 1988.

Bravo, María Celia, and Vanesa Teitelbaum. "Entrega de niños, infanticidios y la construcción de una imagen de la maternidad en Tucumán (segunda mitad del siglo xix)." In *Temas de mujeres: Perspectivas de género.* Tucumán: Universidad Nacional de Tucumán, 1998. 81–96.

Brinton, Crane. *French Revolutionary Legislation on Illegitimacy.* Cambridge, Mass.: Harvard University Press, 1939.

Broder, Sherry. *Tramps, Unfit Mothers, and Neglected Children: Negotiating the Family in Late Nineteenth-Century Philadelphia.* Philadelphia: University of Pennsylvania Press, 2002.

Bullrich, Eduardo J. *Asistencia social de menores.* Buenos Aires, 1919.

Bunge, Alejandro E. *Una nueva Argentina.* Buenos Aires: Hyspamerica, 1940.

Bunge, Carlos Antonio. *Estudios pedagógicos.* Madrid: Espasa-Calpe, 1927.

Caimari, Lila M. *Apenas un delincuente: Crimen, castigo y cultura en la Argentina, 1880–1955.* Buenos Aires: Siglo Veintiuno Editores, 2004.

——. "Whose Criminals Are These? Church, State, and Patronatos and the Rehabilitation of Female Convicts (Buenos Aires, 1890–1940)," *Americas* 54.2 (1997): 185–208.

Camaña, Raquel. "Femeninidad." *Atlántida* 13 (1914): 108–10.

Cámara de Apelaciones en lo Criminal y Correccional de la Capital. *Capital Federal por la Cámara de Apelaciones en lo Criminal Los Tribunales de Menores en la*

Ener, Mine. *Managing Egypt's Poor and the Politics of Benevolence, 1800–1952.* Princeton, N.J.: Princeton University Press, 2002.

Etchegaray, Máximo. *Higiene y puericultura.* Buenos Aires: Imprenta G. Kraft, 1915.

Feinmann, Enrique. *Profilaxis social del delito.* Buenos Aires: Imprenta y Casa Editora de Coni Hermanos, 1913.

Fernández, Maria Esta Alejandra Landaburu, and Flavia Macías. "Esfera pública, moralidad y mujeres de la elite: Sociedad de Beneficencia de Tucumán (1860–1920)." In *Temas de Mujeres: Perspectivas de Género.* Tucumán: Centro de Estudios Históricos Interdisciplinarios sobre las Mujeres, Facultad de Filosofía y Letras, Universidad Nacional de Tucumán, 1998. 120–27.

Feroli, Néstor. *La Fundación Eva Perón.* 2 vols. Buenos Aires: Centro Editor de América Latina, 1990.

Fildes, Valerie, Lara Marks, and Hilary Marland, eds. *Women and Children First: International Maternal and Infant Welfare, 1870–1945.* London: Routledge, 1992.

Fingard, Judith, and Jane Guilford, eds. *Mothers of the Municipality: Women, Work, and Social Policy in Post-1945 Halifax.* Toronto: University of Toronto Press, 2005.

Fitzgerald, Maureen. *Habits of Compassion: Irish Catholic Nuns and the Origins of New York's Welfare System, 1830–1920.* Urbana: University of Illinois Press, 2006.

Flores, María [Mary Main]. *The Woman with the Whip: Eva Perón.* Garden City, N.Y.: Doubleday, 1952.

Foucault, Michel. *Discipline and Punish: The Birth of the Prison.* Trans. Alan Sheridan. New York: Vintage Books, 1979.

Fresco, Manuel A. *Mis mensajes 1936–1940.* Buenos Aires: Talleres gráficos "Damiano," 1941.

Fuchs, Rachel. *Abandoned Children: Foundlings and Child Welfare in Nineteenth-Century France.* Albany: State University of New York Press, 1984.

Gache, Roberto. *La delincuencia precoz (niñez y adolescencia).* Buenos Aires: J Lajouane, 1916.

García Méndez, Emilio, and Elías Carranza, eds. *Infancia, adolescencia y control social en América Latina: Argentina, Colombia, Costa Rica, Uruguay, Venezuela.* Buenos Aires: Ediciones Depalma, 1990.

García Sebastiani, Marcela. "The Other Side of Peronist Argentina: Radicals and Socialists in the Political Opposition to Perón, 1946–1955." *Journal of Latin American Studies* 35.2 (May 2003): 311–29.

Giménez, Angel. *El torno libre.* Buenos Aires: Juan H. Kidd. Cía., 1922.

Giménez, Daniel M. *Gender, Pensions and Social Citizenship in Latin America.* Santiago: United Nations/ECLAC, 2005.

Girbal-Blacha, Noemí. "El estado neoconservador, el intervencionismo económico y la sociedad de los años treinta." In *Estado, sociedad y economia en la Argentina 1930–1997,* ed. Noemí Girbal-Blacha. Quilmes: Universidad Nacional de Quilmes Ediciones, 2001. 27–58.

Gomes, Angela de Castro, Ana Frega, Mónica Campins, Horacio Gaggero, and Alicia Garro. *Estado, corporativismo y acción social en Brasil, Argentina y Uruguay.* Buenos Aires: Fundación Simón Rodríguez, 1992.

González Leandri, Ricardo. *Curar, persuadir, gobernar: La construcción histórica de la profesión médica en Buenos Aires, 1852–1886.* Madrid: Consejo Superior de Investigaciones Científicas, 1999.

Gordon, Linda. *The Great Arizona Abduction.* Cambridge, Mass.: Harvard University Press, 1999.

——. *Pitied but Not Entitled: Single Mothers and the History of Welfare, 1890–1935.* New York: Free Press, 1994.

——, ed. *Women, the State, and Welfare.* Madison: University of Wisconsin Press, 1990.

Gramsci, Antonio. *Letters from Prison.* New York: Harper and Row, 1973.

——. *The Prison Notebooks.* 2 vols. New York: Columbia University Press, 1992.

Gregorio Lavié, Lucila de. *La ciudadana: Para las mujeres que votan.* Buenos Aires: Macagno, Landa and Cía., 1948.

——. *Trayectoria de la condición social de las mujeres Argentinas.* Santa Fe: Universidad Nacional del Litoral, Instituto Social, 1945.

Guy, Donna J. "Feminists, Philanthropists, the Rise of the Welfare State and Child Welfare Policies. *Brújula* 4.1 (2006): 45–60.

——. "Girls in Prison: The Role of the Buenos Aires Casa Correccional de Mujeres as an Institution of Child Rescue, 1890–1940." In *Crime and Punishment in Latin American Law and Society since Late Colonial Times*, ed., Carlos Aguirre, Gilbert M. Joseph, and Ricardo D. Salvatore. Durham, N.C.: Duke University Press, 2001. 369–390.

——. "Introduction." *Americas* 58.1 (2001): 1–6.

——. "Niños abandonados en Buenos Aires (1880–1914) y el desarrollo del concepto de la madre." In *Mujeres y Cultura en la Argentina del siglo XIX*, ed., Lea Fletcher. Buenos Aires: Feminaria Editora, 1994. 217–26.

——. *Sex and Danger in Buenos Aires: Prostitution, Family, and Nation in Argentina.* Lincoln: University of Nebraska Press, 1991.

——. "La 'verdadera historia' de la Sociedad de Beneficencia." In *La política social antes de la política social (Caridad, beneficencia y política social en Buenos Aires, siglos XVII a XX)*, ed. José Luis Moreno. Buenos Aires: Trama Editorial/ Promoteo Libros, 2000. 321–41.

——. *White Slavery and Mothers Alive and Dead: The Troubled Meeting of Sex, Gender, Public Health, and Progress in Latin America.* Lincoln: University of Nebraska Press, 2000.

——. "Women's Organizations and Jewish Orphanages in Buenos Aires, 1918–1955." *Jewish History* 18.1 (2004): 75–93.

Hammond, Gregory Sowles. "Women Can Vote Now: Feminism and the Women's Suffrage Movement in Argentina, 1900–1955." Ph.D. dissertation, University of Texas, Austin, 2004.

Haney, Lynne. *Inventing the Needy: Gender and the Politics of Welfare in Hungary.* Berkeley: University of California Press, 2002.

Hecht, Tobias. *At Home in the Street: Street Children of Northeast Brazil.* Cambridge: Cambridge University Press, 1998.

——, ed. *Minor Omissions: Children in Latin American History and Society.* Madison: University of Wisconsin Press, 2002.

Herrera, Julio (h). *Redención y prevención: Ley orgánica de aplicación de la pena y de amparo social, Código del Niño.* Buenos Aires: n.p., 1949.

Hong, Young-Sun. *Welfare, Modernity, and the Weimar State, 1919–1933.* Princeton, N.J.: Princeton University Press, 1998.

Hurwitz, Samuel I. "Mutualismo y cooperación, bases de la asistencia social." *Judaica* 24 (1935): 273–86.

Ingegnieros, José. "Los niños vendedores de diarios y la delincuencia precoz." *Archivos de psiquiatría y criminología aplicadas a las ciencias afines* 7 (1908): 329–48.

Inter-American Commission of Women. "Report of the Inter-American Commission of Women to the Eighth International Conference of American States on the Political and Civil Rights of Women, Lima, December 1938," mimeograph. U.S. Library of Congress, Washington.

Kertzer, David. "Gender Ideology and Infant Abandonment in Nineteenth-Century Italy." *Journal of Interdisciplinary History* 22.1 (1991): 1–25.

——. *Sacrificed for Honor: Italian Infant Abandonment and the Politics of Reproductive Control.* Boston: Beacon Press, 1993.

Koven, Seth, and Sonya Michel. *Mothers of a New World: Maternalist Politics and the Origins of Welfare States.* New York: Routledge, 1993.

Lago, Carmelo Mesa. *Social Security in Latin America: Pressure Groups, Stratification and Inequality.* Pittsburgh: Pittsburgh University Press, 1978.

Landó, Juan Carlos. *Hacia la protección integral de la minoridad.* Buenos Aires: Editorial Depalma, 1950.

——. "Menores delincuentes." *Infancia y Juventud* 2 (1937): 17.

——. *Protección al menor: Teoría, Práctica, Soluciones.* Buenos Aires: Ediciones Depalma, 1957.

Lapalma de Emery, Celia. *Acción pública y privada en favor de la mujer y del niño en la República Argentina.* Buenos Aires: Alfa y Omega, 1910.

La Rocca, José. "Sobre la necesidad de una ley de adopción." *Infancia* 7.3 (1943): 430–36.

Lavrin, Asunción. *Women, Feminism, and Social Change in Argentina, Chile, and Uruguay, 1890–1940.* Lincoln: University of Nebraska Press, 1995.

League of Nations, Advisory Committee on Social Questions. *The Placing of Children in Families.* Vol. 1. Geneva: League of Nations, 1938.

Lerner, Gloria Rut. *El Asilo de Huérfanas Israelitas.* Unpublished paper, Universidad Nacional de Luján.

——. "La historia del Asilo Argentino de Huérfanas Israelitas." Tesis de licentiatura, Universidad Nacional de Luján, Argentina, 2001.

Levenson, Gregorio, Raúl Zaffaroni, Lucila Larrandat, Elías Newman, Pedro Cahn, and Eliseo Morales. *Chicos de la calle, Niños de la calle: Niños y adolescentes de máximo riesgo social.* Buenos Aires: Fundación Banco Mercantil Argentino, 1995.

Lezica Alucande Priouano, María Rosa. "Profilaxis de abandono en la primera infancia." In Patronato de la Infancia, *Segunda conferencia nacional de la infancia abandonada y delincuente.* Buenos Aires: Peuser, 1944.

Little, Cynthia Jefress. "The Society of Beneficence in Buenos Aires, 1823–1900." Ph.D. dissertation, Temple University, 1980.

Llan de Rosos, Martín. *Del infanticidio.* Buenos Aires: Stiller and Lass, 1885.

López del Carril, Julio J. *Legitimación adoptiva.* Buenos Aires: Abeledo-Perrot, 1964.

——. *Patria potestad, tutela y curatela.* Buenos Aires: Ediciones Depalma, 1993.

Lugones, Leopoldo *La menoría.* Buenos Aires: Biblioteca Policial, 1941.

Luisi, Paulina. *Algunas ideas sobre eugenia: Trabajo presentado al 1er Congreso Americano del Niño, Buenos Aires, 1916.* Montevideo: El Siglo Ilustrado, 1916.

Lynch, Katherine A. *Family, Class, and Ideology in Early Industrial France: Social Policy and the Working-Class Family.* Madison: University of Wisconsin Press, 1988.

MacKinnon, Aron S., and Jonathan D. Ablard, eds. *Unhealthy Interiors: Contestations at the Intersection of Public Health and Private Space. Studies in the Social Sciences* 38 (July 2005): 79–113.

Mazzeo, Victoria. *Mortalidad infantil en la ciudad de Buenos Aires (1856–1986).* Buenos Aires: Centro Editor de América Latina, 1993.

McCauley, Bernadette. *Who Shall Take Care of Our Sick? Roman Catholic Sisters and the Development of Catholic Hospitals in New York City.* Baltimore: Johns Hopkins University Press, 2005.

Mead, Karen. "Beneficent Maternalism: Argentine Motherhood in Comparative Perspective, 1880–1920." *Journal of Women's History* 12.3 (2000): 120–45.

——. "Gender, Welfare and the Catholic Church in Argentina: Conferencias de Señoras de San Vicente de Paul 1890–1916." *Americas* 58.1 (2001): 91–119.

——. "Oligarchs, Doctors and Nuns: Public Health and Beneficence in Buenos Aires, 1880–1914." Ph.D. dissertation, University of California, Santa Barbara, 1994.

Meckel, Richard A. *Save the Babies: American Public Health Reform and the Prevention of Infant Mortality 1850–1929.* Baltimore: Johns Hopkins University Press, 1990.

Medina, Enrique. *Las tumbas.* Buenos Aires: Ediciones de la Flor, 1972.

Meyer Arana, Alberto. *La caridad en Buenos Aires.* Vol. 1. Buenos Aires: Imprenta Sopena, 1911.

——. *Colonias para menores: Bases que han servido para la organización de la Colonia de Menores Varones (Márcos Paz).* Buenos Aires: Talleres Gráficos de la Penitenciaría Nacional, 1906.

Michel, Sonya. *Children's Interests/Mothers' Rights: The Shaping of America's Child Care Policy.* New Haven, Conn.: Yale University Press, 1999.

Moeller, Robert G. *Protecting Motherhood: Women and the Family in the Politics of Postwar West Germany.* Berkeley: University of California Press, 1993.

Moreno, José Luis, ed. *La política social antes de la política social (Caridad, beneficencia y política social en Buenos Aires, siglos XVII a XX).* Buenos Aires: Trama Editorial/Promoteo Libros, 2000.

Moreyra, Beatriz I. "La política social: Caridades, estado y sociedad civil en Córdoba (1900–1930)." Paper presented at the sixth Jornadas de Historia de las Mujeres y I Congreso Latinoamericano de Estudios de las Mujeres y de Género, Buenos Aires, August 2–5, 2000.

Moya, José C. *Cousins and Strangers: Spanish Immigrants in Buenos Aires, 1850–1930.* Berkeley: University of California Press, 1999.

Nari, Marcela María Alejandra. "El hogar, los niños, el esposo y la patria: La creación de la mujer-madre y el surgimiento del feminismo en la Argentina, 1899–1940." Ph.D. dissertation, Universidad Nacional de Buenos Aires, 1991.

Navarro, Marysa, and Nicolas Fraser. *Eva Perón.* London: André Deutsch, 1980.

Nelson, Ernesto. *La delincuencia juvenil.* 3rd ed. Buenos Aires: Editorial "La Facultad," 1941.

Novellino, Norberto José. *Nuevas leyes de familia comentadas y concordadas.* Buenos Aires: Editorial Temis Argentina, 1955.

Nuñez, Richard C. *Derecho penal argentino.* Buenos Aires: Editorial Bibliográfica Argentina, 1959.

Oderigo, Mario A. *Código Penal anotado.* 3rd ed. Buenos Aires: Editorial Depalma, 1965.

Organización de Estados Americanos, Instituto Interamericano del Niño. *Congreso Panamericanos del Niño: Ordenación sistemática de sus recomendaciones 1916–1963.* Montevideo: Organización de Estados Americanos, 1965.

Ortiz, Alicia Dujovne. *Eva Perón: La biografía.* Buenos Aires: Aguilar, 1995.

Pagani, Estela, and María Victoria Alcaraz. *Las nodrizas en Buenos Aires: Un estudio histórico (1880–1940).* Buenos Aires: Centro Editor de América Latina, 1988.

Palacios, Alfredo L. *La defensa del valor humano: Legislación social argentina.* Buenos Aires: Editorial Claridad, 1939.

———. *El dolor argentino: Plan sanitario y educativo de protección a los niños.* Buenos Aires: Editorial Claridad, 1938.

Pan American Child Congress. *Eighth Pan American Child Congress, Washington D.C., May 20, 1942.* Washington: U.S. Government Printing Office, 1948.

Passanante, María Ines. *Pobreza y acción social en la historia argentina.* Buenos Aires: Editorial Hvmanitas, 1987.

Patronato de la Infancia. *Cien años de amor: Centésimo aniversario del Patronato de la Infancia.* Buenos Aires: Patronato de la Infancia, 1993.

———. *Memoria de la Comisión Directiva del Patronato de la Infancia, 1897–mayo 1898.* Buenos Aires: Imprenta Argos, 1898.

———. *Memoria de la Comisión Directiva del Patronato de la Infancia correspondiente al período 10 de enero al 31 de diciembre de 1931.* Buenos Aires, 1932.

——. *Protección a la Infancia: Antecedentes para el estudio de una ley reunidos por los doctores Faustino Jorge y Alberto Mayer Arana, Vicepresidente 1° y Secretario del Patronato de la Infancia.* Buenos Aires: Imprenta Coni Hermanos, 1908.

Patronato Español. Instituto Nuestra Señora del Pilar Patronato Español. *"El pasado nos cuenta,"* 1912–2002: *90 años al servicio de la comunidad.* Buenos Aires: Asociación Civil Patronato Español, 2002.

Patronato Nacional de Menores. *Memoria de la Comisión Honoraria de Superintendencia de la Colonia Hogar Ricardo Gutiérrez, Instituto Tutelar de Menores y Patronato de la Infancia.* Buenos Aires: Imprenta Colonia Hogar Ricardo Gutiérrez, 1925.

——. *Primera conferencia nacional sobre infancia abandonada y delincuente.* Buenos Aires: Imprenta Colonia Hogar Ricardo Gutiérrez, 1934.

——. *Segunda conferencia nacional de la infancia abandonada y delincuente.* Buenos Aires: Peuser, 1944.

Peña Méndez, Carlos. "Proyecto de modificación a la ley 5010 de la provincia de Buenos Aires: Sobre asistencia de embarazadas indigentes." *Boletín del Instituto de Maternidad de la Sociedad de Beneficencia de la Capital* 12.1–2 (1943): 278–81.

Penna, José, and Horacio Madero. *La administración sanitaria y Asistencia Pública de la ciudad de Buenos Aires.* 2 vols. Buenos Aires: Guillermo Kraft, 1910.

Peralta Ramos, Alberto. "Concepto y organización del Instituto de Maternidad de la Sociedad de Beneficencia de Buenos Aires. "In *Primer Congreso Médico, Hispano-Lusitano-Americano, Sevilla, Octubre de 1924.* Buenos Aires: El Policlínico, 1924.

——. *El Instituto de Maternidad: Su historia, fines, construcción, costo y sostenimiento, organización, funcionamiento, etc.* Buenos Aires: Sociedad de Beneficencia de la Capital, 1935.

——. *Obstetrica, ginecología, puericultura: Documentos-memorias.* 3 vols. Buenos Aires: Mercatali, 1939.

Perón, Eva. *La palabra y el pensamiento y la acción de Eva Perón.* Buenos Aires: Editorial Freeland, 1973.

Petriella, Dinisio. *Los italianos en la historia del progreso argentino.* Buenos Aires: Asociación Dante Alighieri, 1985.

Plotkin, Mariano. *Freud in the Pampas: The Emergence and Development of a Psychoanalytic Culture in Argentina.* Stanford, Calif.: Stanford University Press, 2001.

——. *Mañana es San Perón.* Buenos Aires: Ariel Historia Argentina, 1993.

——. *Mañana es San Perón: A Cultural History of Perón's Argentina.* Trans. Keith Zahniser. Wilmington, Del.: Scholarly Resources, 2003.

Podestá, Manuel T. *Niños: Estudio médico-social.* Buenos Aires: Imprenta de la Patria Italiana, 1888.

Ponce, Aníbal. *Ambición y angustia de los adolescentes: Psicología de la adolescencia.* Buenos Aires: L. J. Rosso, 1936.

Premo, Bianca. *Children of the Father King: Youth, Authority, and Legal Minority in Colonial Lima.* Chapel Hill: University of North Carolina Press, 2005.

Primer Congreso Médico, Hispano-Lusitano-Americano, Sevilla octubre de 1924. Buenos Aires: El Policlínico, 1924.

Proceedings and Report of the Columbus Day Conferences Held in Twelve American Countries on October 12, 1923. New York: Inter-America Press, 1926.

Puiggrós, Adriana, ed. *Discursos pedagógicos e imaginario social en el peronismo (1945–1955).* Buenos Aires: Editorial Galerna, 1995.

Ramacciotti, Karin Inés, and Adriana María Valobra, eds. *Generando el peronismo: Estudios de cultura, política y género (1946–1955).* Buenos Aires: Editorial Proyecto, 2003.

Ransel, David L. *Mothers of Misery: Child Abandonment in Russia.* Princeton, N.J.: Princeton University Press, 1988.

Rawson de Dellepiane, Elvira. *Apuntes sobre higiene en la mujer.* Buenos Aires: Pablo E. Coni é Hijos, 1892.

Rébora, Juan Carlos. *La familia (Boceto sociológico y jurídico).* 2 vols. Buenos Aires: Juan Roldán and Cía., 1926.

Reca, Telma. *Delincuencia infantil: Delincuencia infantil en los Estados Unidos y en la Argentina.* Buenos Aires: Talleres Gráficos de la Penitenciaría Nacional, 1932.

Recalde, Héctor. *Beneficencia, asistencialismo estatal y previsión social.* 2 vols. Buenos Aires: Centro Editor de América Latina, 1991.

Remorino, Jerónimo. *La nueva legislación social argentina.* Buenos Aires: Ministerio de Relaciones Exteriores y Culto, 1953.

Rodríguez, Ana María. "Mujeres, estado y filantropía." Primer informe de avance, Beca de Iniciación, Consejo Nacional de Investigaciones Científicos y Técnicas, July 1996.

Rodríguez, Oscar. *Protección social del recien nacido: Bases para una legislación en la República Argentina.* Córdoba: Aniceto López, 1936.

Rodríguez de Ginoccio, Mercedes. "El Consejo de Mujeres de la República Argentina se preocupa de la mujer y del niño." In *Memoria del VII Congreso Panamerican del Niño reunido en la ciudad de México del 12 al 19 de Octubre de 1935.* Vol. 2. Mexico City: Talleres Gráficos de la Nación, 1937.

Rooke, Patricia T., and R. L. Schnell. *Discarding the Asylum: From Child Rescue to the Welfare State in English-Canada (1800–1950).* Lanham, Md.: University Press of America, 1983.

Ross, Peter. "Policy Formation and Implementation of Social Welfare in Peronist Argentina, 1943–55." Ph.D. dissertation, University of New South Wales, Sydney, 1988.

Rueda, Pedro. *Maternidad: Lecciones de puericultura e higiene infantil.* Rosario: Imprenta de la Universidad Nacional del Litoral, 1938.

Ruggiero, Kristin. "Honor, Maternity, and the Disciplining of Women: Infanticide in Late Nineteenth-Century Buenos Aires." *Hispanic American Historical Review* 72.3 (1992): 353–73.

——. "Not Guilty: Abortion and Infanticide in Nineteenth-Century Argentina." In

Reconstructing Criminality in Latin America, ed. Carlos A. Aguirre and Robert Buffington. Wilmington, Del.: Scholarly Resources, 2000. 149–66.

Sainsbury, Diane. *Gender, Equality and Welfare States*. London: Cambridge University Press, 1996.

Salessi, Jorge. *Médicos, maleantes y maricas: Higiene, criminología y homosexualidad en la construcción de la nacionalidad (Buenos Aires 1871–1914)*. Rosario: Beatriz Viterbo Editora, 1995.

Salvatore, Ricardo. "Stature, Nutrition and Regional Convergence: The Argentine Northwest in the First Half of the Twentieth Century." *Social Science History* 28.2 (2004): 297–304.

Saravia, Guillermo Alberto. *La adopción: Estudio de doctrina y de legislación comparadas y del proyecto de reforma del Código Civil Argentino. Bases para una legislación argentina de la adopción*. Buenos Aires: Editorial Depalma, 1943.

Schafer, Sylvia. "Between Paternal Right and the Dangerous Mother: Reading Parental Responsibility in Nineteenth-Century French Civil Justice." *Journal of Family History* 23.2 (1998): 173–89.

——. *Children in Moral Danger and the Problem of Government in Third Republic France*. Princeton, N.J.: Princeton University Press, 1997.

Scobie, James R. *Buenos Aires: Plaza to Suburb, 1870–1910*. New York: Oxford University Press, 1974.

——. "Buenos Aires as a Commercial-Bureaucratic City, 1880–1910: Characteristics of a City's Orientation." *American Historical Review* 77.4 (October 1972): 1,035–72.

Siri, Luis. "Bases para la elaboración del plan general de protección a la infancia en la República Argentina." In *Actos y trabajos del Primer Congreso Nacional de la Puericultura, 7–11 octubre de 1940*. 2 vols. Buenos Aires: Imprenta Alfredo Frascoli, 1941.

Skocpol, Theda. *Protecting Soldiers and Mothers: The Political Origins of Social Policy in the United States*. Cambridge, Mass.: Harvard University Press, 1993.

Sociedad de Beneficencia. *Origen y desenvolvimiento de la Sociedad de Beneficencia de la Capital, 1823–1912*. Buenos Aires: Tipografía M. Rodríguez Giles, 1919.

——. *Reglamento de la Casa de Expósitos: Aprobado en las asambleas del 3 de noviembre de 1936 y 15 de setiembre de 1937, con las modificaciones introducidas por las del 19 de abril, 23 de junio y 29 de junio de 1938*. Buenos Aires, 1940.

——. *Reglamento de la Casa de Huérfanas*. Buenos Aires, 1920.

——. *Reglamento del Instituto de Maternidad: Aprobado en la asamblea del 31 de agosto de 1939, con las modificaciones introducidas por las del 20 de diciembre de 1940, 24 de abril de 1942 y 31 de julio de 1944*. Buenos Aires, 1944.

——. *Reseña de la obra realizada por la intervención en la Sociedad de Beneficencia de la Capital, en su primer año, 1946 setiembre 1947*. Buenos Aires, 1947.

——. *Sociedad de Beneficencia de la Capital, 1823–1936*. Buenos Aires: Jacobo Peuser, 1936.

——. Instituto de Maternidad. *Escuela de Nurses: Reglamento y plan de estudios.* Buenos Aires: Asilo de Huérfanos, n.d.

Socolow, Susan M. "Women and Crime in Buenos Aires." *Journal of Latin American Studies* 12.1 (1980): 387–405.

Stepan, Nancy Leys. *"The Hour of Eugenics": Race, Gender, and Nation in Latin America.* Ithaca, N.Y.: Cornell University Press, 1991.

Sussman, George. "The End of the Wet-Nursing Business in France, 1874–1914." In *Family and Sexuality in French History,* ed. Robert Wheaton and Tamara K. Hareven. Philadephia: University of Pennsylvania Press, 1980. 224–52.

Taylor, Julie M. *Eva Perón: The Myths of a Woman.* Chicago: University of Chicago Press, 1979.

Tenti Fanfani, Emilio. *Estado y pobreza: Estrategias típicas de intervención.* 2 vols. Buenos Aires: Biblioteca Política Argentina, 1989.

Tercer Congreso Provincial del Niño y Conferencia Nacional de Psicotécnica: Actuaciones y Trabajos, Rosario, agosto de 1938. 3 vols. Rosario, Santa Fe, Argentina: Talleres Gráficos R. T. Suárez, 1941.

Tilley, Louise A., Rachel G. Fuchs, David I. Kertzer, and David L. Ransel. "Child Abandonment in European History: A Symposium." *Journal of Family History* 17.1 (1992): 1–23.

Twinam, Ann. *Public Lives, Private Secrets: Gender, Honor, Sexuality, and Illegitimacy in Colonial Latin America.* Stanford, Calif.: Stanford University Press, 1999.

Valobra, Adriana. "¿Del hogar a las urnas? Una aproximación a los discursos de Eva Perón sobre los derechos politicos de las mujeres en el contexto de debate, promulgación y aplicación de la ley 13010/47." Unpublished paper.

Viale, Cesar. *Estadística de los menores de que "dispuso" el Juzgado Correccional entre los años 1923 a 1928.* Buenos Aires: n.p., 1933.

Villanueva, Ricardo. *Breve estudio sobre los delitos de aborto e infanticido.* Buenos Aires: Universidad Nacional de Buenos Aires, 1898.

Ward, W. Peter. *Birth Weight and Economic Growth: Women's Living Standards in the Industrializing West.* Chicago: University of Chicago Press, 1993.

Zamora, Nurith. *Orphanages Reconsidered: Child Care Institutions in Progressive Era Baltimore.* Philadelphia: Temple University Press, 1994.

Index

Patria potestad: adoption and, 173; cases, 24–26; defined, 16; foster parents and, 172; juvenile delinquency and, 27, 32, 95–96; as legislated, 19; mother's custody and, 21–23; state custody and, 21–22. *See also* Custody rights

Patriarchy: Argentine feminists on, 7; custody and, 13, 16; immigrant traditions of, 191; juvenile delinquency, 83, 97; protection and, 23; state, 20

Patronato Asistencia de la Infancia, 52

Patronato de la Infancia: abandoned children and, 104; as ambitious, 43, 101; bonding with charges and, 77; as critical, 56; founding of, 28; juvenile delinquents and, 111; Peronism, 181–82; retarded children and, 53; as sponsor, 182; subsidies to, 53–55, 133

Patronato de Recluídas y Liberadas, 138

Patronato Español, 182; Briones de Sáenz and, 71–72; Comisión de Damas Españolas and, 71; Ortiz de Bayona and, 71–72; Sociedad Español de la Virgen del Pilar, 71

Patronato Nacional de Menores, 21, 121–22, 125, 139, 143–44, 146, 168; child welfare survey by, 53–54

Paz, José María, 33, 81

Pellegrini,Carlos, 46, 94

Pendè, Nicolà, 127. *See also* Biotypology

Pensions. *See* Social security system

Perlinger, Luis César, 162

Perón, Eva, 11; as actress, 171; as champion of poor, 163, 174, 177; Confederation of Labor tribute to, 93; as Dama de La Esperanza, 78, 81; emotive philanthropy and, 78–82; marriage of, 152; mythology of, 187; photographs of, 60, 92; pro-child activities, 190; revenge of, 159; role in legislation, 156–60; social justice

and, 188; Society of Beneficence and, 79, 161. *See also* Eva Perón Foundation

Perón, Juan Domingo: alliance with labor, 10; confrontation with Sociedad de Beneficencia, 159–65; creation of welfare state, 11, 123, 162; election of, 158; on Eva, 80, 152; female suffrage and, 157; ideology of, 184; limited adoption law and, 171–72; policies of, 5; redefinition of child welfare, 169; removal from power, 1, 152; rise of, 150–52; Second Five-Year Plan of, 176–83; Society of Beneficence and,161–64; as vice president, 155

Peronism: child-focused welfare state and, 9, 123, 188; collective benevolence and, 168–71; effect on laws, 191–92; female suffrage and, 154; Jewish relations and, 177–78; opponents to, 189–90; rise of welfare state and, 5–6, 8, 11, 58, 187–88; Sociedad de Beneficencia and, 159–65

Philanthropic organizations: Catholic, 10; child welfare programs and, 27; Jewish, 49–50, 72–78; Spanish, 71–72; subsidies to, 6, 134, 148, 157, 168, 170. *See also* Charitable organizations

Philanthropists, female: feminists and, 1, 58–82, 192; pre-welfare state and, 13–35; social policies and, 56–57, 186; social status of, 8–9; welfare state and, 5, 120–21, 157, 191

Piaget, Jean, 93

Pinedo, Federico, 147

Piñero, Horacio, 34

Plotkin, Mariano, 159, 166

Politics: charitable organizations and, 4, 58; maternalist, 4, 8; personalistic, 10; repression and, 151; of subsidies, 51–53, 187. *See also* specific parties; specific regimes

Ponce, Anibal, 93
Poverty, immigrant, 37–42
Primera Conferencia Nacional sobre
  Infancia Abandonada y Delincuente,
  63, 121, 146
Property rights, 27, 31, 171, 192
Prostitution, 104, 116, 136, 142, 177
Public health: feminists and, 65–66;
  programs, 42–48; specialists, 4, 7
Puente, Susana Fernándes de la, 122

Quijano, Juan Hortensio, 160
Quiros, Carlos Bernaldo de, 128, 148

Ramirez, Pedro, 157
Ramos, Alberto Peralta, 127
Rawson de Dellepiane, Elvira, 14, 66–
  69, 89, 153
Rawson, Guillermo, 42
Reca, Telma, 138–39
Recirculation. *See under* Children
Records, falsifying, 18, 24
Reform schools, 20, 84, 109–12, 118–
  19, 121
Refugio de Menores, 112
Registry of Social Assistance, 132
Religious organizations, and female
  charity work, 3
Rights, women's: equal rights, 8–9, 14,
  65, 66–67, 153, 193; feminists on, 1,
  13; increased, 7; unmarried mothers
  and, 16
Rio Negro (territory), 126, 144
Rivadavia, Bernadino, 9; appointment
  as minister, 45; as founder of Society
  of Beneficence, 19, 160; as a liberal,
  147; reforms of, 9
Roca, Julio, 9
Rodriguez, Martín, 109
Romero, Luis Alberto, 156
Rosas, Juan Manuel de, 9, 42
Rossi, Arturo, 127
Ruggiero, Kristen, 38

Salesian Brothers, 115–16
Salta (province), 131
Salvation Army, 52
Sampay, Arturo, 169
San Juan earthquake (1944), 171
San Martín, José de, 80
Santa Cruz (territory), 144
Santa Fe (province), 51, 145–46
Santiago del Estero (province),
  131–32
Sarsfeld, Dalmacia Vélez, 16–17
Saturnino Unzué Asylum, 30
School of Social Work, 154
Schools: access to, 82, 136; kinder-
  gartens, 69, 87; military education
  and, 106–7; Montessori, 70; refor-
  matories, 20, 84, 109–12, 118–19,
  121; for retarded, 53, 115, 116; as
  workshops, 106–9
Scobie, James, 37
Sebastiani, Marcela García, 169
Second Five-Year Plan, 176–83
Second World War. *See* World War II
Secretaría de Trabajo y Previsión,158,
  161, 171
Serres, Blanca Azucena Cassagne, 90,
  138, 154–55; School of Social Work
  and, 154
Sex education, 34, 69
Siri, Luis, 133–34
Sisters of Charity, 3
Skocpol, Theda, 4–5
Social Institute of the National University of the Litoral, 155
Socialist Party, 22, 123, 130, 169; femi-
  nists and, 193; formation of, 28
Social policies: female philanthropists'
  effect on, 56–57, 186, 194; juvenile
  delinquency and, 83–84; liberal politics and, 19; origins of, 186; Peronist,
  177–78, 191; professional women
  and, 120–21, 138, 150, 191, 193; shifts
  in, 9–10; welfare state and, 3, 5–6,

Donna Guy is the Distinguished Professor of Humanities in the Department of History at Ohio State University. Her books include *White Slavery and Mothers Alive and Dead: The Troubled Meeting of Sex, Gender, Public Health, and Progress In Latin America* (2000); and *Sex and Danger in Buenos Aires: Prostitution, Family, and Nation in Argentina* (1991). Edited collections include *Feminisms and Internationalism* (1999), with Mrinalini Sinha and Angela Woolacott.

Library of Congress Cataloging-in-Publication Data
Guy, Donna J.
Women build the welfare state : performing charity and creating
rights in Argentina, 1880–1955 / Donna J. Guy.
p. cm.
Includes bibliographical references and index.
ISBN 978-0-8223-4347-9 (cloth : alk. paper)
ISBN 978-0-8223-4330-1 (pbk. : alk. paper)
1. Women in charitable work—Argentina.
2. Women philanthropists—Argentina. 3. Feminists—Argentina.
4. Welfare state—Argentina. 5. Women in politics—Argentina.
I. Title.
HQ1532.G86 2009
361.6'50982—dc22 2008042247